Trails of Hope and Terror

Trails of Hope and Terror

Testimonies on Immigration

Miguel A. De La Torre

ORBIS BOOKS

Maryknoll, New York 10545

Founded in 1970, Orbis Books endeavors to publish works that enlighten the mind, nourish the spirit, and challenge the conscience. The publishing arm of the Maryknoll Fathers and Brothers, Orbis seeks to explore the global dimensions of the Christian faith and mission, to invite dialogue with diverse cultures and religious traditions, and to serve the cause of reconciliation and peace. The books published reflect the views of their authors and do not represent the official position of the Maryknoll Society. To learn more about Maryknoll and Orbis Books, please visit our website at www.maryknollsociety.org.

Published by Orbis Books, Maryknoll, New York 10545–0308.
Manufactured in the United States of America.
Manuscript editing and typesetting by Joan Weber Laflamme.

Library of Congress Cataloging-in-Publication Data

De La Torre, Miguel A.
    Trails of hope and terror : testimonies on immigration / Miguel A. De La Torre.
        p. cm.
    ISBN 978-1-57075-798-3 (pbk.)
    1. United States—Emigration and immigration—Religious aspects—Christianity. 2. Emigration and immigration—Religious aspects—Christianity. 3. Illegal aliens—United States. I. Title.
    BR517.D32 2009
    277.3'083086912—dc22
                                                                    2009015110

In memory of my father
Miguel De La Torre, Sr. (1926–2007),
originally an undocumented immigrant
who now finds his bones interred in foreign soil,
far from the land that witnessed his birth

Contents

Preface

Why would people in their right mind pack up their family and their meager belongings to cross hazardous borders in order to enter a country with different customs, traditions, and language? A country that will more than likely misappropriate their labor and simultaneously blame them for all the woes of that host country? If there is crime, if there is high unemployment, if there is litter, the immigrants will be blamed.

Usually this xenophobia is expressed in repressive laws and oppressive living conditions. At times, it might also manifest itself in the form of physical violence, and even violence for economic gain. Take the example of "Sylvia" from Ungheni, Moldova. An unemployed teenager with a baby and no husband or job, she was enticed by a neighbor with employment in Moscow as a sales clerk. But when she arrived at the Moldovan capital of Chisinau to meet the two men who were to arrange her travels to Russia, she was beaten and raped. Eventually, she and eleven others did make it to Moscow, but only to work as sex slaves.[1]

Even when migrants are not physically abused, they are still economically and psychologically abused. A twenty-three-year-old Zimbabwean woman recalls her arrival in England: "The first six months in this country were very hard and no one wants you when you first arrive, you have no employment, no money, you can't get work, you're desperate. . . . When you come you need to register with a college to get your papers, but how when you have no money? No papers means no work."[2]

As difficult as it may be for most of us to imagine leaving behind the country that witnessed our birth and the family that defined us for a new life in a strange land, more than two hundred million migrants (almost half women) throughout the world made this very decision in 2008. And they sent back an estimated $283 billion in remittances to their countries of origin. The two hundred million migrants in 2008 represent approximately two and one-half times the number of migrants in 1965, a rate of increase in excess of the global population growth.³ The modern movement of people across international borders, as a consequence and component of globalization, may very well become a defining characteristic of the new millennium.

But as the globalization of the economy, also known as neo-liberalism, has facilitated the movement of capital, goods, and services across borders, it has also created barriers—at times deadly barriers—to the movement of people. Often their labor in the form of finished goods can cross borders, but not their bodies. This book is an effort to understand why this is so. We must ask what circumstances can explain or justify this major movement of people. Why, knowing the risk, would anyone *choose* to migrate?

A multitude of factors help explain why individuals will risk all, even their lives, to cross a border. This book explores some of these reasons in detail, but here is a brief list:

1. a disparity in income between their country and the potential host countries;
2. increasing demographic imbalances where populations of low-income countries grow significantly when compared to high-income countries;
3. the globalization of the economy in which the flow of goods, capital, and services creates a need for labor;
4. the need in economically advanced countries for low-skilled service-based workers;
5. a decrease for the need of migrants within economically advanced countries creates pressure for outward migration;
6. advances in technology in the form of affordable travel and real-time global communication systems that makes the sharing of opportunities possible;
7. the consequences of foreign policies of economically advanced nations, especially when they lead to political upheaval; and
8. armed conflicts in less economically advanced nations in the form of civil wars, revolutions, and ethnic cleansing.⁴

Because migration in this new millennium is so multifaceted, it doesn't lend itself to easy analysis or uniform policy. As we explore migration, we discover that its causes and its consequences are noticeably different throughout the world. In Africa, migrants are more likely to move to another African country, with Southern Africa, the Maghreb, and West Africa being the regions most affected. Asia, from

Bangladesh to the Philippines, provides the largest source of temporary contracted migrant labor worldwide. In addition, there are vast internal migrations, especially in China and India. Europe is a major receiver of migrants. The European Union attempts to create a common migratory space through a joint effort of managing external borders. The Middle East is also a major receiving region, mostly of contractual workers from Asia. Oceania has two large destination countries, Australia and New Zealand. Although Oceania contains the smallest number of migrants, only five million, because of the region's small population migrants represent the highest percentage of the population (15.2 percent) among the world's regions. And finally, there are the Americas, characterized by a prevalent south to north migratory pattern. Not only are the United States and Canada major receiver nations from the southern hemisphere but also from the entire world.[5]

In 2005 the Americas hosted 51.1 million migrants, of whom 44.5 million were in North America. Not surprisingly, the United States is the main destination for many migrants, hosting about 38.3 million migrants. Of these migrants, the majority, 55 percent, were from Latin America, with the most coming from Mexico (10.8 million), followed by the Caribbean (3.2 million). By 2007 these migrants were responsible for about 60.7 percent of the remittances sent back home.

Migration is destined to be a major global issue with which nations must wrestle. As Christians, we must ask if Christianity has anything important to say about the causes of migration, the process of crossing borders, and the treatment of the alien within our midst. As a Christian ethicist who lives in Denver, Colorado, I cannot avoid this question. In exploring migration, I am focusing on just one aspect of the migration story—the one I know best—migration from Latin America to the United States. Latin American migrants, the largest incoming group to the United States, are being used and abused throughout this nation. Could this be another incredible violation of human rights on U.S. soil?

Introduction

These people don't come here to work. They come here to rob and deal drugs. . . . We need the National Guard to clean up our cities and round them up. . . . [Mexicans and Central American immigrants] have no problem slitting your throat and taking your money or selling drugs to your kids or raping your daughter and they are evil people.
—Chris Simcox, co-founder of the Minuteman Project and president of the Minuteman Civil Defense Corps[1]

September 11, 2001, has become, in the American psyche, a day of pure terror. To simply say "9/11" signifies a day of panic, horror, shock, death, destruction, and above all, terror. Probably for the first time, Euroamericans found themselves vulnerable to forces bent on their harm and destruction. This state of being is nothing new for many within the U.S. population. African Americans experienced it for generations, and terror has been and continues to be the daily companion of most Latino/as in this country, specifically for the undocumented. The use of the word *terror* to describe the experience of Hispanics in the United States may sound like hyperbole to some, but for undocumented immigrants, no other word exists that clearly expresses the situation in which they find themselves. They have embarked upon a trail of terror with no end. At any moment, the sojourner can be separated from loved ones and can face harm, illness, imprisonment, and/or death. Hispanic migrants set out on this trail with some illusions of achieving the so-called American dream, yet deep inside most are resigned to live in the shadows, hoping to send some money home and hoping they won't meet with deportation or death.

As of March 2008, approximately 11.9 million undocumented immigrants were living in the shadows of U.S. society; they represented 4 percent of the U.S. population. Four out of every five undocumented immigrants come from Latin America, with approximately seven million from Mexico and just over two and a half million from other Latin American or Caribbean nations. Most of the others arrived from Asia, Eastern Europe, and Africa. The year 2008 saw a significant drop in

1

the flow of undocumented immigrants. From 2000 through 2004 a yearly average of 800,000 undocumented immigrants entered the United States. Since 2005, the annual average dropped to 500,000. Nevertheless, in spite of the recent decline in immigration, the undocumented immigrant population in the United States experienced a 40 percent increase since 2000, when it was estimated at 8.4 million.[2]

In spite of the recent decline, many still embark upon the trails of terror. Their journey may start in Altar, Mexico, where they first have to avoid becoming prey to government officials, *coyotes* (smugglers), and criminals trying to take advantage of their desperation. Women and children face the additional hazard of becoming victims of physical or sexual abuse. And they need money to live on the Mexican side of the border while they wait to cross—for many this is an event that must be repeated.

If they make it to the border, they must spend several days walking through mountains and deserts. Men, women, and children follow trails where at any turn they can be robbed, beaten, raped, or murdered by drug-smuggling gangs, U.S. anti-immigrant vigilante groups stationed on the border, racist ranchers, and rogue Border Patrol or Mexican law enforcement agents. A foot blister or a sprained ankle can be a death sentence because those who cannot keep up are left behind. Unless they receive help, they die of exposure. Thousands have already died in this way. Those who elude the border vigilantes or the official Border Patrol and make it to a major city quickly try to blend into the community's fabric. But they still live with the daily terror of being detected, arrested, and deported, being forced to leave behind parents, spouses, and children.

Even those of us who have proper documentation share in the constant threat faced by our community. Laws have been enacted that make us accomplices if we give food to the hungry, water to the thirsty, or provide care for the alien within our midst. Many of us within the Hispanic community feel powerless when faced with the full force of the present immigration debate that is being used by politicians to create fear in order to consolidate their power.

With this reality in mind, in the fall of 2007 I accepted the invitation of three women active in their local congregation, St. Andrew Methodist Church in Highlands Ranch, Colorado. Heidi Parish, Laura Dravenstott, and Terri Lowe asked two border-based activists (Gene Lefebvre and John Fife) and two scholars (Dana Wilbanks and myself) to begin a discussion on how to raise consciousness among church laity concerning ongoing human rights violations against migrants.

We gathered to discuss immigration a few months before the Iowa presidential caucus and the New Hampshire primary, the official start of the 2008 presidential election. Without incumbents running for re-election, the field in both parties was crowded. The majority of the Republican contenders for the nomination made opposition to immigration central to their strategy. Democratic contenders were mainly silent on the issue. Throughout the countless debates within the Republican camp, it appeared that each politician was attempting to outperform his colleagues in demonstrating his anti-immigration stance. Just as the Southern politicians of a previous generation attempted to "out-segregate" their political opponents, the Republican presidential hopefuls of 2008 tried to "out-immigrant" one another.

As I drove to the first discussion, I was fully aware of how rancid the political dialogue on undocumented immigrants had become, particularly when coupled with the economic downturn. It made any honest appraisal of the undocumented immigrant situation nigh to impossible. Instead, the issue became a race-based attempt to win votes during the state primaries. This strategy began to emerge among Republican candidates even during the 2006 midterm election.

Throughout the 2006 midterm election the targets of fear shifted toward immigrants, specifically Hispanic immigrants. As targets of fear, they provided motivation for political conservatives and the Religious Right to get out the vote. To this end the Republican-controlled Senate Budget Committee held a series of so-called national fact-finding sessions on immigration. The sessions were held only in congressional districts that seemed vulnerable to a Republican win that year. In the end, few facts were gathered as the committee spent taxpayer dollars to hear from those hostile to the presence of Hispanics. Missing from the hearings were experts on immigration, social workers who were in contact with the undocumented, or anyone who was Latino or Latina. When some of us requested to speak before the hearings held in Aurora, Colorado, we were prevented from addressing our elected representatives.

The night before the hearing, community workers, outraged at being shut out of the political process, held an alternative hearing on immigration at a downtown Denver church. As a member of this panel I heard from gifted young teenagers unable to attend college because they lacked a Social Security number. I heard from local farmers who testified that half of their crop was rotting in the fields because they could not find Euroamericans willing to do the back-breaking work. I heard from economists who demonstrated that immigrants produced more in taxes than they absorbed in social services. In addition to solid information from experts, we also saw the human face of the immigration issue.

The next day, during the Senate Budget Committee hearing, a few of us held a news conference, only to have members of an anti-immigration group aggressively crash the news conference to hurl racial slurs at us. We saw that the twenty-plus police officers present to keep an eye on us seemed to disappear when we were being harassed and our safety was threatened. Then again, the police were there to watch us, not those who threatened us.

Testing the political waters during the 2006 midterm election led some within the Republican Party to conclude that a candidate's anti-immigration rhetoric could be effectively used during the 2008 Republican presidential state primaries. Its appeal to xenophobia would undoubtedly get out the base vote. Sadly, fear of the other was used as an effective political motivator as Republican candidates attempted to win the debate by arguing over who could build a higher and longer wall at the U.S.-Mexican border.

Ironically, even though the anti-immigrant rhetoric intensified in the primary presidential campaign, the general public failed to respond. Americans simply did not consider the immigration issue to be that important. According to a *Los Angeles Times*/Bloomberg poll conducted in December 2007 (one month before the Iowa caucus and the New Hampshire primary) only 15 percent of those surveyed listed immigration as a top priority for presidential candidates. And over 60 percent favored allowing undocumented immigrants who have not broken any laws to become U.S. citizens (64 percent of Democrats and 62 percent of Republicans).[3]

As the primary elections progressed and the field narrowed to one candidate from each party, the once hot issue of immigration moved to the back burner. Both campaigns seemed to avoid immigration, likely from fear of getting caught between anti-immigrant groups and Latina/o voters. But while John McCain and Barack Obama ignored the issue when addressing Euroamericans, both parties made it the centerpiece of their Spanish-language advertising. Curiously, neither candidate translated his so-called pro-immigration advertising into

English or ran it in major Euroamerican markets. To make matters worse, while no thoughtful comprehensive reform was proposed, both candidates disparaged their opponents as anti-immigration and anti-Hispanic. Did they indeed think that Hispanic voters could be swayed by such pandering?

McCain accused Obama of favoring "No guest worker program. No path to citizenship. No secure borders. No reform" based on Obama's support of an amendment that supposedly led to the defeat of a 2007 bipartisan immigration reform bill. However, the bill was actually defeated not by the amendment but by McCain's own party, which led a filibuster against it. The Republicans were aided by right-wing radio talk-show hosts like Rush Limbaugh, who whipped up xenophobic sentiments among many white Americans. Ironically, even though McCain had co-sponsored the bill (along with Edward Kennedy), during the primaries he insisted to white audiences that he would vote against it.

Obama also distorted the facts in hopes of gaining Hispanic votes. In his Spanish-language advertising Obama linked McCain with anti-Hispanic, anti-immigrant radio personalities such as Limbaugh. In reality, Limbaugh consistently attacked McCain for not being anti-immigrant enough. Obama also attempted to downplay the role some Democrats had in helping Republicans defeat the bill in an effort to win over organized labor. Obama did allude to immigration in a throwaway line in the litany of major problems facing the nation during his acceptance speech at the Denver convention.

Hispanics were truly disappointed to discover that politicians from one party increased their anti-immigration rhetoric to score votes while politicians from the other party went out of their way to avoid the issue altogether.

Even worse than avoiding the issue was using the issue to score points with constituents, as did legislation introduced to Congress by North Carolina Democrat Heath Shuler. The Secure America through Verification and Enforcement Act (SAVE) of 2007 was intended to provide more funds to underwrite a mandatory employment verification system for the nation's labor pool. The current program, which is voluntary, has a 4 percent rate of error. This may not sound significant, but when applied to the nation's laborers, it would mean that 240,000 documented workers would appear undocumented and would be responsible for correcting the error with the Social Security Office, a bureaucracy not necessarily known for its speed and efficiency. It would have forced many workers, documented and undocumented, to work off the books. According to the Congressional Budget Office, SAVE would lose over $30 billion in tax revenues as employers and employees would resort to operating outside of the tax system. Congressman Shuler assured his Democratic colleagues that no action would take place on his bill, that it was never the intention to pass this legislation; instead, the purpose was to provide proof during the 2008 general election that Democrats in red states could be just as tough on the undocumented as the Republicans.[4]

While politicians stroke the xenophobia of their constituents to score points, tragically, official statistics (which are probably underestimated) indicate that ten times more people died in nine years trying to cross the U.S.-Mexican wall than died trying to cross the Berlin Wall during its twenty-eight-year existence.[5] I'm particularly shocked that a deafening silence to this humanitarian crisis prevails in most churches, churches dedicated to the message of life they proclaim can be found in their Lord and Savior, Jesus Christ. Yes, although a few prophetic religious leaders, including Cardinal Roger Mahony of Los Angeles, have spoken out in words and action for a more humane approach to immigration, the vast majority of ministers and laity have either ignored that the issue demands a Christian response or else they have chosen a false sense of patriotism over the message of the gospel.

As I drove to that first discussion on immigration on a warm fall day in 2007, I was deeply concerned that much of the Christian church had remained silent on immigration for too long. Had the anti-immigrant rhetoric of the politicians seduced Christians away from their bibles and the traditions of their churches? Was there a way in which we could avoid rhetoric and turn to the issues and the people involved? By the end of that day's discussion we had agreed to organize a seminary class and a church forum on the issue. Both events came about, and both were well attended. At some point along the way it was suggested that a book on immigration should be written to assist the churchgoing layperson in understanding the complexity of the current immigration debate. The book's focus would be on what most affected us in Colorado, the southern border separating the United States from Latin America.

I agreed to spearhead this project because I was convinced that such a book is desperately needed. Many local pulpits have fallen short in discussing with their members the responsibilities churches have in the present immigration situation. A civil conversation that might lead to humane immigration reform must replace the politics of fear that has been used to scapegoat immigrants as threats to the American way of life.

One reason the churches have fallen short is undoubtedly because many Christians have fallen into the trap of anti-immigrant rhetoric, rhetoric that reduces immigrants to objects or the unknown and threatening other. Absent are the stories of real people, their voices, their testimonies.

Through a description of economic and social factors *and* the first-person accounts of migrants this book attempts to provide information that can help Christians participate confidently in the immigration discourse and enable them to discern God's will. Each chapter brings together different voices—the voices of experts, the voices of those who suffer under the current policies, and the voices of those who actively engage in pro-immigrant praxis.

The book is structured around *testimonios,* an approach favored by many Hispanic theologians. A *testimonio* allows a person to

- voice his or her trials and tribulations to the faith community, thus giving the church the opportunity to be used by God to minister to the needs of the troubled soul;
- be a witness to how God is moving within the faith community in spite of the struggles voiced;
- create solidarity with the rest of the faith community, who become fellow sojourners through difficult times;
- realize that despite the hardships faced, he or she is not alone, for God and the faith community are participants in the immigrant's disappointments and victories; and
- enter the reality of the metaphysical presence of the Divine in the everyday, a presence that can lead to deliverance and/or physical or emotional healing.

The use of testimonies allows the discourse on immigration to come alive (to be incarnated) for the reader. What is currently an abstract debate about defending borders and keeping some faceless unknown at bay takes on a human face. While the testimonies chosen do not include all voices and experience, they do represent a majority of the undocumented and those who stand in solidarity with them.

At this point it is important to provide a disclaimer. As the author of this book I do not claim to be an expert on the suffering of the undocumented, although during my earlier years of life my family and I were undocumented after overstaying our tourist visa. Nor is this book an attempt to exploit or romanticize the tribulations faced by the undocumented. Rather, I have simply attempted to put into words the testimonies and perspectives that are usually kept silenced—magnifying the usually ignored voices of those who are most affected by the present immigration policies of this nation. Employing another Hispanic principle, *teología en conjunto* (theology in conjunction), I have attempted to allow the voices of both the undocumented and their allies to emerge. While most of the actual words are mine, it is they who informed this work and provided the resources.

This book is the product of the labor of many. I am deeply grateful to Heidi Parish, Laura Dravenstott, and Terri Lowe, who called for that original meeting. I am also indebted to Gene Lefebvre and John Fife who helped me locate some of the book's contributors and were my hosts and guides when a group of us provided humanitarian aid in the Sonora deserts—an inhospitable terrain that many die attempting to cross. I am also grateful to the "Iliff Eleven" who joined me in the desert, students with a passion for justice with whom I shared parts of this manuscript and from whom I received constructive feedback. Special thanks go to my administrative assistant, Debbie McLaren, who transcribed many of my interviews and assisted me with proofreading. Last, but certainly not least, I offer my thanks for my friend and editor, Susan Perry.

1

Creating Borders
and Their Consequences

*Illegal immigration is a threat to the safety of Missouri families
and the security of their jobs.*

—GOVERNOR MATT BLUNT (R-MO)[1]

In the public square at Altar, Mexico, I came across a group of
eleven migrants preparing to journey north. Some had made the trip
before, but were caught and returned. Others were heading north for
the first time. I did my best to answer their questions about the journey they were about to undertake. "Yes, expect about three days to
cross the mountains. No, Tucson is not a day's walk once you get over
the mountains. Expect heavy rain." And so on. At one point it was my
turn to ask them some questions. "Why are you crossing the border?
Why not go through the proper channels?" Almost unanimously they
answered that they had families who lacked food. Their economy had
spun so out of control that they could no longer feed their families. To
wait for proper documentation would take decades. They had hungry
mouths to feed now. In their minds they had no choice but to risk their
lives in the hope that they could save the lives of their children.

If they succeed, they can send money home to feed their hungry
family. According to the best estimates, remittances home amounted
to $45 billion in 2006.[2] With the worsening U.S. economy, however,
less money is being sent back home as traditional jobs in construction
usually filled by migrants are drying up. At this point one of the young
men said: "Please tell the Americans that I am sorry for entering their
country like this. Please forgive us, but we are simply desperate."

The 1,833–mile border separating the United States from Latin
America has been called a scar caused by the encounter of the First and
Third Worlds. Other than the Rio Grande River that runs between Texas
and Mexico, the United States is not separated from its neighbors to the

south by a natural boundary. Instead, this border was imposed as a direct consequence of the U.S. territorial conquest of northern Mexico at the end of the Mexican-American War (1846–48). Prior to its creation, Mexicans lived both north and south of this line drawn across the sand. Those living north of the new border—an estimated eighty thousand Mexicans—woke up one morning in the mid-nineteenth century to find themselves in a new country. This also happened to Puerto Ricans when their island was absorbed into the emerging American "empire" at the close of the nineteenth century. Like the Mexicans before them, the U.S. borders enclosed them with the conclusion of the Spanish-American War in 1898.

Territorial Expansion

Territorial expansion—always a goal, even from the first colonists—gathered full steam in the early nineteenth century when it became a controlling ethos of the emerging nation of the United States. Undergirding the young nation was a theological and political ideology known as Manifest Destiny, which gave a name to the belief that the United States, due to its racial superiority and its election by God to represent the "New Israel," was manifestly ordained to occupy and inhabit the entire northwestern hemisphere from the Arctic north to the Isthmus of Panama in the south. In 1843 Andrew Jackson used the expression "extending the area of freedom" to describe this expansionism. Manifest Destiny also expressed the post-millennialism[3] of the time, suggesting that God's kingdom would be realized through U.S. history; that is, only after the United States accomplished its apocalyptic mission of occupying the new "Promised Land" given to it by God would Christ be able to return in all his glory.[4]

This doctrine found real expression during the U.S. expansionist war against Mexico. Presidential candidate James K. Polk ran on the campaign promise of annexing Texas and engaging Mexico in war. Shortly after taking the oath of office, he deployed troops into Mexican territory to provoke the Mexican army to fire first upon U.S. troops. This provided Polk with the excuse to request a declaration of war from Congress. Not all members of Congress supported Polk's military adventures. Former president and then congressman John Quincy Adams denounced Polk's request for military aggression against Mexico. During the congressional debate, Adams remarked, "The banners of freedom will be the banners of Mexico; and your banners, I blush to speak the word, will be the banners of slavery."[5]

Those who served as young officers during the Mexican-American War would within a decade fight as generals on opposite sides of the American Civil War. One young officer, Ulysses S. Grant, eventually became the commanding general of the federal armies and eighteenth president of the United States. Decades later, destitute and dying of throat cancer, Grant wrote his memoirs as a means for providing for his family. When he wrote about the Mexican-American War, he questioned its justification. Grant saw the conflict as a war forced upon Mexico for the singular sake of acquiring another people's land. In fact, he saw the American Civil War as God's punishment for the U.S. territorial conquest of Mexico. He wrote, "The Southern rebellion was largely the outgrowth of the Mexican War. Nations, like individuals, are punished for their transgressions. We got punished in the most sanguinary and expensive war of modern times."[6]

The Mexican-American War ended with Mexico's capitulation. The signing of the 1848 Treaty of Guadalupe-Hidalgo ceded half of Mexico's territory to the United States. A surveyor's line was drawn across the sand in an area that, according to archeological evidence, had historically experienced fluid migration. The land transfer comprised 55 percent of Mexico's territory, including present-day Arizona, New Mexico, California, and parts of Colorado, Utah, and Nevada. One immediate consequence of this 1,833–mile border was that the United States acquired gold deposits in California, silver deposits in Nevada, oil in Texas, and all of the natural harbors (except Veracruz) necessary for commerce.

Immediately after signing a peace treaty with Mexico, the U.S. government either abrogated or ignored certain provisions of the treaty, including the rights of Mexicans living in that territory to U.S. citizenship and the rights of Mexicans to retain their historic titles to the land, many of which went back for generations. The United States gained the natural resources embedded in the land as well as cheap labor from Mexicans who lived on the land. Most Mexican Americans became a reserve army of laborers, allowing the overall southwestern economy to develop and function. Likewise, the loss of Mexico's richest land doomed that nation's ability to capitalize on its resources.

Economic Expansion

The consequences of creating the new border extended to more than just conquering and occupying another's nation territory. By the start of the twentieth century the United States was less interested in acquiring territory than in controlling peripheral economies to obtain financial benefits. At the start of the twentieth century President Theodore Roosevelt introduced "gunboat diplomacy" and the concept of "speaking softly but carrying a big stick." While most Americans remember these sayings from grade school, few connect this foreign policy with Latin American history.

Roosevelt's foreign policy placed the full force of the U.S. military at the disposal of U.S. corporations to protect their interests abroad. Any nation in "our" hemisphere that attempted to claim sovereignty to the detriment of U.S. business interests could expect the United States to invade and set up a new government (the term *banana republic* came from countries beholden to the United Fruit Company) or have their country covertly overthrown.[7] Throughout the twentieth century eleven countries experienced twenty-one U.S. military invasions and twenty-six covert operations. During most of the twentieth century no country was allowed to determine who would serve as its leaders without the permission of the U.S. ambassador assigned to that country. The U.S.-installed "banana republics" created poverty, strife, and death in all of these countries.

During the 1980s, for example, U.S. foreign policies designed to safeguard established "banana republics" in Central America led to military conflicts in El Salvador and Guatemala. By 1980, over ten thousand people, including Archbishop Oscar Romero and four churchwomen from the United States, were murdered by the Salvadoran military. Church leaders and workers were commonly targeted for arrest, rape, torture, and disappearance (a euphemism for killing). Meanwhile, in Guatemala over fifty thousand deaths, more than one hundred thousand disappeared, and 626 village massacres took place. Many escaped these death zones by leaving their homelands in search of a safe haven in the United States, usually as refugees.

According to the legal definition, refugees are those persons who fear persecution due to their race, religion, nationality, political views, and/or their association with political or social organizations. Unfortunately for most victims fleeing oppression in Central America, the Reagan administration refused to grant them refugee status, taking the stance that these migrants were simply coming to the United States to seek economic opportunities. After all, how could they be victims of persecution by U.S.-backed governments?

The Reagan administration determined refugee status on the basis of the government of the asylum seekers. Was their birth country on good or bad terms with the U.S. administration? Because Cuba and Sandinista-led Nicaragua had hostile relationships with the U.S. government, people leaving those nations were routinely granted refugee status. They were welcomed because they were fleeing the communists and socialists. But because El Salvador and Guatemala were receiving military aid from the Reagan administration—which interpreted these armed conflicts as a front in the Cold War—applicants for political asylum from these nations were routinely denied refugee status. Unable to meet U.S. legal requirements for migration as refugees, these applicants, who were usually poor peasants, migrated north without the necessary documentation, in most cases fleeing for their lives. If caught and deported they faced certain persecution or death.

Although Manifest Destiny and gunboat diplomacy originally described the relationship between the United States and the rest of the western hemisphere, the latter years of the twentieth century witnessed the globalization of this foreign policy. Following the collapse of the Eastern Bloc, symbolized by the fall of the Berlin Wall (1989), the United States emerged as the world's only superpower, and the system of capitalism (also called neoliberalism) became the undisputed economic model. Profits of transnational corporations could now increase by pitting workers in one country against workers in another. Free trade came to be defined as moving goods freely across borders—free from tariffs or taxes. However, while workers looking for better jobs were *not* intended themselves to cross borders freely, the products of their cheap labor did, as goods were produced and exported. While people were expected to stay in place, factories moved across borders in order to maintain their high profit margins by paying the lowest possible wages. The quest for low wages meant that many industries relocated south of the 1,833–mile border between the United States and Mexico.

NAFTA and Its Effects

Although large numbers of U.S. jobs moved to Mexico,[8] in general Mexicans did not experience a windfall. While numerous factories, known as *maquiladoras*, opened along the border after the implementation of the North American Free Trade Agreement (NAFTA) in 1994, Mexicans sank deeper into poverty. Many Mexican farmers were forced to abandon their lands because they were unable to compete with U.S.-subsidized imported agricultural goods. At first they saw salvation in the *maquiladoras*, but this proved to be an illusion.[9] After

NAFTA, real income for Mexicans dropped 25 percent in purchasing power. In 1975 Mexican production workers earned 23 percent of U.S. wages. Since the relocation of U.S. jobs to Mexico, that number dropped to 11 percent. Women fared worse, and the poverty rate for households headed by women increased by 50 percent.[10]

The impact of NAFTA on Mexican lives continues to be profound. Increased poverty south of the border means dissatisfied workers attempt the hazardous border crossing to the north. From 1990 to 2000 unauthorized migration from Mexico doubled. While the owners and managers in the United States and Mexico benefited from NAFTA, the majority of Mexico's citizens suffered. In its 1993 report prepared for the U.S. House of Representatives, the Government Accounting Office, a government agency, reported "that the flow of illegal aliens across the southwest border is expected to increase during the next decade because Mexico's economy is unlikely to absorb all of the new job seekers that are expected to enter the labor force."[11] The report anticipated the devastating impact NAFTA would have on the Mexican economy and labor market and indicated that it would trigger an increase in immigration. Is it any wonder that the implementation of NAFTA in 1994 corresponded with the start of Operation Gatekeeper?

Securing U.S. borders became a priority. Until Operation Gatekeeper was implemented, an immigrant simply crossed over at border cities or towns. The only danger to face was getting caught and being deported. The primary strategy of Operation Gatekeeper was to disrupt the migration through the San Diego area. Militarizing the border forced migrants away from the popular routes through San Diego and east toward the harsh and desolate areas of the 120,000 square miles of the Sonora Desert or the mountains north of Tecate. It is not surprising that over two thousand immigrants a day and the responding enforcement patrols funneling through these fragile desert ecosystems caused severe damage to the environment.

The Dangers of Border Crossing

An intentional consequence of Operation Gatekeeper was to give the Border Patrol a "strategic advantage" by forcing migrants eastward into far more dangerous terrain, with extreme temperatures in both the desert and the mountains. The possibility of death would hopefully serve as a deterrent preventing others from attempting the dangerous crossing. Since the implementation of Operation Gatekeeper, there has been a 20 percent increase in known deaths associated with unauthorized border crossing. However, no significant decrease in the number of unauthorized crossings since the start of Operation Gatekeeper has been reported.[12] Even the Government Accounting Office blames Operation Gatekeeper for creating a humanitarian crisis.[13] A resolution passed by Amnesty International–USA in 2000 noted that the Gatekeeper strategy is an abuse of the right to control the border "in that it maximizes, rather than minimizes, the risk to life."[14]

The unforgiving and harsh terrain toward which Hispanics are presently funneled can have daytime temperatures in excess of 115 degrees Fahrenheit, higher during summer months, and frigid nighttime temperatures that pose the risk of hypothermia. The majority of deaths, almost 60 percent, are caused by exposure to the elements, specifically hyperthermia, hypothermia, and drowning. Most who perish are in the prime of their lives; around one-third are between the ages of eighteen and twenty-nine, and almost 20 percent are thirty to thirty-nine. Even if death does not claim the life of a border crosser, many still suffer permanent kidney damage caused by dehydration. Women are nearly three times more likely to die of exposure than men, and those women who do not succumb to the cruelty of the desert face the cruelty of sexual assault. It is now common practice for women preparing to make the crossing to use a method of birth control prior to the journey as they are more than likely to be sexually assaulted.[15]

It is difficult, if not impossible, to determine how many people have actually perished attempting to cross the border. Seldom are these deaths reported by the media. It is conservatively estimated that over thirty-six hundred bodies were recovered on the U.S side of the border between 1995 and 2005. The official numbers reported by U.S. governmental agencies are much lower. According to an investigative report conducted by the *Tucson Citizen*, the Border Patrol undercounted border deaths by as much as 43 percent, a charge also made by the U.S. Government Accounting Office.[16] Under-counting occurs because some migrants perish on the Mexican side of the border, and others who do make it across are never found in the remote and inaccessible terrain or predatory desert animals have consumed or scattered their remains.[17] The desert is very efficient at cleaning itself. Thus, the bodies recovered do not accurately represent the number of actual deaths occurring along the border.

However, if only one person were to die a horrific death as a direct result of the policies or procedures of the U.S. government, then that is one death too many. It is all too easy to justify the death of a border crosser by blaming the victim for attempting the crossing in the first place. Once when I was detained for placing water in the desert, Border Patrol Officer D. Koenneker told me, "They made the choice to come, and they came unprepared."[18] Before we can assuage any guilt we might feel by blaming victims for their predicament, it is important to realize that a person would risk death by crossing a desert only for a very powerful reason.

Why Do They Risk Their Lives?

As we ask ourselves why so many risk death to cross this 1,833–mile border, we must acknowledge that the reasons migrants risk their lives today are rooted in the historical relationship between the United States and Latin America, and more specifically Mexico, that has led to economic and trade inequities. Contrary to popular opinion, they do not come looking for a better life in America, or because they plan to deplete American social services. Most would certainly prefer to remain at home with their families and friends, their own music and languages, their own culture and traditions, but they attempt the hazardous crossing because our foreign policy has created an economic situation in their home countries in which they are unable to feed their families.

For over a century, as we have seen, the U.S. military protected U.S. corporations as they built roads in developing countries throughout Latin America to extract, by brute force if necessary, their natural resources and make use of cheap labor. Some of the inhabitants of those countries, deprived of their livelihood, followed the same roads as their countries' resources. They are following what over time was stolen. They come to escape the violence and terrorism left behind. The ethical or moral question we should be asking about the undocumented is not *why* they come, but what responsibilities and obligations exist for the United States in causing the present immigration dilemma.

U.S. policies, first of territorial and then economic expansion and finally of Operation Gatekeeper, represent one of the grossest violations of human rights of our time. And these deaths are either ignored or legitimized generally by our culture and society. Not since the days of Jane and Jim Crow have the deaths of people of a particular race or ethnicity been normalized by the overall U.S. culture. Today the immigration debate rages on, yet it is safe to say that all sides agree that the present system is broken. Operation Gatekeeper is a failure that has resulted in death for many created in the image of God.

Eleven migrants in the main plaza of Altar, Mexico, preparing for their journey north. One of the men offered an apology for being forced to enter the United States under the cover of night.

Testimony from a Border Crosser
"Ignacio"

Ignacio was clean shaven, well dressed, and about thirty years old. A slim man with a light complexion, he entered the room with confidence, carrying a cup of hot coffee. After polite introductions, he began sharing his journey.

It is crazy to cross the desert by foot. It is suicidal. If the extreme heat and lack of food and water don't kill you, accidents, snake bites, or crooked *coyotes* set on robbing you of your entire life's possessions will. You think that it's just a flat desert that needs to be crossed, but mountains need to be surpassed and rivers crossed. This sounds ironic, but drowning in the desert happens. We knew the danger before we set out. We pinned our names and pictures to our clothes in the event we would die; if our bodies were found, we could at least be identified.

We risk death not because we want to, or because we are foolhardy. We risk death for the families left behind. Would you not cross a hundred deserts to feed your child? It may be crazy to cross, but we are not crazy, we are desperate. Even though I'm a believer and put my trust in God, I'm still desperate. I come from a family of eight brothers and sisters. All are educated and are professionals. Still, I simply could not provide the basic necessities for my children. I had to cross for their sake.

If you're going to cross the desert, it's best to do it before summer. In the summer the heat is so bad it feels as if your brains are broiling. Unfortunately, many cross when the opportunity presents itself, regardless of the danger. I was lucky. It was in March 2005 when I crossed over. The days were not as hot, and the evenings were cool. Nevertheless, the entire trek took three long and grueling days and nights. Mostly we walked in the evening when the temperature was cooler and the Border Patrol was less vigilant. In the darkness of the desert the stars are awe inspiring. They reminded me that God had not abandoned me. They also provided the little light we had to navigate through the hazardous terrain. During the heat of the day we rested

---

"Ignacio" is Subject #7, interviewed and taped by Miguel A. De La Torre on June 20, 2008. His story was translated, transcribed, edited, and then written by the interviewer.

and attempted to blend in with the surroundings so as not to be detected.

There were seven of us in the group led by a *coyote*. We paid the *coyote* five hundred dollars[19] up front just to get us across. We were lucky—this one was honorable. Not all are. Before we started he told us that if any of us got hurt we could decide to either go back or turn ourselves in, or we could split up, with him staying behind with the injured person. Many *coyotes* don't care and simply leave stragglers behind to fend for themselves. These are the ones who end up walking in circles, eventually succumbing to the elements and dying.

The *coyote*'s job was to smuggle us across the border and deliver us to a safe house. There we would be charged an additional five hundred dollars. For that fee we could rest for about two days, be fed, have the opportunity to wash up, and be provided with new clothes. From there we would either be picked up by a friend or family member or pay an additional five hundred dollars to travel to another city, preferably a city in the north. This may not seem like a lot of money for those living in *el norte,* but for those of us who have lived in poverty, this sum is a small fortune. Some of us in the group sold our homes or took out "shark loans" in order to pay for this service. Before we risk our lives, we must risk all we have in the hope of working at a job no one else wants to do.

The *coyote* told us what to bring, mainly food and water for three days. Carrying heavy water jugs through the desert slows you down so, as expected, none of us brought enough. On the trails you can see the discarded water bottles, as well as clothing and other personal items that must have gotten too heavy to carry. Thank God we came across water tanks. They literally saved our lives—at least for the moment. Before we continued our trek, we usually left notes by the water tanks describing what we were wearing and our names in the event those following us on the trail would discover our bodies.

In the pitch-black night, with stars as our only light, we walked north. At dawn we would find a place to hide. Although we might walk a bit during the day, we mostly stayed hidden. We were instructed to lie on the ground and not move if we heard or saw a helicopter. We were told we would usually spot them approaching before they would spot us. If we started running, they would notice us and send ground support. But if we quickly dropped and remained motionless, we might not be detected and the Border Patrol would pass over us. That is what happened to us once.

On the third night we reached a stretch of Highway 10 in a town called Deming somewhere in New Mexico. There the *coyote* told us that our meeting place was at a certain mile marker about a mile away at five in the morning. Before going there, he wanted to make a call to make sure he didn't have any messages. He left us there and never returned. We didn't know if he had been caught or if he just took off. If he was caught, he didn't turn us in. After some time passed and the rendezvous time approached, we simply walked to the mile maker that served as our meeting place. At the assigned time a van stopped and picked us up. As we entered the van we paid the driver the five-hundred-dollar fee to take us to the safe house.

It took eight days before the pain of the walk ceased, but I could only stay there for two days. We brought lotion to use during the walk for our feet and thighs, and this did soothe the pain of blisters and chafing. Still, it was not enough. The only way I can describe my feet is by saying that they looked like raw hamburger. Three days and nights of walking is very hard and tiring. You have to fight the desire to just curl up somewhere and die. Still, we made it, but we didn't have time to recover. At least I was able to take a shower and rid myself of the smell of desert and death.

Based on what we saw at the safe house, we became concerned that the people there might also be dealing in drugs. At least the people who took us there were doing drugs. We wanted to leave that place as soon as possible. Still, they did warn us of what we would undergo in this country. They prepared us for the hardships that still awaited us. They told us how we would be treated, as if we were either invisible or dogs. At first I didn't believe them, but after being here for three years, they were right. Frankly, I'd rather be treated as a dog than invisible—at least a dog's existence is recognized. They told us that we would be seen as criminals. And, yes, I go to work and I give my labor for less than it is worth. But that is not enough, they also take my dignity.

After two days in the safe house I gave my last five hundred dollars to be moved further north. I immediately starting working in construction, doing my best to learn English. Learning English is important because it opens doors of opportunity. I even used some of my earnings to learn how to do work with computers in order to advance myself.

Still, I live in fear, fear of being caught, fear of being returned, and of course, fear of having to cross that desert again. We say that to jump the border *es una ventura* (is an adventure). For some, like me, the adventure has been somewhat positive, because I am able to work hard to advance and to support my children whom I haven't seen in three years. That's the hardest thing about this adventure, not being able to hug my children, knowing that they will grow up not knowing who I am. It's enough to drive you mad. That's why for many, the adventure is also a nightmare. If the desert doesn't kill us, racism might. We are humans who work for our food. That should earn us some respect. That's not to romanticize us. Obviously, as in all races, there are those who do drugs and engage in violence. Some who cross over lose their morals and become too liberal. But do not treat all of us based on the actions of a few. Most are like me—just wanting to work and survive.

Testimony from a Border Activist
Dan Millis

Recently three young volunteers and I were on a No More Deaths[20] patrol in a remote desert canyon. We were dropping off water, food, blankets, shoes and socks along some remote migrant trails. Walking up the canyon, I saw some green shoes and, thinking they looked pretty new, began to yell, as we always do, *"Hola, hola! Tenemos agua, comida, somos de la iglesia . . . "* (Hello! Hello! We have water, food; we are from the church). I only got to the second *hola* before I saw her teeth. I quickly spun around and told my friends to stop.

In my three years of volunteering with No More Deaths, I had never before found someone dead in the desert. The feeling is horrible—so ugly, so frustrating, so tragic. I looked at my feet and said, "Goddammit." I'm still mad. Josseline was only fourteen years old. From El Salvador, she was heading to the West Coast to reunite with family members. I can't stop thinking of all the freshmen I taught at Verde Valley School. She could have been one of them.

The idea behind No More Deaths is to provide humanitarian aid such as water, food, and medical care to migrants in need. Every day a large number of people cross the border in search of work. Many of them find themselves in emergency situations as the result of becoming

---

Dan Millis was a high school Spanish teacher for five years before quitting to work as a full-time volunteer with No More Deaths.

lost, injured, or dehydrated. The climate near the border is harsh, especially during the rainy season, when nearly record high temperatures are interrupted only by violent, sometimes freezing, afternoon and nighttime thunderstorms. One such Saturday night while at the Arivaca camp, I saw the most incredible storm of my life. It would have rivaled any overdone and exaggerated lightning storm scene from a scary movie. For more than two hours I sat under a canopy and watched the wind, rain, and lightning. The lightning flashes were so rapid, intense, and frequent that it could have been a strobe light gone haywire. And it wasn't just sheet lightning—crazy loud thunder and big fat bolts of lightning hit just as hard, often, and close as a Flagstaff afternoon monsoon! Despite the comfort provided by the big huge canopy, I was scared, cold, and tired. Migrants who move at night don't have rain jackets, much less a canopy. They have to negotiate flooded washes, muddy trails, and a pitch-black sky (following the lightning) in addition to cactus, varmints, and unscrupulous humans occupying the border desert. I cannot even imagine.

During the summer of 2007 we found many people crossing over the border. Here are a few examples spanning just a couple of weeks: Guillermo whistled at me as I was driving down a dirt road. He had been drinking green, buggy water from a cow tank and had bloody blisters as big around as baseballs on both of his feet. Margarita, from Central America, had been wandering alone, moving during the hottest hours and hiding at night for fear of rape, when some of our volunteers stumbled upon her. She was far from a trail or road. Alfredo was also wandering alone in the desert and flagged down one of our trucks. He wanted to go back to Mexico, so we called the Border Patrol for him. He cheerily joked with our volunteers for the four hours it took the Border Patrol to show up and "arrest" him. Juan Carlos, eighteen years old, wandered into our camp alone after having looked for the "frihway" for four days (including during the Saturday night storm). All of these people ended up being deported.

Christian, whom our volunteers found on a trail, took all the food and water we could give him, gave a "thumbs up" and a smile, and continued on his way. Another volunteer and I stumbled on a group of two men and three women who had been out for five or six days but had been separated from their larger group and their guide for four or five of those days. For two days they were without water. One of them turned his ankle, another had blisters, and another had blood pressure problems and felt ill. Still they wanted to continue! The other volunteer and I hiked back to the truck to fetch as much food and water as we could carry. We gave it to them, along with some basic first aid, and as far as I know they kept going!

These people are amazing. It is not enough simply to recognize the humanity of migrants, to defend them from those who try to turn them into a statistic or something foreign that doesn't count. To me, the argument that "migrants are people too" is almost wrong. What they go through every day out here is totally beyond what I think people like you and I could endure. Nearly every migrant I mentioned above was totally cheerful and positive, despite the dire circumstances. These people are my heroes.

Not long ago a group of five or six migrants wandered into our camp, looking for help for a young woman who was feeling ill. She didn't have any serious problems that I could find, just a sore throat. But the rest of their group was hiding out in a nearby wash, and there were eighteen or nineteen of them. The smaller group took me to visit the wash, as several among the larger group were also sick.

I don't quite know how to describe my visit to a migrant camp, if you can even call it a camp. I'll tell you what I saw. The young woman held her boyfriend's hand. I followed them and their companions across open desert, carrying food and medical supplies. We walked quietly, listening for helicopter sounds. A helicopter had scattered them the day before, they said, but, miraculously, no one was caught or lost. We came to several barbed wire fences that they easily passed over, under, or through. I wondered how many dozens of fences they had come across during their nighttime hikes. We got to the wash and the relative safety of the trees, where people sat, stood, and squatted, looking mostly calm and very tired.

They hadn't eaten in two days, and the heavy box of food we brought was quickly emptied. *"Son uno por dos"* or something like that—one lunch pack for every two people. A chubby man was feeling ill, thirsty, and weak. He was diabetic. He was taking his meds, he said, and showed me a bottle of some sort of glucose-type pills. He said they were his insulin. I did not know what to tell him, except drink water, eat food, and rest. Earlier a slim young man with silver teeth and curly hair had drunk water from the creek. Since then, he had vomited a few times. Another guy had diarrhea. I also told them to rest, drink water, and eat food.

They didn't all look like hardy farm workers, but more like random people from the street—young adults who could be my buddies. There were at least three women, two of whom were young and pretty, like the ones you see at the mall. That is what I thought as I gave everyone the same advice, the same Tylenol and Emergen-C, and asked the same questions. They insisted no one had blisters or wounds, but I was doubtful. Everyone just wanted a magic pill and a big truck. This group was not far from the road, and they were waiting for their ride to come and take them further north. The ride was supposed to have come the day before but still had not shown. They were anxious. I was anxious. I am still anxious.

Their ride was supposed to be there at 12:30. It was 12:45, and I wasn't of any particular help, so I went back to camp, leaving instructions to come again if they needed anything. They said they would. That afternoon and night it rained. It rained steadily all night. Even my North Face tent wasn't keeping me dry. Those folks barely had trash bags, much less tents or sleeping bags. I really hoped their ride had come. When no one had come back to our camp for more food by the afternoon after the storm, I was pretty sure they were fine. It was time for the volunteers to move on, but we left a box of food out on the table with a note, just in case.

The next day a volunteer told me he went back to our camp. He had forgotten his shoes there. When he arrived he saw that the food we had left on the table had been eaten! A dozen and a half people sat in the rain all night in a wash. This is the same wash that flooded and flowed so strongly a week before that our volunteer campers were stuck at camp. Even the Border Patrol could not cross the brown, choppy waters. I don't know what happened to these folks, but I hope they are all right. My only consolation is knowing that they got some food and provisions that they otherwise might not have received.

Because obtaining a visa through official means is next to impossible, the majority of those who wish to come north cannot cross the border at a port of entry. Instead, our government builds walls to force them into the furthest, most inhospitable stretches of desert. As crossing without documents becomes more difficult, the price of the journey rises. Smuggling people is as profitable as smuggling drugs, so cartels are more involved and violence is increasing. "Securing the border" is a term that just means speeding up this vicious cycle. Each year hundreds of people die trying to cross the southern borderlands, walking north for a better life. People like Josseline. It is very rare for humanitarian aid organizations like No More Deaths to find a dead migrant in the desert. It happens about once a year. This year my friends and I are the unlucky ones.

Josseline Hernandez, age fourteen, was left behind because she could not keep up. Her body was found three weeks after she disappeared. According to the coroner, she died from exposure one week before her body was found.

TAKEN FROM A "LOST" POSTER.

I'm not writing this to ask for sympathy. I'm asking for action. Though the many calls and kind words I've received since finding Josseline are appreciated, I don't feel comforted. How can I take solace when finding a dead body in the desert is a regular occurrence in the United States? These deaths reveal the racism and inhumanity that is consuming our country. How can we feel secure when our neighbors are being rounded up as scapegoats in our own communities far from the border? How can anyone feel comforted when a kangaroo court called Operation Streamline[21] is forcing poor and hungry people to beg a judge for forgiveness for their "crime" of trying to feed their families, or face jail time and criminal records? The U.S. border policy is designed to neglect, berate, scapegoat, humiliate, torture, and kill innocent people. Let's change it. Now, goddammit!

Josseline's death is not counted by the Border Patrol because they did not participate in the discovery or recovery of her body. To them, she is a (no)body. Under her cross appear the following words: "When you feel that the path has become hard and difficult, do not give in to being conquered but continue forward and look for God's help. We will always carry you in our hearts."

Testimony on Being a Good Samaritan
Rev. Daniel G. Groody

During midsummer, while traveling in the southern part of Arizona, I found myself driving down the road near the town of Arivaca. I was about thirty miles north of the Mexican border when I passed a man on the side of the road. He was waving empty water jugs in his hands and obviously in need of help. I did not stop but kept driving. As I traveled down the road, I could not stop thinking about his situation. All at once the complicated laws at work on the border began to rush in on me. I realized I was not only at the border between Mexico and the United States, but at the border between national security and human insecurity, sovereign rights and human rights, civil law and natural law, and citizenship and discipleship. In the face of his need I knew I couldn't deliberate long and had to make a decision. Even as the summons to higher laws began to challenge me, I also began to consider the many good reasons why it would not be a good idea to stop and help.

If the Border Patrol pulled me over and found me aiding and abetting this person's entry into the United States, I would face one to ten years in prison. From the perspective of the gospel, if I ignored this person in need, the consequences could be graver. For one long mile three images went through my mind, each of which shaped my vision of pastoral theology and the immigrant. The first was the parable of the Good Samaritan (Lk 10:25–37). The second was the Last Judgment (Matt 25:31–46). And the third was that of an elderly priest, a good friend and a mentor who spent many years working with immigrants. Once, in a very similar situation, we drove by someone and he said, "I never take chances with people like that." Surprised by his words, I said, "What do you mean?" He replied, "That's Jesus over there, and we need to welcome him."

These three stories made me turn the car around to go back to help this person. The man I met was winded and weathered, and his voice was weak and weary because he had gone days without food and a day

Daniel G. Groody is an assistant professor of theology and director of the Center for Latino Spirituality and Culture at the University of Notre Dame.

without water. His name was Manuel, and his first words to me were, "I just want to turn myself in to the Border Patrol." He said he had looked death in the face, and he wanted to exchange his freedom for a ticket back to Mexico. He began his journey with a few friends, but later he had trouble keeping pace with them, so they left him behind. They knew he would get lost, even die, but they kept going. "At that point, I was lost and disoriented," he said. "I didn't know which direction was north, or if I ever would get to a road and find some help. So I just prayed and prayed."

Manuel's story is all too common on the border. Desperate to survive the long and arduous journey, some immigrants resort to drinking out of livestock feeding troughs or drinking their own urine. For many it is a journey to the very margins of life. In the midst of heat exhaustion, within hours of dying, one immigrant said:

> My body started doing crazy things. I couldn't hear right and I had this loud, buzzing sound in my head. I felt dizzy and had terrible headaches. Blisters covered my feet, and then my arms and legs began to feel numb. My throat swelled up, and my heart began to beat real slowly, until everything felt like it was moving in slow motion. Everything turned black and white, and, at that moment, all I wanted to do was die, for I felt only death could liberate me from my suffering.

Some describe their situation in terms of living in between *guatemala* and *guate-peor* (between a bad state and a worse state). As one man put it, "The desert is dangerous, but my need is great. The fact is, I'm already dead in Mexico. By crossing the border I have a chance to live, even if I die."

These are glimpses into the stories of thousands who try to cross daily, who walk for days in a no man's land, trying to avoid detection by the Border Patrol. Since Operation Gatekeeper and similar border-control initiatives began in 1994, migrants have been diverted into more dangerous areas like the Sonoran Desert to make it into the United States. Desperate in their misery, they are forced to travel through hellish territory in order to get jobs in America that, ironically, no one else wants to do—jobs that entail stoop labor in scorching fields, deboning chicken in poultry plants, cleaning bathrooms in restaurants, and other menial work. In addition to helping immigrants with immediate needs and fighting for more just and humane legislation, the pastoral challenge resides in learning to see immigrants in a different way. It means going beyond the labels of *undocumented, illegal,* and *alien* and seeing in each and every person an inner dignity and a God-given worth.

In its own story of migration Israel was delivered not only from a specific geographical place (Egypt, *mitsrayim,* which in Hebrew means "narrow places") but also from a narrow way of thinking. Liberation at Sinai was not simply about taking off the shackles, it meant taking on a new mindset, adopting a new way of looking at the world, living out a different vision, and ultimately learning to love as God loves. The migration of Israel after the Exodus was meant to help Israel reenvision how to live in the world, which proved more challenging than the geographical migration. It was easier to take Israel out of Egypt than to take Egypt out of Israel. After coming to power and prosperity, Israel frequently forgot its history and subsequently mistreated those who came to it as strangers and immigrants. Seeing Christ in the eyes of the immigrant and seeing the immigrant with the eyes of Christ involve a different kind of movement, a cognitive migration. It means not only speaking about God to people like Manuel, but letting Manuel reveal something of who Christ is today.

One way to think about Christ in immigrants is to think about them in terms of what Ignacio Ellacuría called "the crucified peoples of today." Many immigrants experience an economic crucifixion as a poor man, a political crucifixion as an illegal alien, a legal crucifixion as a border crosser, a cultural crucifixion in coming to a new country, and, above all, a social crucifixion in piercing loneliness. One of the most difficult parts of immigration is not the physical journey but the feeling that you are no one to anybody.

Another way of seeing immigrants is to contemplate ways in which they embody the presence of Christ. Matthew 25:31–46 speaks not only about the judgment of individuals but the judgment of nations and the response to those deemed the most vulnerable and insignificant. Hungry in their homelands, thirsty in the deserts, naked after having been robbed, sometimes at gunpoint, of their possessions, sick in the hospitals, imprisoned in detention centers and, if they make it, estranged and marginalized, those stranded by the side of the road leave us with questions about the ways Christ is present in those we are so ready to ignore or reject.

In my encounter with Manuel and others like him I was often surprised by the strength of their faith in God, even after having to undergo such a godless journey. Amid his trials he said he depended more than anything else on his faith: "I thought the people I left with were my friends, but they really weren't. When I was all alone I realized that the one and only friend who will never abandon me is God. He was the only one with me in the desert when everything else was taken away." When asked what parts of the Bible spoke to him, he said it was Job who gave him insight and helped him through his trials. "Job lost everything: his friends, his family, his livestock, his house, and his health. Job's story is my story. I've lost everything, and about all I have learned is how to suffer. But in Job's case, he never cursed God. And I've always been inspired by him, because I want to be faithful to God as Job was, even with all my struggles."

As difficult as the physical struggles are, however, many immigrants say that the most difficult part of the journey is the indignities they face. When talking with one immigrant in a detention center, he said, "I've walked across deserts in the scorching heat. I've slept in the mountains in the freezing cold. I've stowed away in buses and trains and known what it is like to go without food or water for days on end. But what is the worst is when people treat you like a dog, like you are the lowest form of life on earth. Nothing hurts more than feeling like you are not even worthy to be a human being." Pastoral ministry to the migrant begins with recognizing that the greatest hunger of the migrant is not only for food but to be valued as a human being.

Saint Augustine interpreted the parable of the Good Samaritan in light of the incarnation. He saw the wounded man as a symbol of a broken humanity and Jesus as the one who reached out to his neighbor in need. In the act of God becoming human, God redraws the borders between people, making strangers into neighbors, and aliens into members of a common family. The Last Judgment brings out new possibilities for encountering God when we cross the borders of our own comfort zones and meet Christ in the poor and insignificant. Paradoxically, to close ourselves off from those in need not only deprives the needy but dehumanizes those who have the opportunity to help.

Testimony about the Border Patrol
Gene Lefebvre

No More Deaths volunteers encounter Border Patrol agents in the desert south of Tucson, Arizona, on a daily basis. Sometimes it causes us to wonder about the origins of this militaristic force and what its role is today. It's barely more than one hundred years old. As early as 1904, mounted watchmen of the U.S. Immigration Service patrolled our country's borders, working as far west as California to restrict the flow of illegal Chinese immigration. This short-lived effort failed as workers came into demand to work on the railroads and in the mines needed to build the West.

The Immigration Act of 1921, followed by the Labor Appropriation Act of 1924, officially established the U.S. Border Patrol to secure the U.S. borders between border inspection stations. In those first days, and continuing today, two of the basic values that shape the Border Patrol are professionalism and respect for human life.

In Arizona, where I was born and grew up, the Border Patrol had to come to terms with the reality of the ever-present back-and-forth flow of migrant workers from Mexico and other southern nations. I remember as a child standing at the main port-of-entry in Nogales (now called the DeConcini Port-of-Entry, after one of Arizona's senators). Just a hundred feet away people came and went through a hole in the chain-link fence carrying shopping bags full of goods. Of course, some of the men were actually migrants heading to the inner country of the United States to work—picking apples in Washington, harvesting strawberries in California, slinging meat in packing plants in the Midwest. During their work period they sent home remittances via Western Union so their mothers and wives and children could survive. At the end of the season they reunited with their families.

No doubt the situation was frustrating for the Border Patrol. If a migrant made the sixty miles to Tucson, he was home free, because in those days the Border Patrol stayed along the border. In addition, if the

---

Gene Lefebvre is a retired Presbyterian minister who lives in Tucson. A co-founder of No More Deaths, he serves as an active volunteer in that movement. He was active in the Sanctuary Movement in the 1980s.

migrant was captured, he (there were few or no women in those days) could turn around and try again the next night. To the Border Patrol agents, it was all a game—and at times a dangerous game when drug-trafficking was in the mix. In short, Border Patrol agents felt ineffective and inadequately supported.

After 9/11 the federal government began to pour resources into what is now U.S. Customs and Border Protection in an attempt to cut the flow of unauthorized migration. When 9/11 happened, those of us in Arizona knew the threat of terrorism would be used as a rationale for further militarization of the border. In truth, the Border Patrol has doubled in size in the past eight years, and enormous sums of money have been spent to patrol the border and to build both real and virtual fences. At this writing, contractors are asking Congress for an additional $400 million for these barriers to add to the already-appropriated $2.7 billion.

The militarization process has not gone smoothly. Mandated and funded by Congress to increase their numbers, the Border Patrol suddenly had to train three thousand additional agents a year when five hundred was the norm. The Border Patrol has an academy, but recruits need not be high school graduates; however, they must have a GED, the equivalent of a high school diploma. The rush to put boots on the ground has led to substandard training. For example, when working in the hilly desert lands in southern Arizona, they should know how to use a global positioning system (GPS) and to read a topographic map. Nonetheless, No More Deaths volunteers encounter many agents who can do neither. I remember contacting the Border Patrol to come pick up some exhausted migrants who simply wanted to return to Mexico. It took the Border Patrol several hours to locate us because they did not understand what map coordinates were. They were unable to get to us without a lengthy process that ended with them sounding their siren and my yelling, "Yes, I can hear you; now you're closer, keep coming," until finally they arrived.

When the agents placed the migrants in their vehicle, they asked me how I was going to find my way home. When I told them I would take "this road" and it would quickly lead me to a paved highway, they wanted to know how to get to another highway where a Wackenhut bus, contracted by the Border Patrol to carry migrants, was stationed. Using a topographical map, I laid out a route for them. I was surprised they had never seen one. Their crude map showed only major roads in the area. They and other agents have been sent into unforgiving terrain without the necessary skills to function effectively.

More disturbing examples demonstrate Border Patrol agents' lack of preparation. They are frequently first at the scene of migrants in distress, with deep blisters, broken limbs, dehydration, exhaustion, and sometimes illnesses like diabetes or heart disease. During the winter I came upon a rollover automobile accident with residents of Arivaca, the main town near our No More Deaths camp. Eventually, eight Border Patrol cars showed up, none, apparently, with first aid kits. Fortunately, I was riding with a paramedic who took over the situation and helped the injured boy whose grandmother had died. I was disappointed that the Border Patrol agents seemed unprepared and didn't have ordinary first aid equipment or skills.

It really doesn't matter though. These particular agents probably won't stay in the area for more than six months before they are rotated to a different location. This prevents them from being subjected to possible bribes and from getting too close to the residents of the area. Not surprisingly, morale is low and turnover rates high; the Border Patrol has had turnover rates of over 30 percent for some time now. Much of their work is boring; in some cases, they are asked to sit on the top of a hill in blistering hot weather and keep an eye out for migrants. Often they are asked to patrol where there is little activity. Still, in an instant their job can become dangerous, with angry ranchers, terrified migrants, and armed drug smugglers populating the land.

Today's Border Patrol is under tremendous pressure. The agents know that much of their work fails in its mission to secure our borders. They also know that since they have been watching the borders more closely since 9/11, we have heard of no terrorist being caught in their net. In addition, they know the desperate migrants, determined to find a better life, will keep coming. We detect agents' frustration at checkpoint stations where encounters are brief, or when we run across them in the field, where sometimes we have a chance to converse at greater length. Ninety percent of my encounters have been positive. Recently, at a checkpoint near Arivaca, as one agent was passing us through, another agent jogged around our car and asked, "Are you the people who put out water? You're needed over by Hopkins Peak. There are lots of trails, and someone just died there." He recognized me by my bright blue FJ Ford Cruiser, which he'd seen before.

In the field I have had several agents tell me they respect and appreciate our work to end the deaths. In August 2008 the Border Patrol raided our humanitarian aid camp near Arivaca. Two agents who guarded me during my two-and-a-half-hour detention told me privately that they respect the work we do. I told them we respect their work also, but we are at cross purposes on interpreting the law about how far humanitarian organizations can go to aid the migrants. No doubt all of the agents there, at least fifteen of them, several on horseback (just like the old days), including a public-relations officer, would have no problem following orders, arresting me, and putting me in jail. But individual agents are beginning to understand that policies of our own government send migrants into a dreadful corridor. Desperate people willing to risk their lives in the desert make it difficult for the agents to halt their attempts at a better life. In fact, it is impossible.

We also see a dark side to the work of the Border Patrol. During the past two years No More Deaths and other humanitarian organizations have documented a long list of abuses of migrants, some of them egregious, while in Border Patrol custody. At this writing a report is being released, and hearings are being held in Washington with members of Congress and immigration rights groups. The coming election, of course, takes all the media attention.[22]

When working in the desert, No More Deaths volunteers do not think of the Border Patrol as an enemy (well, one of our volunteers flipped one agent the bird—we sent him home). But we are not naive. Over the past five years we have felt the noose slowly drawing tighter around the edges of our work. First, we were able to take the sick and wounded to the hospital in Tucson, but then we couldn't. We could give food and water to migrants waiting to board the bus, but now we can't. This summer [2008], three humanitarian aid workers have been cited with various crimes (putting out water is considered littering). The raid on our camp, the first such raid, was just the latest attempt to shut us down.

I believe that over the long run we will be successful in stopping the frequent tragedy of border deaths and the daily misery of hundreds of migrants racing through the 100-degree-plus heat to find safety. The passage of more humanitarian laws to meet the U.S. need for workers and to provide ways for migrants currently residing in the United States to become citizens will begin to address the deliberate efforts by our government to stem the flow of migrants by causing people to die.

Some Americans are pausing in their rhetoric against migrants. Law enforcement officers and others who have opposed our work in the past are becoming more sympathetic with what we do. No More Deaths' recent fund-raising appeal for money to fund gas and food packs and medical supplies brought in more than twice the amount of our previous appeal. We are encouraged by the support. Still, we recognize we are on thin ice with government strategists and at any moment could be jailed. I don't want to go to jail, but neither will I be shut down from providing humanitarian aid to nearby people who are at high risk of dying. Helping migrants is *my* cause. Everything I stand for, most of all, my faith, calls me to this place and this work at this time.

Voice of the People
Gene Lefebvre

SUE LEFEBVRE

Mother and Child

We met them on the square in Altar, a small town sixty miles south of the border, a crossroads for people crossing illegally into the United States. The young parents and their two-year-old daughter, Jennifer, were preparing to cross the next day. They would board a van to be taken to the Arizona border where a guide or *coyote* would lead them on their seventy-mile hike to Tucson. We talked with the parents, "You won't make it with your two year old.

The weather is very hot, and the trail is rough. You cannot carry enough water and your daughter for the five-day journey. It's five days if you don't get lost, injured, or arrested by the Border Patrol."

They looked straight at us and said, "We have no choice. There is no work and so no food for us to eat where we live. We know it will be hard, but what else can we do?"

People in our group bought walking shoes for the mother because she was wearing high heels. We continued to discourage them from going, but it was the only course they could imagine. We think of them often. What happened? Did they make it by some miracle? Or are they back home in their poor village in Chiapas, returned by the Border Patrol? They were one family among hundreds of migrants in the square that day, many with stories just as tragic.

2

Economic Realities

My message to them is, not in two weeks, not in two months, not in two years, never! We must be clear that we will not surrender America and we will not turn the United States over to the invaders from south of the border.
— REP. VIRGIL GOODE (R-VA)[1]

At [the present] rate of arrests, it would still take 2,943 years to deport the estimated 12 million undocumented immigrants.
— REP. ZOE LOFGREN (D-CA)[2]

Throughout 2007, tens of thousands of people demonstrated on the streets of Mexico protesting a 60 percent hike in the price of tortillas. The price increase was a direct result of the soaring international price of corn. But Mexico is not alone in its difficulties with the rising cost of food. The international increase in corn prices is causing havoc in many developing countries where inhabitants struggle to acquire sufficient food to maintain and sustain life. In the first decade of the new millennium, many poorer nations have experienced sharp spikes in food costs, especially corn. But what is causing the price of corn-based food products to rise? And more important for our purposes, how are corn prices affecting the rise of undocumented immigrants in the United States?

Before answering these questions, it is important to first understand that when Mexicans took to the streets in 2007 to protest, they were underscoring the significance of corn in Mexican society. Corn has historically been the lifeblood not just of Mexico, but of all the Americas. After all, it is estimated that 98 percent of U.S. Hispanics eat either corn tamales or corn tortillas every day. Tortillas are the second-highest-selling packaged bread product—selling at a rate of one tortilla a day for every American. Throughout Latin American, almost every country has its own unique national dish based on corn.

The Importance of Corn

It is difficult to determine when corn became a basic food substance for the Americas. Fossils of corn pollen discovered in lake sediment beneath Mexico City date back more than eighty thousand years. Still, it is believed that corn, as used today, was developed some fifty-six hundred to seven thousand years ago in the Tehuacán Valley and from there spread to southern Mexico and Central America. It was introduced to North American Indian communities, probably by way of the indigenous nations of the Chihuahuan and Sonoran deserts. Eventually, it became part of the staple diets of most indigenous people throughout the Western Hemisphere. A plant that does not naturally exist in the wild, corn was developed by humans from wild grass called *teosinte;* it survived because humans cultivated and protected it. A resilient crop, corn grows in areas below sea level and at altitudes of twelve thousand feet in the Andes Mountains. It can grow in areas that receive as little as twelve inches of rainfall each year and also those that record four hundred inches of yearly rainfall.

As ancient rock paintings demonstrate, the indigenous people who first grew corn regarded it as a sacred crop. It was honored in its various forms of maturation (seed, sprouting plant, and fully grown crop). Corn served as an appropriate sacrifice to several of the Aztec agricultural deities. To this day Mexican farmers sprinkle cornmeal on their fields during the planting season while chanting and praying for a successful crop so that it can provide health for the family and unity for the community. It was believed by the Mayans that the deities created humanity out of corn; hence, they came to be known as the "people of corn."

Corn became the major source of energy in the Meso-American diet. Corn, beans, and squash were known as the Three Sisters by Native peoples. These three crops, planted together, were the main source of food. To a great extent, the entire culture revolved around their cultivation and consumption. Maize, as corn was called by the Taíno indigenous people of the Caribbean, was eventually introduced to Europe by the colonialists, with Columbus first taking corn back to Europe. From there, it spread throughout the rest of the world.

Until recently, Mexican farmers cultivated corn the way their ancestors did for centuries, using a burro on a small plot of land and relying on the rain to irrigate the fields. A third of the crop was reserved to feed the family, and the rest sold at local markets. This simple formula kept the people fed during good and bad economic times. But, since the passage of NAFTA, at least 1.7 million Mexican farmers, unable to compete with cheaper imported subsidized corn from the United States, have lost their small plots of land. They have been forced either to emigrate to large Mexican cities where there is already high unemployment or to risk the dangerous border crossing to the United States. Ironically, NAFTA did not translate as a windfall for small U.S. farmers either; they too were negatively affected. More than thirty-eight thousand farms in the United States, primarily small family farms, have also gone out of business since NAFTA's passage.[3] To survive, U.S. farmers must mechanize their farms and employ fewer people. It seems as if the only winners of NAFTA are a handful of multinational corporations, especially those who had a hand in drafting the agreement.

Because the United States provides subsidies to U.S. farmers to underwrite the cost of producing their crops, U.S. farmers were able to sell their crops at a lower price than that of the international market. It is estimated that from 1995 to 2004, the U.S. government spent $41.9 billion on corn subsidies.[4] By contrast, the World Bank imposed structural adjustments upon Mexico in 1991 that eliminated all government price supports and subsidies for corn production. When U.S. subsidized corn is exported to developing countries, such as Mexico, local farmers who receive no subsidies from their government are unable to compete. Imported U.S. subsidized corn is thus sold at a lower price than corn grown in Mexico.

One would think that the availability of cheaper corn would benefit the Mexican people. Unfortunately, this has not been the case. In fact, the suspension of price controls on tortillas and tortilla flour caused their prices to triple. During the first decade of NAFTA, rural Mexican farmers witnessed corn prices plunging by as much as 70 percent, while the cost of food, housing, and other essential services skyrocketed by as much as 247 percent. The prices of some products—tortillas, for example—increased by more than 483 percent from January 1994 to January 1999. According to the Mexican Agricultural Ministry, one million Mexican farmers abandoned their farms a year after the initiation of NAFTA.[5] Studying the impact of ten years of NAFTA, the Carnegie Endowment for International Peace concluded that NAFTA has brought hardship to hundreds of thousands of subsistence farmers.[6] Not surprisingly, many of the farmers who abandoned their lands have since made the journey north.

For centuries corn has been used mainly to feed humans and animals. It has also been converted to sugar and alcohol (the cause of the 1792 U.S. Whiskey Rebellion). Recent attempts to find new energy sources that do not depend on foreign oil have led to the profitable venture of converting corn to ethanol to run engines. This new use of corn is rapidly changing the role corn has historically played in the Americas. For the ethanol industry to operate at full efficiency, larger shares of corn production must be acquired, diverting corn from human and animal consumption and causing steep rises in corn prices, which in turn, negatively affect the poor of the world. For example, to fill a twenty-five-gallon SUV tank with pure ethanol requires 450 pounds of corn—that is enough corn to provide the calories to feed one person for an entire year.[7]

The rising price of corn is further exacerbated by transnational agribusinesses like Cargill (U.S.) and Maseca (Mexico) that are able to speculate on future prices. With Mexican farmers squeezed out because of their inability to compete with U.S.-subsidized corn, U.S.-owned transnational traders are able to step in and monopolize the corn sector. They can use their power within the market to manipulate movements on biofuel demand and thus artificially inflate the price of corn many times over.[8]

The Effects of NAFTA

The end result is quite ironic. Thanks to NAFTA, the land where corn was first domesticated has now become dependent on U.S. corn imports. Take the example of Francisco Javier Ríos, a farmer from Bahia de Banderas in the State of Nayarit. Each year he has planted fifteen acres of white corn. Depending on prices and weather, his profit margin ranges from three thousand dollars to four thousand dollars. But with the final lifting of the last tariffs on corn (as well as beans, sugar, and milk) on January 1, 2008, Ríos worries that he will not be able to stay in business. And he's one of the lucky ones. According to Mexican officials, four-fifths of the nation's 2.6 million small farms have similar small plots and produce just enough to live on. Is it any wonder, then, that on January 30, 2008, tens of thousands of farmers took to the streets in Mexico City, protesting the end of corn tariffs? One of the main concerns voiced during the protests is that the elimination of trade barriers will drive many farmers off their lands, thus "inviting" more Mexicans to migrate north.[9]

The United States is in no rush to change the present system. Agriculture is one of the few sectors of the economy where the United States runs a trade surplus. But often American agricultural profits cause economic devastation on the developing nations of the world. Former World Bank president James D. Wolfensohn has connected the $1 billion a day wealthy nations "squander" on farm subsidies with their devastating impact on poor nations. To make matters worse, many wealthy nations place tariffs (at times exceeding 100 percent) on agricultural imports from developing nations, turning any attempt at giving them market accessibility into a "sham."[10] This has led Ian Goldin, the World Bank's vice president, to conclude that "reducing these subsidies and removing agricultural trade barriers is one of the most important things rich countries can do for millions of people to escape poverty all over the world." C. Fred Bergsten, director of the Institute for International Economics in Washington, was even more blunt: "Our American subsidy system is a crime, it's a sin, but we'll talk a good game and get away with doing almost nothing until after the [2008] presidential election."[11]

Undocumented workers are in the United States because of what immigration experts call the push-and-pull factor. The economic conditions existing in their homelands, due in part to our agricultural subsidies, "push" them out, while the U.S. need for cheap labor "pulls" them in. The presence of undocumented workers in the United States results primarily from economic conditions created, in good measure, by U.S. trade policies geared, thanks to subsidized corn (as well as other agricultural goods), to profit U.S. businesses at the expense of farmers in other countries.

Farmers who can no longer compete in the market with subsidized produce have little choice but to abandon their lands, the land of their ancestors, and venture into the cities with the hope of finding jobs in the factories. The former farmer, who now works for about $5 a day, can look out the window of the factory and see a McDonald's on the other side of the border where a high school student can make more in a few hours than the former farmer can make in a week. If only the former farmer could cross the border, then he or she could again feed a family. NAFTA has changed the equation for the poor. Working on someone else's land in a different nation now becomes the hope for survival.

Still, it would be a mistake to assume that the majority of those crossing the border are seeking employment in agricultural sectors. The continuous mechanization of U.S. farms is reshaping the types of jobs the undocumented are filling. Although the agricultural sector was once the predominant employer of migrants, it has been displaced by construction, industrial manufacturing, and the service sector. Still, the constant factor is that the undocumented continue to occupy the least-skilled and lowest-paid jobs, regardless of where they work. And there is high demand within the United States for unskilled workers. Nevertheless, the lack of documentation makes them susceptible to unscrupulous employers who hire them for dangerous jobs at or slightly above minimum wage where injuries are frequent and death a common occurrence.

The present immigration policies that have been devastating to Mexican farmers have also created chaos among U.S. farmers. This was not always the case. Since the military acquisition of what would become the southwestern United States, U.S. employers have imported foreign manual labor to develop the economic prosperity of the region and the nation. The increase of fruit production in California during the 1850s and 1880s established a close relationship between U.S. farmers and Mexican field hands. Whenever workers were needed, for example, during the construction of the transnational railroad in the 1880s and 1890s and during the First and Second World Wars, Mexicans were welcomed. However, during economic uncertainty, the United States has attempted to respond to the situation by deporting anyone with Central American indigenous features, specifically those with Mexican ancestry.

During the depths of the Great Depression, anywhere from half a million to one million Mexican immigrants and U.S.-born citizens with Mexican ancestry were rounded up and deported in an attempt to reduce welfare rolls. A similar immigration policy appeared in 1954 when the Immigration and Naturalization Service (INS) implemented Operation Wetback, responsible for deporting over 1.3 million immigrants and U.S. citizens of Mexican ancestry. We should not be surprised, then, that the present anti-immigrant sentiments that have arisen throughout the country correspond to the expanding economic downturn characteristic of the George W. Bush administration coupled with the increasing economic difficulties faced by many Americans due to the globalization of the economy. Deportation, then and now, was based on who looked Hispanic, a judgment that is particularly disturbing because all Latino/as are seen first as *not belonging*, as foreign, and thus in need of proving that they really do belong.

Most people have forgotten that documented immigration existed from 1942 through 1964. Over four million Mexicans worked on U.S. farms under the Bracero program. At the height of the program, during the late 1950s, an average of 438,000 workers with proper documentation crossed the borders to work on U.S. farms. They mostly traveled back and forth across the border, with few settling in the United States. Their brown hands made the United States the agricultural center of the world. A multitude of reasons, including abuses of farm workers, eventually brought an end to documented immigration. Regardless of the change in the law, since 1964 farm workers have continued to enter the country during the harvest, only now without documentation, to continue picking American crops. Between 1965 and 1985 millions of undocumented workers crossed the border for work and returned home after the work was completed. Out of the millions who came to work, only about 150,000 a year actually settled in the United States, with about an additional 59,000 with proper documentation arriving to stay.[12]

Using this informal system, U.S. farmers posted their need for workers in local Mexican newspapers. The laborers simply crossed the border. If they failed, they would simply try again the next day. It might take a few tries, but eventually the border would be crossed. The workers would then make their way to the fields in need of field hands. Once the work was done, the migrants returned home. Sometimes, employers actually called the Border Patrol so they would get a free ride back to the border. This "wink and a nod" allowed U.S. farmers to get their crops harvested, and it provided Mexican workers with the ability to feed their families back home. The real job of the Border Patrol was to make sure these workers returned at the conclusion of the harvest.

Operation Gatekeeper

The implementation of Operation Gatekeeper to deal with the consequences of NAFTA changed this informal system. As a result, few potential farm workers cross the border to work the fields, and those who do are less likely to return home after the harvest because of the difficulties in returning the following year. Operation Gatekeeper has eliminated the fluid flow of workers across the border in response to a need and put in its place a system that encourages workers to stay in the United States if their hazardous crossing succeeds. What was once a circular migration has become a permanent one that moves in only one direction.

Operation Gatekeeper has had two immediate results. First, the scarcity of field hands is creating chaos in the agricultural industry. In 2006, 20 percent of ripe agricultural products were not picked. In 2007 it is estimated that this figure reached 30 percent. Michigan growers were forced to leave their asparagus in the fields to rot, while North Carolina farmers lost nearly a third of their cucumber crop.[13] Second, those crossing the border to work on farms were forced to pay higher costs, in monetary and human terms, to the *coyotes*—whose power has been strengthened and solidified—because of the trails now moving through the mountains and treacherous deserts.

Nearly all parties agree that current U.S. policies on immigration, and particularly policies dealing with the Mexican/U.S. border, aren't working. Our agricultural trade policies contribute to the economic hardships of Mexicans and end up pushing them out of their homeland. Our present immigration policy actually encourages migrants to stay in the United States once they cross the border because of the life-threatening ordeal of crossing again. Both the foreign and domestic policies that we have developed and implemented make the undocumented within our midst a reality. Yet, rather than deal with the complexities that cause migration, we have instead blamed the victims for being pulled into this country. As long as we continue to ignore the basic economic causes of migration, no progress will occur. Our borders will remain broken, and the undocumented will continue to pay the price—at times with their lives.

Testimony from a Central American Farmer

"Marco"

"Marco" is a young Honduran man who is probably in his late twenties. He has a dark complexion, perhaps signifying some African ancestry. We are both spending the night at a migrant house

---

"Marco" is Subject #1, interviewed and taped by Miguel A. De La Torre on August 29, 2008. His story was translated, transcribed, edited, and then written by the interviewer.

*in Altar, Mexico. Marco is what is known as a subsistence farmer—
one who grows enough food for his family and sells the rest at the
local market. But Marco is now planning to make the dangerous
journey into the United States within a few days. After dinner, we
sit in the courtyard and he tells me why.*

Since I was a child of about ten years, I have been working the land.
Being a farmer is who I am, and what I want to do with my life. I work
the land with my father and with my brothers. We are a large family—
there are twenty brothers. That's a lot of mouths to feed. Raising
enough food is not always guaranteed. There are years when the harvest is not sufficient to sustain us, let alone provide anything extra to
sell at market. When you live on the farm, you can expect a certain
amount of poverty. There are some summers when it is too dry, and
there is a lack of sufficient water. Those summers you can lose your
entire harvest. But the cycles teach us to store during good times so we
can survive the bad ones.

For generations we have planted corn, along with coffee and beans.
In good years we grew enough to feed everyone in the family and had
some left over to either barter for goods we lacked or to sell at the local
market. We always seemed to survive. But since the mid-1990s, things
have become more difficult.[14] It became harder to get loans from the
bank to buy seeds and fertilizer. We began to be seen as a risky invest-
ment. Also during this time it became cheaper to buy corn and beans
grown in the United States rather than grow it ourselves. Poverty has
become more constant for my family. It's not that we don't want to
work the land; it's just harder to make enough when corn prices are
so low. You grow the corn, you grow the beans, you harvest the crop,
you have it there, but then, when the prices drop, it does you no good.
You just cannot make a profit. But regardless of the market, we managed to survive, raising almost enough for us to eat.

Basically there are two types of farmers. There is the farmer who
grows enough to be able to sell some of the harvest, and then there are
those who are able to grow just enough to feed their families. Because
of the low prices, we were no longer able to grow enough to produce
extra to sell at the market, causing our suffering to increase. We were
reduced to forgetting about the market and hoping only to grow
enough to feed ourselves.

But then things got worse. We lost the little we had left when the
hurricane came.[15] At that point we lost it all. The hurricane took away

our corn, it took away our coffee, and it took away our beans. It was total destruction. And with the little bit that was left, no matter how much we planted, there simply was not enough to feed our entire family.

There comes a point when the poverty is so severe, when the desperation is so great, when there is nothing more to lose, that the only option available is to emigrate. After a while, you start getting very hungry. Of course, you don't want to see your family suffering, so you leave. My family didn't send me north. Basically, I saw their suffering and I took it upon myself to try to fix the situation. I left my family in the hope of rebuilding our farm. When there is so much suffering, you begin to dream of going up north. Unfortunately, sometimes, all someone realizes is death. Still, you risk death because you do not want to suffer, and more important, you don't want to see your family suffer. Who would not sacrifice his life for his family? That is why I am here in Mexico with the desire to get to the other side.

It has been nine months since I left my country, and I still have not achieved my dream of getting to the other side. When I get to the other side, I plan to work hard to make some money so I can eventually come back and expand our land, rebuild the farm, and work the land. Basically, I want to do what I have always done: I want to work the land, but that dream seems to have turned into a nightmare. Three times I have made it across the border, and three times they caught me and sent me back. The first time I crossed over, I arrived in the morning in the United States, and by the afternoon they caught me and sent me back. The last time when I was there, we were caught in Tucson and our *coyote* just disappeared. He abandoned us. Now I'm going to have to pay a *coyote* $2,500 just to get me across to the other side. Because I am poor and I come from poverty, I will have to pay off the debt to the *coyote* by working in the north. This may take some time, but the arrangement is if I do not get across safely, I do not pay him.

My dream is to go to the north, work hard, and provide for my family. Of course, there are those in my country who do not even have this possibility, who do not even have land that they can work. They work just in order to get enough so they can buy food and live one more day. And here is the tragedy. Many people are afraid to explain the reasons why they are trying to cross over to the north because they are afraid that they will be seen as failures.

If I could say anything to the American people, what I would say is that we are coming because of the poverty that we are forced to live in and that we just want to try to reach that dream, the dream of being able to work and provide for our families. Each one of us that you find in the desert has left behind a family that we loved. Many of us end up lost in the desert, and some of us die. Our families will never hear from us again or know what has happened to us. We who are called wetbacks are just coming to work, so please have some compassion for us when we are risking our lives in the desert. I have twenty brothers and all of us work hard on the farm. They work the land just as I do. Look at my hands. You can see the calluses on them from working the land. My hands are the proof that what I am saying is true.

Testimony from a Euroamerican Farmer

Andy Grant

When I was a boy and my father had a small farm in Fort Lupton, Colorado, we never had "illegal" immigrants; they were just called migrant workers. I remember that the same migrant families would come up every year, work the land, and return home. I always looked forward to their return in the spring to hoe Dad's sugar beets. When they arrived, I once again played with their children while our parents worked in the fields. As a young boy it was all quite mystical for me to hear a different language; their clothes were different, and the food always smelled and tasted very good. Mostly I was amazed when their pickup truck with a camper shell on it came filled with all of their belongings—but also with watermelons—which at that time was an unusual treat so early in the summer. This was a time when produce for the most part was available only in its season.

But recently, our society has found a more evil term to make them seem like something different from hard-working people doing honest work. It is a politically polarizing term that makes these people appear to be "less than" in today's society, something to get people riled up politically. Yet we ignore that migrant workers are the lifeblood of

Andy Grant operates Grant Family Farms in Wellington, Colorado, a few miles south of the Wyoming state line. The farm was the first in the state to be certified as an organic farm.

Colorado. Our society prospers on their backs. It is really a shame how society has used migrants for the past four or five years for political gain. Instead, our society should be grateful for the work these people do. They work the fields under harsh conditions, standing and stooping twelve hours a day—regardless of whether it is cold and rainy or 100 degrees. It is not pleasant work; in fact, it is very hard work, and work that is boring. They are feeding America, yet Americans lack gratitude for the people responsible for putting food on their table. We turn around and snap at the people who feed us, work in our restaurants, and clean up after us. The scapegoating and villainization that my country and its citizens are inflicting on these people is absolutely wrong; it is immoral. Rather than address the real problem, that nobody in our culture wants to work in the fields, we blame someone else for everything. We fail sorely as a country to take personal responsibility for ourselves and the world around us. There is something profoundly disturbing here. Any culture that attacks the people who are feeding it is a culture that is really in trouble.

Two years ago, right before the 2006 elections, the Colorado Supreme Court struck down two ballot measures that were anti-immigration. The Republicans desperately wanted those measures on the November 2006 ballot, so that the party faithful would come out and vote on Election Day. When the state's Supreme Court struck down those two ballots in June, the Republican governor called the House and Senate back into a special session to get the Colorado legislature to place these measures back on the November ballot. Nor did the Democrats stand up to this injustice because it was getting too close to the election. So the Democrats bowed down to the Republicans, resulting in the toughest immigration laws in the country. Every Spanish-speaking television and radio station in the country carried stories about Colorado's anti-immigrant laws. This was devastating to us farmers.

Many workers who traditionally migrated to Colorado from Texas or Florida in the summer did not bother to return. They went to Wisconsin; they went to California. They were afraid to come back to Colorado. There were rumors and fear that the moment they crossed the Colorado state line, the police would be waiting to round them up and kick them back to Mexico. Most of our very steady year-in and year-out workers did not return to our farm. Even those who had proper documentation stayed away because they did not want to immerse themselves in a situation they felt was dangerous. Because I had fewer people working the fields, I lost over 50 percent of my crop! I grew it but left half of it in the field because I did not have the bodies to go out and pick the produce. Millions of dollars of good food went to waste, even after the gleaners from the food bank took all they could. Because there were no workers to weed the fields, some of the crops were never able to mature properly.

It really bothers me to see how hard these people work on my farm and other farms, and yet have to be fearful about their place in society. They work hard and pick the food Americans eat, yet they are denied secure sleep with the knowledge that they are safe. First there was the moral debate over gay marriage—a debate whose real purpose was to get people politically energized. Now we have the moral debate about illegal immigrants, but the real morality in this debate is how our actions are breaking apart families. How dare the pious in America talk about family values! Before, the migrants would come, work, and return to their families in Mexico. But we have "closed" the border.

The truth of the matter is that the door at the border is not closed. It has simply become a one-way door. We have not sealed the border coming this way; we have only sealed the border going back. Before, they would come up to Colorado in the summertime and make money, returning to their own farms in Mexico in September and October when the rains started. Now, decades go by without our workers being able to return and see their families or work their lands. After years of not returning home to their families, they start getting lonely and they start new families here. Our immigration policies are responsible for fostering this immorality and destruction of families.

Why don't I just hire Anglo Americans to do the work of migrants? No "American" person is going to come to my farm and work ten to twelve hour days picking spinach or onions. The offer is always open. We will give anybody a job any time to work in the fields. Yet I have not had an Anglo person work in the fields for the past five years. Why? Not only is it backbreaking work, but our culture does not respect or honor those who work on farms and in fields. We are becoming Rome!—a fat, lazy society that cannot even feed itself. We focus on material things, consume more, and look down on those who serve us. In the last twenty years I cannot think of an Anglo person who has come to work in the fields who has lasted longer than a week.

When we speak about NAFTA, we need to also keep in mind how it affects U.S. farmers. The problem I'm having is that I am forced to compete with produce grown in Mexico, where workers receive far lower wages. On our farm we pay our workers a guaranteed minimum wage. On greens and on onions, we also have piece-rate systems over and above minimum wage. I'm happy with the minimum wage going up. It's hard to live on $5.15/hr. Let's just say that the minimum wage is $7.25, but the worker's overall average is closer to $8.50 or $9.00 an hour. I cannot compete with Mexican agriculture when the minimum wage there is around $6.00 *a day*! For example, Mexico is delivering cilantro into Houston for $7.00. When I'm paying between $8.50 and 9.00 an hour for labor, Mexico's prices are below my cost of production. So in this case, NAFTA is actually working against me as an American farmer. My prediction is that in ten years a majority of the vegetables and fruit we eat will be grown in Mexico. Once American farmers quit, generations of know-how will be lost, never to return. One does not just start growing things and find success—it takes years, decades, even generations to master the skill of growing vegetables in local climates. But Mexican agriculture cannot compete on commodity crops like corn and beans, which are the staples of the Mexican diet. By mechanizing American farms, American farmers are able to produce corn and beans more efficiently than Mexican farmers.

Because of the labor shortage we are farming two thousand acres, half are in corn and wheat, which is mechanized, and the other half in vegetables. We need 250 employees at peak season to bring in the harvest. Three years ago we were farming two thousand acres of vegetables, and we had about five hundred employees. But because of the revised immigration policies, we have had to change the crops we grow so that we could cut in half the number of workers we need. The writing is on the wall. We will continue to downsize our non-mechanized acreage.

Testimony from a Rancher on the Border

Joseph Arachy

For fifteen years I have owned and operated an eighty-acre ranch that sits about ten miles from the U.S.-Mexican border. By horseback,

Joseph Arachy is a rancher whose land is close to the Mexican border.

it takes me about five hours to get to the border. I love living out here. It is peaceful. When I purchased this land I knew nothing about the illegals. In fact, I never saw any illegals for the first five or six years. Today it is a different story. So many are coming through my land that it is causing difficulties for us ranchers.

The illegals affect us ranchers without realizing it. For example, they carry food wrapped in plastic and liquids in plastic bottles. When they finish eating or drinking, they drop their plastic on the ground. They don't exactly come over with trash bags to pick up after themselves. There is a problem when one of our livestock comes by and eats this plastic. Some of them die because the plastic gets stuck in their digestive tracts. Also, the illegals come to our water tanks and carelessly use our entire supply. They have done it a couple of times to me. They turn the water faucet on and forget to turn it off. I come out to get a drink of water in the morning, and there is no water. They drained my tank dry, and they did this about 1 or 2 o'clock in the morning.

But in spite of the problems they cause, I do not blame them. I blame our government, Republicans and Democrats alike, for the mess they created and their refusal to legislate humane immigration laws. Now it is important to note that I believe in the ideals of this country. I am a patriot and served my country in Vietnam. My duties there have resulted in medical issues and my present state of being disabled and retired. But being a patriot does not change the fact that these illegals are human beings. I have one neighbor that figures the water being left on the trails somehow attracts them. So he goes out and punctures holes in the water jugs. I think what he is doing is wrong. Somebody could be out there starving and thirsty. Not long ago we had a girl die not far from my home who was only fourteen years old. Ironically, she was near a water tank. She was dehydrated and simply died. That is uncalled for. I just don't understand how we can have Christians who believe that giving them food and water is wrong. You don't have to go too far into the Bible before discovering that you have to take care of your brethren.

My house is among those closest to the border. It sits on top of a hill. When I have my dining room light on, it is like a lighthouse that shines out into the dark mountains. Many come out of the mountains, hungry and thirsty, see the light, and follow it to my house looking for help. Before, whoever knocked on my door looking for food or water was always welcomed. But now the new law says that I cannot bring them into my house. What am I supposed to do when winter comes? I may just have to take an electric heater and put it outside for them or give them blankets. You are not allowed to put them in a building because you would be accused of providing safe housing or harboring illegals. I just thought I was responding to a fellow human in need. How can I, or any one of us, turn our backs on a human being who needs a cup of water or some food?

I let one guy who came to my door into my air-conditioned house; he was so overcome by the coolness that he just passed out. He came knocking on my door. I asked him if there was anybody else, and he said no. He just could not go any further. His feet were real bad. The soles of your feet are pretty thick, but when they bubble up with blisters, it becomes very painful. You don't want to drain the blisters because then they get infected. And a lot of them think that by lacerating the blisters they release the pressure. What they need to do is stay off their feet. But they simply do not have the luxury to just rest. They persevere and keep going to the extreme limits of endurance.

The present system is just broken. What we should do is have an open border. Of course there needs to be restrictions. We should not let criminals enter. I would be happy to see some kind of workers' program in place. That would stop this unauthorized flow of people into our country. Under such a system they would pay taxes, have Social Security when they retire, and go to Mexico and live a decent life. Unfortunately, some of my fellow ranchers have a misconception about all of these illegals. Yes, you have your bad elements, but you have your bad elements among Americans too. Some senators living in Pennsylvania or Idaho or Kansas might know a little bit about immigration, but they really don't understand the situation. They may see the Mexicans working in their hometowns and see them as cheap labor. And in the event you don't want to pay them much, you simply don't pay them. The Mexican has no recourse because if he complains, he'll get reported and deported. It's like some form of slave labor.

When people talk about the border, they are literally speaking about my backyard. It is so easy to blame the illegals for the problems we ranchers are facing with the flow of humanity that crosses our lands. But the real culprit is our government, which refuses to enact comprehensive immigration reform to provide a safe and humane passage for the laborers we need to do those jobs white America will not do.

Testimony from a U.S. Day Laborer
"Alberto"

"Alberto" has worked as a documented day laborer in the United States for about eight years, but a trip home to El Salvador resulted in losing his status. Sitting in the public square in Altar, Mexico—the gathering place for those attempting to cross the border—Alberto prepares to return to the United States, but this time as an undocumented. He appears to be in his mid-thirties and possesses strong Mayan features.

The first time I went to the United States was toward the end of 1999. I left behind my family in El Salvador so that I could earn enough money for them to eat and for my children to go to school. If they do not get an education, they will not be able to succeed and have a better life than mine. When I crossed the borders that first time, I did not have any documents. But by 2001, I attained the proper papers to be able to stay and work. I lived in Washington DC, where a large Salvadoran community exists. I worked in construction. Each day we would gather at certain locations around the city where those needing our services would drive by and offer us a job. Toward the end of my stay in the United States, I was making about $60 a day. The work was hard and most of the time we were treated poorly, as if we had no dignity. We were usually given the worst jobs at a construction site. Nevertheless, I saved my earnings, living frugally so that my family back in El Salvador could survive.

I lived in the United States with documentation for eight years, but then in October 2007, I returned to El Salvador because my daughter, who was then fifteen years old, became gravely ill. It was bad enough that I was separated from her for eight years. As a father, I just needed to be there. Thank God, she got better. At first I thought of staying in El Salvador with my family, but knowing that the country is very poor and few opportunities exist, I decided in March 2008 to return to the United States.

"Alberto" is Subject #3, interviewed and taped by Miguel A. De La Torre on August 30, 2008. His story was translated, transcribed, edited, and then written by the interviewer.

Even though I had been documented, I lost that documentation because I left the country without notifying the proper authorities. Frankly, I let the forms lapse and was thus denied reentrance. I crossed the border anyway but was caught in Texas, where I was arrested. After thirty-seven days in jail I was deported back to El Salvador. A few months later I crossed the border again and went back to Texas. But once more I was caught, this time in Houston. I was arrested and deported for the second time. So, basically my plan is to attempt a third return to the United States. My only motivation is to be able to provide for my family, which is having economic difficulties because the economy in our country is very, very bad. With the money I made when I worked in the United States, my family was able to buy a house. I'm to the point that I have placed my house up as collateral to pay for my passage into the United States.

My only hope right now is that God will listen to my prayers and have mercy on me and my family. I pray that God will allow me to return to the United States so that my family can become more financially secure. Even though I know that once I arrive in the United States we could lose our house in El Salvador, I am hopeful that in the long run it will be for the best. The way I worked the deal is that once I arrive, the man there will go ahead and pay off the *coyote* that got me across the border. In return, I will give him the house as collateral, and then I will work and pay off this man what I owe plus interest. After I pay him off, I get back the house. The deal is that this will not happen until I actually get into the United States and start working again. Basically, my wife in El Salvador will sign off on all the papers and sign the mortgage once I'm in the United States and once I'm working.

The fee to the *coyote* will not be so high because I will make most of the journey myself. Many think that we just have to cross one border. But for those of us in Central America, we have to cross many borders. In each country we pass through, we get harassed by the police authorities or beaten and robbed by bandits. There are those who are called the "pull-downs" because they pull down all your clothes and leave you naked on the trails to make sure they took everything of value you might be hiding. To get from El Salvador to the United States costs anywhere from six thousand dollars to seven thousand dollars. Fortunately, because I have done this several times, I know the route between El Salvador and Altar, Mexico. By jumping onto trains and pretending I was an Indian from whatever country I was passing through, I was able to once again make it to this point. In reality, that was the hardest part of the journey. This last leg of crossing into the United States is easier. Coming on my own from El Salvador saved me a great deal of money. I did not have to pay anywhere close to the six thousand dollar to seven thousand dollar figure. The cost will only be two thousand dollars to pay the *coyote* to get me across the border and to the United States. I know I am gambling everything—but what other options do any of us here have?

Testimony from a Labor Organizer
Rev. Daniel Klawitter

At my ordination as a deacon in the United Methodist Church, I was "set apart for the ministry of love, justice, and service; of connecting the church with the most needy, neglected, and marginalized among the children of God" (*United Methodist Book of Discipline*, par. 319). In fulfilling this sacred charge, I have exercised a somewhat unique ministry in the Labor Movement. From 2002 to 2007 I was a full-time union organizer with the Service Employees International Union (SEIU) Local 105 in Denver. Although I worked primarily in the Health Care Division of that union, representing mental-health-care employees, I also spent some of my time supporting SEIU's low-wage immigrant janitors.

The Justice for Janitors campaign actually began in Denver in 1985 and was characterized by nonviolent civil disobedience and street theater in order to attract attention to the plight of these low-income workers. Many immigrant janitors are from Mexico, and no one knows exactly how many might be undocumented. You would think that undocumented workers would be afraid to engage in high-risk public actions that might lead to deportation, but in 1990 janitors in Los Angeles held a three-week strike to improve their wages and benefits.

Daniel Klawitter is the religious outreach organizer for the Front Range Economic Strategy Center.

On June 15 the L.A. police beat and injured twenty-four janitors who were engaged in a nonviolent demonstration with approximately four hundred of their fellow workers.[16] The media videotaped the assault and the police department was found guilty in court of causing a riot. As a result, SEIU Local 1877 was able to win a 25 percent pay raise for the janitors and fully paid health-care benefits, the best labor contract any janitors in the United States had won in the previous two decades.

My first exposure to the struggle of janitors occurred while I was still in seminary at Iliff School of Theology in Denver. In the summer of 2000 I was accepted into an innovative religion and labor internship program sponsored by the AFL-CIO (American Federation of Labor-Congress of Industrial Organizations) and the National Interfaith Committee for Worker Justice (www.iwj.org). The program sends seminarians around the country to work with labor unions for the summer and to build relationships between union leaders and religious communities. I was assigned to build religious support for SEIU Local 105 in Denver.

At that time SEIU Local 105 represented two thousand low-wage immigrant janitors who cleaned the largest office buildings in the downtown area. At the beginning of the campaign for a new contract, many janitors worked only part-time and made $6,500 a year. At the end of the campaign janitors had the opportunity to transition to full-time work, earning $18,928 a year *plus* health insurance and family prescription-drug benefits. The economic impact of this contract on the lives of janitors in Denver was amazing. In some cases it meant an end to the choice of paying rent or buying groceries for their families.

While much of the labor movement is losing members, SEIU has grown to be one of the largest unions in the United States, representing over 1.8 million members. Much of this growth has been due to SEIU's willingness to organize immigrant workers. And thankfully, they are not alone. Other unions in the agricultural, food service, hotel and laundry industries are aggressively organizing immigrants to fight for their rights on the job.

As our national economy moves from a manufacturing base to a service-sector economy, it is my belief that immigrants are the future of the labor movement and hold the greatest promise for organized labor's return to influence. However, not everyone in the labor movement shares my positive analysis of immigrants and their potential to revitalize organized labor. Particularly in some of the more conservative building trades, some unionists still see immigrants as the enemy: illegal aliens who drive down wages for everyone else. But the "low-wage effect" of immigrants on native-born labor is often grossly exaggerated. The National Academy of Sciences did a study in 1997 that concluded that the increase in low-wage immigrant workers in the 1980s *may* have cut pay by 1 to 2 percent for all competing native-born workers. Furthermore, this effect was strongest on the 10 percent of U.S. workers who had dropped out of high school. In other words, immigrants tend to take jobs that are classified as unskilled and do not require a high level of education and training.

Another fact that is often overlooked is how U.S. economic policy itself is largely responsible for driving immigration patterns from the South in the first place. For example, after implementation of NAFTA in the early 1990s, more than 1.5 million Mexican farmers lost their sources of income and were forced to give up their farms. In 2005 Mexican farmers earned 70 percent *less* for their corn than they did before NAFTA, while at the same time they were paying 50 percent *more* for tortillas! No wonder so many people are willing to cross the border and risk their lives to support their families.

In conclusion, if the labor movement is to survive in the twenty-first century, it must organize all workers according to the work they perform, not according to their country of origin. In the 1950s union membership in the United States stood at a high of 35 percent. Today, only 12 percent of the work force is unionized. This is frightening because back when unions were strong they were able to negotiate social policies that helped *all* working people rise out of poverty, not just union members. Social Security, the eight-hour work day with paid overtime, vacations, and pensions all came about because of the power and influence of organized labor and its allies.

But today, 1 percent of the richest Americans own almost *half* of the country's wealth, and perhaps most shocking of all, the average CEO in America today makes over 360 times what the average worker makes. If organized labor wants to reverse this trend, it must rely on the passion, courage, and self-sacrifice that immigrants have always brought to this country.

Voice of the People

This family rests in Altar prior to crossing the border.

CROSSING THE BORDER
Daniel Klawitter

It is a crime to be criminalized
for crossing a border
that crossed you first.

When will they realize
that walls made of mortar
can't contain the desperate thirst

for a better life
and a heavier purse
in the land of milk and honey?

It is a crime to be cursed
for speaking a language
that doesn't fit their Story.

And as for those who worship
the red, white and blue
of Old Glory . . .

well, let's just say it's usually true
that the people waving that flag
at you are neither red nor blue—

which leaves only one hue
that is, in fact, the absence
of pigmentation.

That no human being is illegal
in the eyes of the angels
seems to escape their imagination.

And as the cries of "Go back to Mexico!"
arise with religious indignation,
I wonder what these patriots will do

when they finally cross through
the door of death and come at last to
the guarded gate of God's own town . . .

And discover to their horror,
that Jesus crossed the border
and Jesus Christ is brown.

3

Demythologizing the Immigration Debate

The brown toxic cloud strangling Los Angeles never lifts and grows thicker with every immigrant added. . . . The streets of L.A. shall sink into a Third World quagmire much like Bombay or Calcutta, India. When you import that much crime, illiteracy, multiple languages and disease—Americans pick up stakes and move away.

—FROSTY WOOLDRIDGE[1]

Juana Villegas lay on a bed in Nashville General Hospital giving birth to her son. One of her feet was cuffed to the bed post. In the room, standing guard, was a sheriff's officer. Her husband was barred from being present at the birth of his son and wasn't even allowed to speak to his wife. After giving birth, she was separated from her nursing infant and returned to jail. She was prohibited from taking to her cell a breast pump that had been given to her by a hospital nurse. As a result, her breasts became infected, and her son developed jaundice.

What horrific crime did Mrs. Villegas commit to warrant this level of security, this violation of basic human dignity? She was pulled over on July 3, 2008, in the Nashville suburb of Berry Hill for careless driving. Rather than getting a citation for driving without a license (a misdemeanor), which is standard procedure when non-Hispanics are pulled over, she was arrested and taken to Davidson County Jail where a background check revealed that Mrs. Villegas, who was nine months pregnant and had lived in the United States since 1996, was undocumented.[2]

This raises disturbing questions about the racial profiling of Hispanics. If a Euroamerican motorist was stopped and failed to be carrying a driver's license, would she also be arrested? Would she have been taken back to the station to have her documentation checked? If not, why would there be such different treatment between Latina/os and non-Hispanics? Are Latina/o-looking people being arrested on flimsy charges in order to verify their documentation status? In other words, based on ethnic characteristics, are all Hispanics guilty of being un-documented until proven innocent? The predicament of Mrs. Villegas clearly illustrates what happens when local police who lack proper training in federal immigration laws supersede their authority.

Fear and suspicion of the stranger, the foreigner, the alien, the other is not a new phenomenon in U.S. history. Arguments made today about the refusal of Hispanics to assimilate into the mainstream culture are the same arguments that were made against the Germans in the eighteenth century. In 1753, for example, Benjamin Franklin lamented that a "swarm" of "swarthy" German immigrants was pouring into Pennsylvania, making the entire state into "a Colony of Aliens," because they would "never adopt [Anglo] language or customs."[3] During the mid-nineteenth century the Irish were seen as a subhuman race prone to crime and disease—an inferior people at the evolutionary level of African Americans—who were incapable of assimilating. By the start of the twentieth century it was the Italians and Eastern Europeans who were seen as inferior. Nativist sentiments led President Warren G. Harding to sign the first immigration Quota Act in 1921. A fear existed among nativists that unrestricted immigration of "undesirable" groups would lead to the adulteration of America.

This continued fear of the alien within our midst has led to over fifteen hundred anti-immigrant legislative bills introduced in state houses throughout 2007—a clear indication that the federal government has failed to deal adequately with the present immigration crisis. Of these, 244 became law, three times more than in 2006.[4] To pass these legislative bills, an anti-immigrant frenzy had to be maintained—a frenzy that often suggests that Hispanics are a subhuman race prone to crime and diseases, an inferior people incapable of assimilating. The rhetoric used by anti-immigrant groups and politicians often consists of the following arguments.

1. They are using up our services and contributing nothing financially.

A major component of anti-immigrant rhetoric is the assumption that the undocumented are fleecing the resources of our social services and that their presence is an economic burden on the country. Like parasites, they use the social services to which U.S. taxpayers are entitled.

However, most researchers agree that the economic contributions made by the undocumented, through stimulating labor and purchasing consumer goods and services, outweigh any costs of needed social services. According to economist William Ford of Middle Tennessee State University, the majority of economists agree that the undocumented are a net benefit to the U.S. economy. Ford calculates that they contributed $428 billion dollars to the nation's $13.6 trillion gross domestic product in 2006.[5] As was demonstrated by the testimony of farmer Andy Grant in the previous chapter, their absence would definitely have a negative impact on local economies.

As the undocumented leave, communities suffer. Mesa, Arizona, illustrates this point well. Reed Park, a predominately Hispanic neighborhood in Mesa, is feeling the effects of anti-immigration legislation coupled with a sagging economy. The families and businesses of central Mesa are disappearing. Although it is still too early to provide reliable data, 2007 witnessed more vacant houses and apartments, a sharp drop in business catering to Hispanics, and a decline in church and school attendance. According to Cynthia Garza, a city Neighborhood Outreach coordinator, "From what you hear in the neighborhood, people have packed up and left and have gone to other states, or have gone back home to their country." It is estimated that the neighborhood's vacancy rate is as high as 40 percent, driving landlords, out of desperation, to put up "For Rent" signs that read "Gratis Renta" [Free Rent].

As Hispanics leave, businesses catering to them become more vulnerable. Luis Campos, who owns a music store, estimates a 60 percent drop in business. Harry Kirakosia, who owns a small shopping strip mall, was forced to close one of his stores and is now contemplating closing the laundromat. According to Kirakosia, "The city councilman comes by and asks us what he can do to improve the area and we keep telling him he's got to protect us from the sheriff [Joe Arpaio] and immigration because those are the people we cater to right now. Nobody listens."[6] Central Mesa's predicament is one that could become the norm in other communities with substantial Latina/os as communities continue to get swept up in the anti-Hispanic hysteria prevalent throughout the nation.

State economies are also affected by anti-immigrant legislation. Many states stand to lose billions of dollars in lost sales and business revenues, as well as tax revenues collected from the undocumented in the form of sales taxes, property taxes, and excise taxes. Oklahoma is a good example. A state bill written by Republican Randy Terrill that took effect on November 1, 2007, prevents undocumented immigrants from obtaining driver's licenses and public services. As a result, many foreign-born workers fled the state, taking their local spending dollars with them. Since the law took effect, school enrollments have declined, construction work has slowed for lack of workers, and rental units have emptied. A study commissioned by the Oklahoma Bankers Association estimates that this new anti-immigration law will create a $1.8 billion economic loss for the state. These projections are based on fifty thousand workers, documented and undocumented, leaving the state, thus causing a 1.3 percent reduction in gross state production over the next few years.[7]

In 2006 the neighboring state of Texas was the first state to conduct a comprehensive financial analysis of the impact of undocumented immigrants on the state's budget and economy. According to Carole Keeton Strayhorn, the Texas comptroller, "The absence of the estimated 1.4 million undocumented immigrants in Texas in fiscal 2005 would have been a loss to our gross state product of $17.7 billion. Undocumented immigrants produced $1.58 billion in state revenues, which exceeded the $1.16 billion in state services they received."[8]

Nebraska has calculated that if immigrants were to disappear, the state would lose seventy-eight thousand jobs, some of which are held by U.S.-born workers.[9] Even though immigrants represent 5.6 percent of the state population, they comprise 7 percent of the working-age population. In certain sectors they represent the majority of the work force; for example, 80 percent of those who process meat and poultry. Additionally, state production would drop by 9 percent, or by about $13.5 billion. According to a study done by the University of Nebraska in Omaha, immigrants pay $1,554 per capita in taxes (property, income, sales, and gasoline) and cost the government $1,455 per capita in services (food stamps, public assistance, health, and education).[10]

According to a study conducted by Adelphi University's Center for Social Innovation, Latina/o immigrants on Long Island, New York, contribute $5.7 billion a year to the economy as a result of consumer spending and create about fifty-two thousand additional jobs.[11] The study concludes that immigrants contribute $614 more per person in taxes and government fees than they require through schools, health care, and law enforcement.[12] The New York–based Council of the

Americas estimated that the average immigrant's lifetime tax payment will exceed the cost of services he or she will use by $88,000. In addition, we can expect by 2010 to have 3.2 million Hispanic-owned businesses generating a total of $465 billion in revenues.[13]

Even the federal government benefits by the taxes paid by the undocumented. Because many undocumented immigrants use false Social Security numbers to obtain employment, taxes are removed from their paycheck. These taxes are neither refunded nor used for their benefit. According to the IRS, federal taxes were withheld on $40 billion in 2004 that are believed to have been generated by the undocumented. If we look only at Social Security withholding, there exists a net benefit to the American public of $9 billion annually.[14] Ironically, as the seventy-eight million baby-boomer generation starts to retire and draws Social Security checks, it will be the undocumented who will contribute to the economic health of Social Security and Medicare for this generation of documented Americans.

2. They are taking away our jobs.

If we are pro-business and pro-economic growth, then we must also be pro-immigration because we, as a country, do not have enough low-skilled workers. Instead, we accuse the undocumented immigrants of taking away jobs from U.S. citizens. Blaming the undocumented provides easy answers to the economic hardships faced by many Americans during the first decade of the new millennium. As Americans face record-level foreclosures of homes, spiraling gasoline prices, greater unemployment, and a downturn in stock prices, it isn't surprising that we seek to blame someone for the economic situation. Rather than focus on our economic structures that continue to contribute to the increasing gap between the few who are rich and the many who are poor, we focus our attention on the foreigner, the outsider, the Hispanic other for our economic woes. *They* are taking away our jobs. If only we could send *them* all back, we would begin to solve our economic situation.

Regardless of the rhetoric, scant evidence exists that the undocumented have caused any significant reduction in the wages of documented Americans. In 2004 undocumented workers held 6.3 million out of 146 million jobs, or about 4.3 percent of all U.S. jobs. The growth in undocumented immigrant jobs, according to the U.S. Bureau of Labor Statistics, occurred in service occupations and other industries requiring minimal education or skills. In the coming decade the number of low-skilled jobs is expected to grow by 700,000 per year. Most undocumented immigrant labor tends to be low skilled when compared to the labor of native-born workers and seldom threatens their jobs. In addition, over the past quarter century the number of Americans without a college education, including high school dropouts, has sharply declined. The pool of workers who would be most vulnerable to competition from the undocumented has been substantially reduced. Generally speaking, undocumented immigrant labor contributes to economic growth while having a minimal impact on unemployment or wages paid to U.S.-born workers.

A study conducted in 2005 by economist David Card of the University of California, Berkeley, bears evidence to this effect. When Dr. Card compared cities with high numbers of undereducated immigrants to cities that had few immigrants, he found no wage differences that could be attributed to immigrants. What Dr. Card discovered is that industries that employ immigrant labor tended to grow economically.[15] When all sectors of the labor force are examined, undocumented labor has a positive impact on wages.

A second study in 2005, conducted by Harvard economists George J. Borjas and Lawrence F. Katz, revealed no negative impact on U.S. wages by the undocumented. They discovered, instead, that the presence of undereducated immigrants actually increased the earnings of educated workers because highly skilled workers were able to hire the undocumented at low wages to mow their lawns and care for their children, thus freeing their time to pursue more earnings.[16] Legalizing the current undocumented work force could create a stable labor pool that would actually benefit the country economically in the long run.

3. They increase the rate of crime.

Whenever news reports focus on crimes committed by Hispanics or Latino/a gangs, a reality is being constructed for the American public that says immigrants, specifically Latino/a immigrants, are more prone than native-born Americans to violence. Yet, according to the Department of Justice, only 6 percent of U.S. prisoners (federal and state) are noncitizens (compared with the 7 percent of the population they represent). Immigrants from Mexico and Central America have lower incarceration rates than U.S.-born residents.[17] A study done by the Public Policy Institute of California, a nonpartisan research group on immigration and crime, found U.S.-born American men ages eighteen to forty were at least eight times more likely to be imprisoned for crimes than non-naturalized Mexican immigrants (many of whom are probably undocumented) in the same age range.[18]

From 1994 to 2005 the undocumented population, due in part to NAFTA, has doubled to about 11.9 million, yet Department of Justice statistics show a decline in violent crime by 34.2 percent during that same period. Cities with the highest immigrant populations (Miami, Chicago, New York, Los Angeles) and border cities (San Diego) experienced lower crime rates. Census information, police records, and other sources show that a large increase of undocumented immigration into an area does not contribute to a rise in the area's crime rate. Rather, studies show the opposite; crime is reduced.[19] Those who have faced death in order to cross the border are more likely to engage in productive work rather than crime, for possible deportation serves as a potent deterrent to criminal activities. Nevertheless, conservative politicians and radio talk-show hosts have successfully used the politics of fear and manipulation to define Hispanics as a threat to law-abiding Americans.

Rather than committing crimes, the undocumented are often the victims of criminals. They are easy targets because they are often unable to use banks (which require documentation to open accounts) and thus carry large sums of cash. Also, criminals and race-based hate-crime attackers know that the undocumented avoid contacting law enforcement when they are victimized. Because they are here illegally, think many criminals, they will be less likely to go to the authorities if a crime is committed against them.

4. Because of 9/11 we must secure the border from terrorists.

The fear of terrorists entering the United States through our southern border has been effectively used to secure money from Congress to militarize the border. Yet, the number of terrorists caught crossing the southern border with Mexico remains at zero. It is Congress that has conflated the war on terror with illegal immigration. Who benefits from this merging of issues? Since Operation Gatekeeper has militarized the border, military contractors have benefited from quintupling immigration-control expenditures.

In 2007 President Bush requested roughly $13 billion for the 2008 fiscal year for the express purpose of border control and internal enforcement of immigration law. By the end of 2008 the number of agents on patrol increased to 18,300—a doubling of agents since the start of the Bush administration.[20] It is interesting to note that in 2006

Boeing was awarded a $30 billion Security Border Initiative contract. That same year Lockheed Martin was awarded a $45 billion Eagle Project contract. Other firms, including Blackwater USA, the private security firm that came under scrutiny for its activities in Iraq, is also positioning itself to participate in the lucrative opportunity to protect U.S. borders.

5. They are bringing diseases into the country.

Lou Dobbs, of CNN's popular *Lou Dobbs This Week*, claimed that because of illegal immigration, when there once were "nine hundred cases of leprosy for forty years, [there are now] seven thousand in the past three years."[21] A fear of contagious diseases has effectively been used in the past as well to combat immigration, whether that immigration came from Ireland, Italy, or Eastern Europe. Use of this tactic continues today by describing Hispanics as dirty, if not disease-carrying individuals, a health danger for the rest of America. By accusing Latino/a immigrants of infecting Americans with diseases like tuberculosis, malaria, gonorrhea, syphilis, hepatitis, Chagas disease, and "swine flu," fear of the undocumented can be generated to mobilize people of good will against an ethnic group.

Politicians in search of votes and news pundits in search of audiences commonly make outrageous claims without providing any evidence. In spite of Mr. Dobbs's assertion that seven thousand new cases of leprosy in the past three years was probably an underestimation, the federal government numbers show a total of seven thousand cases of leprosy identified over the past thirty years, not three years.[22] Not only is there no link between the undocumented and leprosy, there is no governmental agency that claims that the undocumented are infecting the U.S. population with any type of contagious disease.

6. They are destroying the environment.

The Center for Immigration Studies published a report in August 2008 that argued that immigration significantly contributes to global warming.[23] The Center for Immigration Studies is one example of a group of nationalist organizations that believe that the present flow of immigrants is undermining U.S. culture, the economy, and society in general. Rather than framing their views in language that might be construed as racist and thus offensive, these organizations attempt to create a more liberal profile by connecting immigration with degradation of the environment, unemployment, population control, the increasing economic crisis, and/or anti-corporate sentiments. They argue that they are not anti-immigrant but rather are opposed to "mass immigration."

They take great pains to avoid racist rhetoric by focusing on the code language of "controlling borders." For example, according to the website of the Center for Immigration Studies, the mission of "the Center is animated by a pro-immigrant, low-immigration vision which seeks fewer immigrants but a warmer welcome for those admitted."[24] Other organizations using similar tactics include NumbersUSA, Americans for Immigration Control, Project USA, Americans for Better Immigration, and the influential Federation for American Immigration Reform (FAIR).[25]

At times, blaming the undocumented for the ills of society borders on the absurd. Take, for example, the government report produced by the Republican-led legislative panel of the Missouri House Special Committee on Immigration. The report argues that undocumented immigration is caused by high U.S. abortion rates. If we didn't have as much immigration, abortion rates would drop. According to the committee's chair, Representative Ed Emery (R), "You don't have to think too long. If you kill 44 million of your potential workers [through the abortion process], it's not too surprising we would be desperate for [immigrant] workers."[26]

7. They don't want to learn English.

A majority of U.S. states have some form of "English only" legislation. Part of the anti-immigrant rhetoric maintains that newcomers do not want to learn the official language because of a hidden agenda to take over the country and impose their own language. In spite of such laws to force people to speak English, the undocumented already know that if they wish to survive in this country, they will have to learn the language of commerce. Both documented and undocumented immigrants are keenly aware that proficiency in English is closely correlated with socioeconomic advancement.

The desire to learn English is evident in the fierce competition for the few seats available in English-as-a-second-language (ESL) classes. In New York City, for example, three out of four ESL applicants are turned away because there are not enough classroom seats. In Boston, 16,725 adults are on waiting lists, hoping to get into a class eighteen months later. Yet, while government bodies are demanding that immigrants learn English, the Bush administration scaled back funding for

ESL classes from $570 million to $207 million for the 2006 fiscal year.[27] The problem is not that immigrants don't want to learn English; the problem is the lack of a sufficient number of classes.

8. *What part of illegal don't you understand?*

According to current immigration laws, those who are already in the country without proper documentation are seldom able to acquire permanent residency. To do so, they must first leave the United States and return to their homeland. Once there, they must apply for a legal visa, which prohibits them from entering the United States for three to ten years. Due to the backlog of applications, they will probably never receive proper documentation. Presently, no administrative mechanism exists that allows the undocumented to "legalize" their status; hence, those who are already here are more than likely to live in the shadows of society.

Lacking documentation is defined in the present immigration debate as being illegal. *Illegal* is not a neutral word; it connotes criminality—that those who are illegal are somehow inherently bad, if not evil. But do we call a driver who is driving without a license an illegal driver? Or do we call a taxpayer who fails to file his documents in time an illegal citizen? Not having proper documentation, either as a driver or when filing one's taxes, does not make the person a criminal. Sadly, criminalizing immigrants can be profitable. From 1994 to 2006 detention of immigrants increased by 400 percent, becoming the fastest-growing prison population and leading to a rush to build more prisons exclusively for immigrants. This has proven to be a windfall for corporations like Geo Group (formally Wackenhut) and Halliburton.[28]

The reason migrants without proper documentation are called illegal has nothing to do with their character or their moral framework; they are illegal because those in power have the legislative authority to impose such a definition on society. This has happened before in this country when Americans in positions of power have legislated conformance to their world view. For most of this nation's history, it was illegal for African Americans to experience the freedom of whites. It was also illegal for women to vote. When such laws restrict humans from participating in their full humanity, it is the prevailing laws that rob a certain group of people of their dignity that are illegal and not the people themselves. And Christians must ask themselves if they have a moral obligation to obey such illegal laws.

In the Book of Acts, the apostles Peter and John stand before the Sanhedrin, the religious and legal authorities of the time. After a formal hearing this court ordered them not to proclaim the gospel message. They chose instead to break the law, to do something illegal. "Whether it is right in God's eyes to listen to you and not to God, you judge," they retorted, "for we are unable not to speak what we have seen and heard" (Acts 4:19–20).

Christians have always had the duty to disobey human laws in favor of the laws of God. The Reverend Martin Luther King, Jr., understood this, and his bold actions to do something illegal and go to jail helped begin an important conversation in this nation concerning race. Today another race issue faces the nation, that of Hispanic ethnicity. How can immigration laws be moral if they dehumanize and bring death to a segment of the population?

Immoral laws are often ignored, not out of disrespect for the rule of law, but because the lack of justice erodes compliance. When the people continuously disregard the law, it indicates a lack of consent, and without the consent of the public, laws cease to hold society together. Christians of all traditions, as well as believers in other religious traditions, recognize that justice and equality for the least must trump the laws of nations that disenfranchise portions of the community. They have a moral obligation to be illegal in the same way as Peter and John, and in the way Martin Luther King, Jr., modeled. The issue is not what part of illegal we fail to understand, but rather what should be our response to policies of our nation that are immoral.

Testimony about Detention

Pramila Jayapal

Since 1996 there has been a dramatic increase in the number of immigrants held in detention in the United States. By mid-2008 nearly thirty thousand immigrants were detained daily across the country, some in local jails and others in privately run detention centers. This

---

Pramila Jayapal is founder and executive director of OneAmerica, an organization based in Washington State that works for comprehensive immigration reform. She is a featured speaker nationwide and a regular guest on local and national television and radio shows on issues of immigrant and human rights.

compares to an average daily population in 1994 of only five thousand. The total number of immigrants detained annually grew from approximately ninety-five thousand individuals in 2001 to over three hundred thousand in 2007.

This growth began in 1996 when Congress passed legislation that dramatically expanded mandatory incarceration without bond provisions for large categories of immigrants, including lawful permanent residents (green-card holders) who sometimes commit minor crimes, as well as refugees escaping persecution. The 1996 laws also established a new provision called Expedited Removal, which allows immigration officials summarily to remove immigrants arriving without proper documentation, including refugees, without a hearing and with extended detention.

Anti-immigrant advocates in Congress used the post-9/11 environment as an opportunity to link immigration to national security, focusing almost entirely on an approach that emphasized harsh enforcement strategies such as detention, deportation, and raids. Members of Congress, most notably Representative James Sensenbrenner, who chaired the House Judiciary Committee, argued that all immigrants—and particularly undocumented immigrants—posed a serious threat to the national security of the country.

In 2004, as Congress was debating legislation to implement the recommendations of the 9/11 Commission, Sensenbrenner argued for the inclusion of a number of contentious immigration enforcement measures that further expanded the government's ability to arrest, detain, and deport immigrants; restrict judicial review and oversight; and reduce the number of documents immigrants may use to establish their identity. He also proposed a provision that would bar states from issuing drivers licenses to undocumented immigrants. Ultimately, these provisions were not included in the legislation, but Sensenbrenner went on to draft his now-infamous bill, HR 4437, which criminalized undocumented immigrants. It passed the House of Representatives in early 2006 and resulted in massive immigration demonstrations and marches in the spring and early summer of 2006.

In 2004 Congress did, however, authorize the creation of forty thousand new detention beds by 2010, which will bring detention capacity close to eighty thousand. Although detention was always supposed to be a short-term strategy, Immigration Customs and Enforcement (ICE) reported that the average stay in 2003 was sixty-four days, with 32 percent detained for ninety days or longer. Asylum seekers granted refugee status spent, on average, ten months in detention, with the longest period being three and one-half years. Clear violations of human rights and constitutional rights occur regularly in the detention centers. Because there are no legally binding and therefore enforceable standards to regulate conditions in the detention centers, there is also no accountability.

Immigrant rights advocates across the country regularly witness the real impact of these harsh enforcement measures on families and individuals. While the focus has been on undocumented Hispanic immigrants because of their large numbers, it is also true that the impact of eroded due-process protections, detention, and deportation has been felt by immigrants and refugees from all over the world, including Cambodia, the Philippines, and Somalia.

Across the country, immigrants live in fear today. Some have gone to appear in court for a traffic ticket and been arrested. Some have been picked up at checkpoints or bus stations. Some work in industries where businesses are raided. One immigrant said, "I keep my head down every day and make sure my kids know what to do if I don't come home from work. I am always living in fear." One apple farmer in eastern Washington State spoke before a panel about how he gets calls from his workers, now friends after years of working together, in the middle of the night. "The rumors of raids are as scary as the raids themselves. The fear is tearing our community apart."

A report published by OneAmerica, an immigrant and civil rights organization in Seattle, Washington, and the Seattle University School of Law Human Rights Clinic, clearly documented these violations of rights and presented a textured picture of what immigrants face that is consistent with national reports from across the country. The following are findings and stories from the June 2008 report *Voices from Detention*, which documents human rights abuses within the Northwest Detention Center in Tacoma, Washington (available online). These findings are similar to those reported from other detention centers.

Lack of Due Process: Many Americans do not know that the immigration system is a civil not a criminal system. Thus, immigrants who have committed immigration violations are not provided with an attorney. While they can get an attorney, it is extremely difficult to find a good one, to find the money to pay for one, or to find one in a hurry when an immigrant is detained unexpectedly. As a result, 95 percent of immigrants go through the immigration system with no legal representation, even though immigration law is extremely complex and arcane.

In many cases detention centers are not in major city hubs, so attorneys must travel hours to see a client, making it extremely difficult and costly to provide good and timely representation. In the Northwest Detention Center, overcrowding had resulted in too few confidential rooms for attorney-client conversations, contributing to long lines or conversations in the hall that others could overhear—violating attorney/client confidentiality.

Being Forced to Sign Papers: Many immigrants, when detained, are transferred to a detention center. Too often, they have no means to notify their families. The person simply "disappears." Upon arrival in the detention center, immigrants are supposed to be told about their rights, but often they are not. Detainees are often coerced into signing papers without consulting with an attorney or even being told what they are signing. Most of the time they are not provided with interpreters or translators. And, almost unbelievably, many times ICE officials make mistakes about the identity of a detainee.

In *Voices from Detention* Hector Pena Ortiz described how he had been asked twice to sign papers that would allow ICE to deport him immediately. The first time he was shackled and taken to the intake room. He told the officials that he had a pending legal appeal and did not want to sign anything. After much convincing, they checked the file and found that he did have an appeal pending. However, shortly after, he was shackled and told again to sign the papers for expedited removal. This time it turned out ICE had the wrong detainee.

Guard Retaliation and Abuse: Detainees regularly report that guards retaliate against them for filing grievances or visiting with their attorneys. For example, one detainee had his bunk searched an inordinate number of times. Others reported strip searches after attorney visits and being segregated from other inmates. Although ICE continues to deny that strip searches are conducted, there are numerous reports of such searches on detainees from across the country.

Detainees repeatedly report verbal abuse, with guards calling them *cucarachas* (cockroaches) and employing intimidation, threats, and even force. Detainees have reported being grabbed by the arm, pushed, shoved, and threatened. One detainee in *Voices from Detention* reported that an officer sprayed her food with chemicals. Because no interpreters are provided and all the signs are in English, detainees often reported being screamed at, even shoved against the wall for failing to follow orders in English. Two of the detainees discussed inappropriate sexual behavior and comments, as well as strip searches that were humiliating and demeaning.

One of the most disturbing events involved a transfer of detainees on two flights to Alabama in the summer of 2007. The detainees were being transferred in anticipation of overcrowding pending an ICE workplace raid in Portland, Oregon. Abuse on the flight included physical abuse (hitting and punching and putting a hood on a mentally ill detainee); refusing to allow detainees to use the restroom for over seven hours, resulting in defecation in their seats and sitting in their own feces; and handcuffing and shackling hands and feet of the detainees so that they could not eat.

Access to Medical and Emergency Care: Detainees are often faced with a short supply of medical-care professionals. Although each detention center is supposed to have a written plan for the delivery of twenty-four-hour emergency health care and internal health clinics are to be staffed twenty-four hours a day, detainees must wait in line for hours to receive emergency care, much less standard care. Outbreaks of food poisoning, such as the outbreak that occurred at the Northwest Detention Center in Tacoma, made over three hundred detainees sick, but no in-house medical clinic or emergency care was provided until the next morning.

In order to get outside care if a doctor deems it necessary, detainees are shackled and transported. Several pregnant women have talked about being seven months pregnant and having to walk shackled in order to see a doctor. *Voices from Detention* told of one detainee who suffered from seizures remaining shackled for the entire five days she spent in the hospital even though she was not considered dangerous. When she was first seen in the emergency room, the attending doctor requested that the shackles be removed in order to treat her, but the officer refused. Detainee deaths have increased, and even though ICE is supposed to release the names of those who have died in detention, this often does not occur without intervention from Congress or the filing of a Freedom of Information Act request.

Access to Mental Health: Inadequate mental-health-care treatment is perhaps one of the most difficult issues to hear about from detainees. Many detainees suffer from depression. Some who are refugees and have fled wartorn countries find themselves suffering from post-traumatic stress disorder after being locked up again. Even though detainees may exhibit signs of severe mental illness, they are regularly placed in living quarters with the rest of the detainee population. Officers are supposed to be trained to recognize mental health problems, but few are. Often, they resort to the use of solitary confinement rather than treatment.

Living Conditions: The living conditions in many detention centers are substandard and violate basic rights. In *Voices from Detention* detainees spoke of food that was rotten, cold, and of minimal quantity and not nutritious. Since many detainees are in detention for months or even years, the lack of food poses an enormous human rights violation. One detainee, who was not overweight, lost fifty pounds and became so weak that he was unable to do any exercise.

Detainees are often housed in dormitories that are overcrowded and unsanitary. In one case detainees must eat their meals in their bunks because there is simply no room at the tables. Toilets do not have doors or any privacy, with sometimes over eighty people sharing six or seven toilets that are infested with rats. In the Northwest Detention Center, because of overcrowding, dining tables are kept near the bathroom, and toilet water sometimes sprays onto the food.

One of the hardest things for detainees to bear is the lack of visitation. Unlike many prisons where contact visits are permitted, visitation takes place behind a glass partition that separates the detainee from his or her family. Visits typically last no more than thirty minutes, and sometimes families must wait hours to see a detainee. One wife of a detainee tries to visit her husband at least once a month. Their daughter has a debilitating chronic illness. It takes them three hours to drive from Oregon to see him. They typically wait up to an hour for a fifteen-minute, no-contact visit. A few times she has waited nearly two hours to see her husband. The visits have been traumatizing for her, her children, and her husband. Some detainees say that the short, no-contact visits make them even more depressed.

Language creates enormous barriers for detainees, and interpreters are rarely accessible. Detainees have reported being unable to communicate with their officers, unable to read signs that are in English, and unable to discuss problems with others. Detainee handbooks, which are supposed to be provided to each detainee upon arrival, are available only in English, with a truncated version provided in Spanish.

Conclusion: When detaining immigrants, the United States has an obligation to comply with both international and domestic legal standards of detainee treatment. Detention without accountability only increases maltreatment and sets aside the most basic values of liberty and dignity. As Americans concerned with upholding our Constitution and ensuring justice, we should remember that America is degraded when the government fails to uphold those very rights that make us a great country. And we should note that once some people's rights are abused, all of our rights can be abused.

Testimony from a U.S. Resident
Minsun Ji

Enrique comes to Denver every April and leaves every November, traveling back to his home state, Chihuahua, after he is able to save about thirty-five hundred dollars. The workers at El Centro Humanitario elected him Denver's first day-laborers' president when the center opened in 2002. Enrique usually stays at a downtown shelter in order to reduce living expenses and seldom spends any money on himself.

An educated man with a college degree and the skills of an electrician, he is still unable to find employment in Mexico. He dreams of opening a brick company with his brother if he ever saves enough money. For now, his funds go to assist his ailing mother. Every morning he comes to El Centro seeking employment as either a skilled or unskilled laborer. Enrique always volunteers his time to El Centro, doing whatever is needed, from janitorial duties to speaking at public events. Why? Because he believes in the mission of the center.

Alberto was a regular worker and leader at El Centro until he became severely ill. His kidneys failed as a result of diabetes. Alberto took care of the physical plant, and he tended to the spirit of the building's inhabitants as well. Everyone recognized him as a spiritual leader, and workers often sought his wise advice. Even when quiet, Alberto emoted natural authority. He was a writer, a poet and a reader with his face always in some political book.

When he was young, Alberto worked as a carpenter. But now he often failed to obtain daily jobs, for they usually went to the younger

---

Minsun Ji is the director of El Centro Humanitario—an organization in Denver that promotes the rights and well-being of day laborers through education, job skills, leadership development, united action, and advocacy.

and stronger workers. Still, he spent most of his days at the center, educating peer workers about their rights, offering construction classes to younger workers, and volunteering to organize yard sales for the center's fund-raising campaign. El Centro became his home away from home. Whenever the staff and workers of El Centro asked him to take a rest, Alberto always joked that "I do not have much time left. I have to help other workers take care of El Centro." Sadly, he was right. Our good friend passed away in 2005.

Vicente used to be a doctor in his native Peru. After a series of unfortunate events, including an illness that cost him his job and led him to the United States in search of better health care, Vicente found himself seeking employment on the street corner. An educated and eloquent speaker, in 2002 he represented El Centro Humanitario at a national gathering of day laborers in San Francisco, and he displayed a natural charisma. Although Vicente was a white-collar worker in Peru, he had to learn menial skills in construction in order to survive.

One day Vicente disappeared. We were worried. But to our delight and surprise, Vicente reappeared three years later as an apartment manager, now living with his children, who had emigrated from Peru. Although financially more secure, he never forgot how he began his life in this country as a day laborer and how El Centro helped him. Today, he and his children assist with many of El Centro's events. An active board member, he insists on cooking Thanksgiving dinner for the workers.

Ofelia stood out more than her quiet husband Pedro. She was the first woman day laborer who walked through the doors of El Centro. After crossing the border, Pedro and Ofelia found themselves with a huge debt. The *coyote*'s fee for guiding them across the border was due, forcing them to work many hours just to pay him back. When Ofelia first attended El Cento with her husband, she discovered that there was no community for women. Many assumed she would simply stop coming to the center, mainly because it was male dominated. But rather than complain, she created El Centro's women's project—a women-centered business cooperative that caters local events, provides cleaning services, and helps care for children.

Even though she was illiterate in her native tongue of Spanish, she showed up for English class every morning. She understood, like most immigrants, that any hopes for economic advancement required her to learn to speak and write English. Everyone loved her big smiles and tamales. It was a sad day when Ofelia had to return to Mexico to care for a desperately ill sister.

Manny is a day laborer who hangs out on the street corners of Aurora, Colorado. One day he found himself standing in front of a criminal court jury with a real possibility of facing jail time. His crime was that he had dared to speak the truth. Manny received a trespassing ticket from the Aurora police, who had become increasingly aggressive about moving Aurora day laborers off city streets. City officials supported these aggressive policies and even considered passing laws banning the right of day laborers to speak up or ask for work in the city of Aurora. When it became clear that such laws unconstitutionally restricted the free speech rights of day laborers, Aurora officials and police worked together on an alternative strategy of citing and arresting day laborers for trespassing on private property near the street corners where they gathered. In many cases police detained day laborers and refused them the right to stand on public sidewalks by issuing citations for trespassing when, in fact, they were not breaking any laws.

Thus in September 2007 Manny stood in front of an Aurora court judge. Threatened with jail time if convicted, Manny's co-defendants agreed to plead guilty, pay a small fine, and stay away from the sidewalks. Manny refused to plea bargain. He believed it was unjust to be cited for trespassing, and he refused to plead guilty and pay a fine for a crime he did not commit. Because he refused to accept the trespassing charge, local prosecutors threatened him with jail time.

Manny was terrified to stand before the jury. A native of El Salvador, he does not speak English. While in Mexico, he worked at a *maquiladora* (factory worker) for four years, enduring low wages and constant abuse. One day he had had enough. He spoke against wage abuses to the Mexican labor department. Receiving no protection from the authorities, he found himself unemployable. Feeling hurt and despondent, Manny decided to journey to the United States with the hope of surviving. And he was promptly ticketed for a trespassing crime that he did not commit.

El Centro Humanitario provided a pro-bono lawyer for Manny. To make his case before a jury, Manny had to miss two days of work, a luxury he could not afford. While four police officers testified to giving trespassing tickets to the workers, Manny kept his head down in silence. When Manny was asked about the police testimony, he said that he felt bad, because "it was not true." After hearing Manny's words and considering the powerful closing argument by our attorney, the jury deliberated. We all thought that the row of uniformed officers staring at the jury for hours would overcome Manny's simple story of truth. When the jury filed back into the room, we were not optimistic, but then the verdict was read—"Not guilty!" The jury had seen past the police uniforms and had stood up for the rights of the very poorest among us. It was a great day for Manny and for the spirit of solidarity, ethical treatment, and justice that represents the mission of El Centro Humanitario.

All of these workers are the immigrant day laborers I work with on a daily basis. These are the poorest of the poor, gathering every day on street corners to seek employment so that they can survive and send money to their families. These are the workers who fled desperate poverty south of the border. They provide Denver with some of its most backbreaking work, often working for minuscule wages and under dangerous conditions. For years these immigrants have lived and worked off the street corners, without shelter in the scorching sun or chilling cold, without protection from unscrupulous employers who sometimes refuse to pay wages, and without access to bathrooms, water, or telephones.

When Miguel suffered permanent nerve damage to his arm at an unsafe construction site and was ignored by his employer, El Centro made sure that he received an adequate personal-injury award so that he could rebuild his life. When Roberto worked for four days straight and then was stiffed by his unscrupulous employer, El Centro provided advocacy and wage-claim services so that Roberto could receive his pay. When Pepe experienced a life-threatening rupture of his appendix, it was El Centro's business to secure medical attention and ensure that his family in Mexico was aware of the situation. When area residents and businesses complain of an unsavory street scene as immigrants gather on the corner seeking jobs, it is El Centro's job to develop solutions, to give workers a place to gather off the street, and to foster healthy dialogue between area residents and the street community.

El Centro is home for immigrant day laborers who are sojourners in our city, and who seek nothing but the barest income necessary to survive and support their family. It is a home filled with the dreams of strong, young men, striving to achieve their piece of the American dream. It is a home filled with the lively voices of the women's collective, working together and lifting each other up to build creative new enterprises in America. It is a home filled with the desperation of the ill and the lonely, who seek a bit of help to locate a hospital, their family, or their "disappeared" best friend. It is a home filled with the tired bones of men past their prime and broken down by years of hard work, now seeking a place to rest, reflect, and have a cup of coffee. Sometimes, sadly, they are seeking only a dignified, final resting place. El Centro is home to all of these travelers—those who are beginning their lives with hope and aspiration and those winding down their lives by sharing the rare wisdom of the years. All these are the workers, and all these are family.

Voice of the People

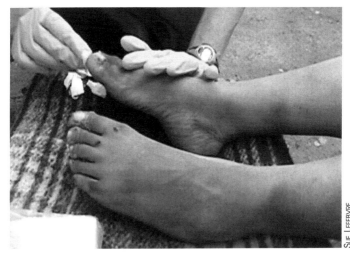

Mending Feet

EL ESPEJO (THE MIRROR)
Laura Dravenstott

Petite and soft-spoken,
Legs bruised and skin broken,
Three days and three nights
In the desert.

Life marked by separation,
Quiet strength and desperation.
Left to the roadside
Mercies of Border Patrol.

Little water, many dangers,
Now relying on strangers
To wash and mend
Your feet.
Rain-slicked rock and
Mountains block
The road to work and
Daily bread.

Your younger child near,
The oldest—where?—not here.
More hungry, more wary than mine.
Two thousand miles more,
Legs tired, feet sore,
To a job
In my husband's hometown.
We visit later; I wonder.

Your age my own,
Two patterns sewn
In life's crazy quilt
Now align.
Will you try a second time—
Be punished for the so-called crime?
Do you know that for grace,
I could be in your place?

4

Family Values

Our enemies are bloodied and beaten. We cannot relent. Our boot is on their throat and we must have the willingness to crush their "throat" so that we can put our enemy down for good. The sovereignty of our nation and the future of our culture and civilization is at stake. The United States is a beacon of salvation unto the rest of the world. Our freedoms, our culture is man's salvation. If we perish, man perishes.
—JOSEPH TURNER, FOUNDER OF SAVE OUR STATE (S.O.S)[1]

The United States lacks a clear, consistent, long-term strategy to improve respect for the human rights of migrants.
—UNITED NATION'S HUMAN RIGHTS COUNCIL, 2008[2]

On the outskirts of Victoria, Texas, a deserted forty-foot-long insulated semitrailer was parked at a truck stop. Police investigating the abandoned vehicle early on the morning of May 14, 2003, made a gruesome discovery. Inside the trailer were the remains of seventeen undocumented immigrants. According to survivors, seventy-four migrants were herded into the unventilated truck in Harlingen, Texas. Among those who did not survive was a seven-year-old boy, who died along with his father. Two migrants who initially survived eventually expired at Citizens Medical Center, a local hospital. According to health officials, they died from asphyxiation and heatstroke.

Temperatures in that part of Texas were close to 90 degrees and it is estimated to have been above 100 degrees inside the trailer. As the temperatures rose and the situation became more desperate, those trapped inside the truck tried to punch holes through it in order to get some air.[3] Among the dead were fathers, mothers, brothers, and sisters. Each was part of someone's family and, more than likely, had embarked on a hazardous journey north out of familial duty and responsibilities.

Unfortunately for them, and the many others who have perished crossing the border prior to and after this event, they belonged to families that some Euroamerican Christians refuse to acknowledge.

During the last decade "family values" has become a battle cry among Christians, specifically conservative Christians, and it has been a decisive component in recent presidential elections. Without a doubt, the Christian organization most responsible for shaping the contemporary definition of *family values* is the organization Focus on the Family, whose spokesman is James Dobson. Focus on the Family's self-declared mission is to "redeem families, communities, and societies worldwide through Christ."[4]

Generally speaking, the endeavor to connect biblical teachings to the difficulties faced by modern families is indeed a noble venture. In fact, several Latino/a conservative religious groups have made alliances with organizations like Focus on the Family to push through political issues identified by the Religious Right as important for the well-being of the American family. Unfortunately, when Latina/os raise the concern that the present U.S. immigration policies are damaging to Hispanic families, their requests for solidarity are met with silence. When Hispanics across this country took to the streets throughout April and May 2006 demanding comprehensive immigration reform, the absence of many leading conservative religious figures was noticeable.

Why do many in the Religious Right avoid focusing on undocumented families? The official website of Focus on the Family notes that while immigration and poverty are worthy issues, the focus must remain on abortion and homosexuality.[5] Relegating immigration to simply another issue—and an issue that then is less important—betrays the bias of the organization. There is no indication at all that Focus on the Family sees immigration policies as violence visited upon Hispanic families. Instead, immigration is an issue to consider only if or when it affects the families of the dominant culture. For example, immigration is discussed in the context of international adoptions. The ministry of Focus on the Family is unambiguously focused on documented Euroamerican families or Latino/a families that have assimilated to Euroamerican values.

Nonetheless, whether documented or undocumented, a family is still a family, and it needs to be strengthened and nurtured. Our present immigration policies, coupled with anti-immigrant, anti-Hispanic rhetoric, have brought tremendous violence to undocumented families.

Such violence includes death in the desert for those attempting to make the hazardous crossing; rape of Latina women and girls; denial of basic medical services; economic abuse in the workplace; and the separation of families, husbands from wives and parents from children.

Contrary to agency practices, Border Patrol agents are threatened with punishment for failing to meet arrest quotas. According to Lombardo Amaya of Local 2554 of the National Border Patrol Council, agents stationed in Riverside, California, were ordered to arrest one hundred and fifty suspected undocumented agents in January 2009.[6] The danger exists that constitutional protections are sacrificed to meet quotas and quickly get the necessary numbers to avoid being disciplined.

Separation of Families

When arrests are made, it is common practice for the Border Patrol to separate families at the time of arrest and to deny migrants information about the whereabouts of their relatives. Separated in custody, they are also routinely repatriated at different times to different ports of entries, and these ports of entry are often far apart, with little likelihood that they are where the migrants actually attempted to cross the border. It becomes almost impossible for family members to find one another and reunite.

The Border Patrol's focus on the family seems designed to cause separation and disintegration. Take the example of "Luis" (age twenty-four), who, along with his brother, was chased through the desert by Border Patrol agents. Once caught, law enforcement agents grabbed his brother's head and slammed it into the ground three times. With the agent's foot on his brother's head, the agent yelled "f___ you" several times. The brothers were immediately separated and repatriated at different times. No one is immune to being separated from family. Even children are separated from adults.[7]

Another family that would be ignored by organizations like Focus on the Family is the Arces. They moved to Phoenix in the early 1990s from Guadalajara. Since that time Adrian Arce worked as a house painter, while his wife Diana cleaned houses. Over the years they were able to save enough to buy two cars and make a down payment on a house. Their eldest daughter, who graduated from high school in 2006, has been going to the community college on a full scholarship. But when Arizona passed the Employer Sanctions Bill in 2007, authorizing county attorneys to suspend or revoke business licenses of employers who knowingly hire undocumented individuals, Adrian Arce lost his $14 an hour job. After much scrambling he was able to find employment at $7.50 an hour. According to his wife Diana, "[Because he was undocumented] the employer knew he would take the job."

In 2007 Arizona passed a proposition banning undocumented students from paying in-state tuition. Their daughter lost her scholarship, forcing her to drop out of college. Adding to their difficulties are the overly zealous tactics of their local sheriff, Joe Arpaio, who has made a name for himself by setting up road blocks to check people's documentation. The undocumented members of the Arce family have become prisoners in their own home. "We used to like visiting the park and the library," says Diana Arce, "[but] everything has changed."[8] The Arce family, like most undocumented families, avoids leaving home except to work or buy groceries, out of fear of being arrested and separated. Why does this family not deserve to be strengthened and nurtured?

The plight of the Ramírez family is also ignored. Juan Ramírez Bocanegra was scooped up during a raid of undocumented workers at the Swift and Company meat-processing plant located in Greeley, Colorado. Because the work is dangerous, it has a high turnover rate; nevertheless, Ramírez was able to make about $12 an hour. He had attempted to get proper documentation six years earlier by applying for a visa, but after two years he realized he was not likely to receive it. He was one of 261 undocumented Swift employees in Greeley who were snatched from their place of work on December 12, 2006. An additional 1,282 workers were arrested at five other Swift plants. At that time the Swift raids constituted the largest workplace crackdown ever conducted by Immigration and Customs Enforcement.

According to Ramírez, the immigration agents harassed the workers, made derogatory statements, forced them to sit for hours on concrete floors, and sleep without blankets (it was cold in December). He wasn't allowed to contact his family until he was expatriated to Mexico. With only $17 in his pocket (all the money he thought he would need that day before returning home from work), Juan Ramírez found himself sixteen hundred miles away from his wife and three children, an eight year old, a three year old, and an eighteen-month-old toddler. "All I do is cry on the phone. I can't even talk. I choke on my words," says Ramírez. "My oldest daughter says 'I miss you so much, Daddy.' I tell her, 'My darling, I will see you soon.' I feel her pain. The sadness is so overwhelming." Now Ramírez must decide what to do next. If he stays where he is, he cannot support his family. If he risks returning and is caught, he could end up in prison.[9] Why does this family not deserve the focus of Christians?

Along with Ramírez, other parents were arrested and deported during the 2006 Swift raids, leaving behind children that are now being cared for by uncles and aunts.[10] According to Greeley Mayor Tom Selders, "By people being arrested, children who were citizens of the United States were left without nurturing parents."[11] Of the nearly 2.2 million undocumented deported from 1997 to 2007, 100,000 were parents of children born in the United States.[12] If any of these children are forced to return to the homeland of their parents, then we must ask if we are deporting U.S. citizens.

It is estimated that there are approximately five million U.S. children who live with at least one undocumented parent. The Swift raids in Greeley and Grand Island, Nebraska (two of the six sites of the raid), along with a raid in New Bedford, Massachusetts, of Michael Bianco, Inc., a textile manufacturing facility that makes U.S. military backpacks, resulted in the arrest of over nine hundred workers. Collectively, the parents among the arrested had over five hundred children. In one of the sites two-thirds of the children were U.S. citizens. Following arrests at two of the sites, 79 and 89 percent of the children left behind were ten years or younger; at one site more than half of the children separated from their parents were five or younger. Hundreds of children, many U.S. citizens by birth, found themselves without a nurturing parent.

Many arrested were "voluntarily" deported before being able to contact either families or friends to care for their children or lawyers to defend their basic rights. They were placed in remote detention facilities with limited access to phones. Many were afraid to say that they had children, fearful that their children would also be arrested. Their children were in a precarious situation, having to rely on the charity of informal family, church, and community networks. Some family members, including children whose primary caregiver or source of support did not return home, hid for days and weeks in basements, attics, and closets. Some teenagers were left without adult supervision, and younger children were left with babysitters.

As funds and savings quickly dried up without a primary wage earner, children were left lacking the basic necessities. Although charity and/or privately funded assistance often lasted for two to three months, most parents were detained for five to six months. Hardest hit were infants in need of baby formula and diapers.

Besides economic deprivation due to the raids, children whose parents had been deported also experience feelings of abandonment and display symptoms of emotional trauma, psychological duress, and mental health problems. Fear, isolation, and economic hardship lead to mental problems as children suffer from depression, separation anxiety disorder, post-traumatic stress disorder, and suicidal thoughts.[13]

To make matters worse, a new and disturbing trend of "legally" removing Latino/a children from their parents is developing. An example is Carlos, a six month old whose Guatemalan mother, Encarnación Bail Romero, was swept up during a raid of the poultry-processing plant in Carthage, Missouri, where she worked in 2007. A year and a half after going to jail, a county court terminated her rights to her child and allowed a Euroamerican couple to adopt Carlos. According to Judge Dally, the couple made a comfortable living while the child's natural mother had nothing to offer. To expedite the process, the biological mother was not informed of losing her child until it was too late to legally protest. The judge stated, "Her lifestyle, that of smuggling herself into the country illegally and committing crimes in this country, is not a lifestyle that can provide stability for a child." Carlos's mother wants her child, but because she is an undocumented Hispanic, her child can be taken from her by any Euroamerican couple of means who wants to adopt a child.[14] It is not enough that Hispanic labor and dignity are taken from them, now their children are too.

To break up families is cruel and inhumane, and yet it is common to find Hispanics separated for years, if not decades, from their children. A U.S. permanent resident can expect to wait a minimum of five years before being able to bring his or her spouse and children to the United States through legal channels. This is a lifetime for a child. Family values cannot solely focus on the families of those privileged by documentation. Members of all families have a basic human right to be united with their loved ones.

Workplace Raids and Families

Raids such as the one experienced by Ramírez are not uncommon, and they are not limited to the work place. The undocumented are also at risk of being deported when at elementary schools, at Hispanic businesses, or at random road blocks. The number of workplace arrests of undocumented workers has recently skyrocketed, increasing from five hundred in 2002 to thirty-six hundred in 2006.[15] Although the official reason for conducting such raids is to arrest undocumented workers, the raids have a secondary effect—one could say a hidden agenda—and that is to terrorize the Latino/a community. The frequency and arbitrariness of these raids seem designed to shock Hispanic communities into submission and to suppress any efforts to organize the immigrant community. Fear forces the undocumented underground. They avoid public spaces like shops, churches, and parks; parents stop sending their children to school; and laborers stop going to work.

While such raids have devastating effects on Hispanic families, they also result in substantial economic losses for the Hispanic community in general. The raids undermine basic workers' rights, including the right to organize, further exposing laborers to exploitation in the workplace. U.S. taxpayers are also burdened by these raids. The cost of the raid of Agriprocessors, Inc., in Postville, Iowa—at that point, the largest federal immigration operation of its kind in U.S. history—was, as of August 21, 2008, $5.2 million dollars. Taxpayers paid $13,396 for each of the 389 undocumented workers taken into custody. It is important to note that at this writing the final bill has not been calculated. As of October 2008, undocumented workers in detention were still working their way through the legal system.[16] Based on these numbers and using similar tactics of law enforcement, it would cost approximately $161 billion to arrest all of the undocumented residing within the United States.

As noted earlier, undocumented workers have always been counted upon to fill jobs at the lowest end of the pay scale, jobs that documented Americans refuse to take and jobs that expose workers to physical abuse and risk. When added to their fears of exposure and deportation, the undocumented often live in the shadows, relegated to an underground cheap labor pool. Their hourly wages are lower on average than U.S.-born workers, and almost half earn less than 200 percent of the minimum wage compared with one-third of U.S.-born residents.[17] Even though the vast majority of workers are law abiding and contribute to society by paying taxes, they are forced to remain silent regardless of the abuse, maltreatment, violence, or crime they face. Their precarious status relegates the undocumented to a servant (slave?) class without the possibility of organizing to demand justice, to petition for change, or to bargain collectively for humane treatment. Denied basic benefits that are standard for any worker within the

United States, their undocumented status makes them vulnerable to all manner of abuse.

Revelations that came to light after the raids at Agriprocessors kosher meat-packing plant in Postville, Iowa, on May 12, 2008, demonstrated the extent of this abuse. Almost four hundred of the plant's nine hundred employees were arrested on immigration charges. With an unemployment rate of 3.5 percent in Iowa, these immigrants were providing a vital service to a state experiencing a labor shortage. Nevertheless, the working conditions they faced were at the least immoral and illegal and at worst inhumane. One undercover immigrant sent to work at the plant by immigration authorities reported seeing "a rabbi . . . calling employees derogatory names and throwing meat at employees."[18] In another episode witnessed by the undercover informant, a floor supervisor blindfolded an immigrant with duct tape. "The floor supervisor then took one of the meat hooks and hit the Guatemalan with it."[19]

Among the undocumented workers arrested during the Agriprocessors raid were more than two dozen under-age workers, some as young as thirteen, a clear violation of child-labor laws. They were forced to work shifts of twelve or more hours, six nights a week, using razor-sharp knives and saws. These children earned about $7.25 an hour and worked without paid overtime or rest breaks and without undergoing any safety training. If they complained, they were threatened with a call to immigration officials.

Sixteen-year-old Elmer L. summed up his experience: "I was very sad, and I felt like I was a slave." During one altercation with a rabbi, he was kicked from behind, causing a sharpened knife to fly up and cut his elbow, a laceration that required eight stitches. When the stitches ruptured the next day, according to the worker's injury report filed at the company, he was given a bandage and sent back to work. A fifteen-year-old Guatemalan, Joel R., was forced by financial needs to drop out of the eighth grade to work a 5:30 p.m. to 6:30 a.m. job at Agriprocessors.[20] These basic human rights violations, made public by the raid, have led the Iowa attorney general to bring 9,311 criminal misdemeanor charges against the company.[21] Unfortunately, the working conditions experienced by the undocumented at Agriprocessors are not an exception but tend to be general practice. Stories of abuses faced by society's most vulnerable families abound throughout the nation.

The institutionalized violence that befalls undocumented families is manifested in many other ways. For example, in Newark, a Hispanic-appearing freelance photographer who reported a dead body in an alley was detained by police and asked about his immigration status. In Durham, North Carolina, police have noticed that undocumented families are increasingly becoming victims in robberies because criminals consider them to be "soft targets" who will not report the crime to officials out of fear of being deported.[22] Women in particular are often victims. Staffers at the Tarirhu Justice Center in Falls Church, Virginia, constantly receive calls from women who have been assaulted but are afraid to report it to the police. And several women at the Agriprocessors plant reported sexual harassment. Women preparing to cross the border are advised to begin taking birth-control pills months prior to their crossing under the assumption that they will be raped by the smugglers, Border Patrol agents, or unscrupulous employers.[23] According to a study conducted from August 2007 to August 2008 by the University of Arizona, some three hundred women at three federal immigration detention centers faced widespread mistreatment and dangerous delays in receiving health care. Some of the women even suffered miscarriages while in detention.[24]

Treatment of the undocumented facing deportation by government agencies illustrates how violence against migrant workers has become institutionalized. According to medical records, internal government reports, and interviews with deportees, Immigration and Customs Enforcement has injected over 250 undocumented immigrants, against their will, with dangerous psychotropic drugs to sedate them during their expatriation. These antipsychotic drugs have been administered to individuals with no history of mental illness or documented history of violence.

One evening in February 2006, five guards piled on a forty-nine-year-old Ecuadorian in a Chicago holding cell to restrain him so that the nurse could punch a needle through his coveralls into his right buttock and administer drugs. The Ecuadorian had no history of a psychiatric disorder. He was sedated just so he could be easily deported. According to a deportation file that contained the nurse's account of the event, government officers stood menacingly over him while taunting him with "nighty-night."[25] To administer chemical restraints to detainees against their will when no medical justification exists is a violation of several international human rights codes, and specifically the Declaration of Helsinki, which emerged in the aftermath of World War II as a guideline regulating biomedical ethical conduct. Yet it appears that such procedures have become routine when it comes to the undocumented.

For Christians, families are the essential building blocks for community. Focusing on their well-being, providing pastoral support, and holding society accountable in preventing their disintegration should be mutual concerns of all believers. To claim a lack of time to deal with the trials and tribulations undocumented families face, as does Focus on the Family, ignores God's image that resides in them and denies any Christian claim to be disciples of Jesus. In *Gaudium et Spes*, an encyclical of the Second Vatican Council, the Roman Catholic Church laid out Christian guidelines on how to treat undocumented families:

> Justice and equality likewise require that the mobility which is necessary in a developing economy be regulated in such a way as to keep the life of individuals and their families from becoming insecure and precarious. Hence, when workers come from another country or district and contribute by their labor to the economic advancement of a nation or region, all discrimination with respect to wages and working conditions must be carefully avoided. The local people, moreover, especially public authorities, should all treat them not as mere tools of production but as persons, and must help them to arrange for their families to live with them and to provide themselves with decent living quarters. (no. 66)

A cornerstone of any reform of immigration policies must focus on the family, specifically on its unity and reunification. All families have worth in the eyes of God. All families deserve to be treated humanely and with dignity. Yet Hispanic families are being torn apart by laws and governmental policies and thus require the full attention of Christians. The Christian mandate is clear: we are required to focus on all families, the documented and the undocumented.

Testimony from a College-bound Young Adult
"Rosa"

Many people tell me that I am as American as apple pie. The funny thing about it is that I am neither a pie nor American. I am not American in the sense that I don't have the documentation to prove it. Yeah, from the outside I appear just like everyone else. I am eighteen years

old, full of life, and anxious about the future that awaits me. Yet there
is something that separates me from everyone else. That difference is a
couple of pieces of paper, documents that keep me from living my life,
keep me from my education, and keep me from my goals and dreams.

My story begins eighteen years ago when, by accident, on a cold
winter night, I was born in Mexico City. I say it was an accident because my mother was living in California at the time, but due to a family tragedy she was forced to return to Mexico and I was born there.
Although ironic, I also find it a little humorous. I was raised in Mexico
by my mother and my older half sister. My parents decided to divorce
soon after I was born. It was hard growing up in the environment and
situations that I faced. We were very poor, I had to deal with abuse,
and my mother was dying of AIDS. I did not have the security, comfort, love, and protection that children need. From my earliest memory
onward, I remember my mother being sick. My memories of childhood
are of going to hospitals, being afraid, and being alone. I watched my
mother's health deteriorate, until finally, two weeks after my eighth
birthday, I watched as she passed away.

As I sit here writing I feel a knot in my throat because I cannot
believe this is my life that I am describing. I knew as soon as my
mother passed away that my life would change, but I had no idea what
would come. A couple of days after my mother's death my father re-
entered the picture; he had come from the United States, and he wanted
me to go back with him. He painted a perfect picture for me. I was
wounded and I wanted to get away from the misery, so I decided to
leave with him. What hurt me most was leaving my half-sister, but I
was told that she would be fine. Soon after I left, my half-sister also
decided to leave. Her own father resided in the United States, so she
soon followed in my footsteps.

So there I was on my way to the United States, filled with hope and
happiness about the new life that I would begin. My hopes were soon
shattered when I found that my father was no father at all. He did not
give me the love and security I had hoped for. Instead I found myself
in another compromising situation where, like before, I had to take
care of myself. There were days when I found in myself so much sadness and anger. I cursed the day that I had decided to travel north.

When I was about twelve my father got really sick and he almost
died. No one ever explained to me exactly what had happened, but it
passed and everything returned to normal. After that my father went
to the doctor more and more routinely, and while he would talk about

his sickness he never mentioned what it actually was. Finally, about a year ago he told me that when he was sick a couple of years before, he was told that he had AIDS. Somehow I already knew or had figured it out, but inside I felt the heartbreak of that illness all over again.

Throughout all of this I was able to focus my energy and dedicate my time to my passion: my education. Starting with the first grade I have kept all my report cards because like a proud parent I am very proud of all my accomplishments. I found my happiness in school. That was the place I felt I belonged. There I found security, love, and I was able to express myself. Most important of all, I found my true love—learning. My eager and curious mind wanted to learn about everything. Even when I had just arrived in this country, I loved going to the school library. I thought it was the most amazing place. I remember looking at all the space books, looking at the planets, stars, and galaxies in amazement. I picked up a book on the first woman astronaut, and I looked at the pictures and I knew from that moment that a fire inside me was ignited. One day I wanted to be like her.

I had finally found the place where I belonged, and I was able to shine like the stars that I watched over my head at night. In school I always got the best grades, and my teachers always said great things about my future. I have always received awards, and I have always wanted to go above and beyond. I loved being involved, and I loved reading everything I could get my hands on. I still have an eager and curious mind that loves to learn about absolutely everything.

Once I got to high school I felt as if I couldn't ask for anything better. I decided to attend a nontraditional high school: a charter school. It was a new school, small in size, but the intriguing thing was that it was offering free college classes. How could I say no? I signed up and soon found out that I had been accepted. When I was a sophomore, about fifteen years old, I began taking college classes. Before I knew it I was fully enrolled in all college classes, and I was a full-time student at our community college. Although I was always the youngest person in my classes, I absolutely loved every minute of it. I was now being challenged, and I was learning amazing things. As before, I succeeded, and as with my teachers in high school, I was able to develop great relationships with my college professors. Then finally the day came when all my work came to fruition.

In May 2008 I graduated from the community college with an associate of science degree two weeks before I was to graduate from high school. Out of all the seniors in my school I was able to share this honor with four of my friends. We were the only ones who had completed our degrees. I graduated from college *magna cum laude*, made president's list, and was a member of Phi Theta Kappa (the honor society of two-year colleges). Then my high school graduation came, and I graduated second in my class. That's when my education ended.

I stood and watched as everyone around me was excited about the new lives they were about to start. By that time I had gotten used to standing on the sidelines. When all my peers and friends were excited about their first jobs, all I could do was watch. When they were excited about learning how to drive and getting their first car, I just watched. When they were excited about being accepted into college and leaving to continue their education, I just watched. I wasn't free to do all the things they did because according to the laws and documents, I had no right to any of those things. I have no right to be here, and some would call me a criminal.

How can I be a criminal? Do people call someone who is passionate about learning and who loves education a criminal?

I have been trying to find ways to continue my education, but it gets very hard when I don't qualify for federal aid, loans, grants, and most scholarships. With my educational record I have found that colleges easily accept me, but the problem is the money. Also, they don't know how to categorize me. Am I an international student or am I a domestic one? Or, as one school put it, am I a domestic student who has to pay international tuition?

It breaks my heart that what I love most in the world has been taken from me so cruelly and coldly. With all the things that I have experienced in my short life, my goal is to use my passion for education to help the world. Since I was a little girl I have always wanted to travel the world to help anyone and everyone. As I got older I realized how wounded the world really is, and somehow in my heart I feel it is my duty to do something. I have always felt that I need to get out there and save the world, but now I see that maybe it is the world that has to save me. Since I was young I knew that I wanted a career where I could help people. I had wild dreams of being an engineer, a scientist, a lawyer, a veterinarian, a jet pilot, an astronaut, and many other things. But how can my dreams come true if I cannot even pursue my education?

I find it funny when people ask me if I speak Spanish, and they are surprised when I tell them that I do and that I am Mexican. Most people cannot tell because I am just like everyone else. They assume I'm just another American. I enjoy going to baseball games, and my favorite sports are football and stock-car racing (NASCAR). My favorite food is mac 'n' cheese. I enjoy the outdoors and love all animals and wildlife. I have recently started volunteering so that I can begin giving back. I even looked into joining the military; I thought maybe in that way this country would finally accept me, but of course I could not.

I didn't ask to be brought here, but here I am. I have embraced my life here and all I want is to succeed and give back. I have never gotten in any sort of trouble; it's never even crossed my mind. People still call me a criminal. I hope that people can realize that I am just like everyone else and that even if I don't have the right papers I should not be treated any differently.

I grew up here and I have made my life here. This is my home. I have nowhere else to go. Imagine waking up one morning and being told to leave, that you don't belong here. It has been a hard struggle, but I have always had angels by my side, my teachers, helping me with every new rock on my path. Even though some days I feel lost in despair I will continue to fight for my true love of education, because the fire and passion I have for learning will never die out. I am just like everyone else, really, and I guess I am as American as apple pie, even if I don't have the papers that prove it.

Testimony about Separated Families
Elise Martins

Yesterday (May 12, 2008), our town was raided by four hundred FBI agents, ICE agents, state troopers, and a variety of other agencies. Helicopters flew overhead for hours, all the roads coming into and going out of Postville, Iowa, were blocked, media crews and cameras were *everywhere*, and there was mass chaos. The federal government had decided to make Postville an example for the rest of the nation to see our so-called Homeland Security at work.

Ironically, as this all transpired, I was at the county courthouse with my government class; the goal was for the students to learn firsthand how our judicial system works. We got more of a lesson than we bargained for. I received calls from the school telling me not to return

---

Elise Martins is a history/government high school teacher with the Postville School District.

because the school "was concerned" about some of my students. (Yes, my class included undocumented students who have been in this district since they were in fourth grade. They speak English clearly. Their parents work here in town and pay taxes. They have tried to file papers to become legal but have been denied because they do not come from a "desirable" country.)

I was told after a few hours that I could come back on the school bus, but that I should expect to be pulled over by the FBI and that under no circumstances was I to let an officer on the bus. I had twelve students who were scared about what would happen, including four students who could possibly be arrested. Basically, I had twenty minutes to get my wits about me and be ready to face ICE or the FBI and tell them to take a hike.

Under federal laws, schools and churches are considered sanctuaries. This did nothing to calm my nerves, for I was afraid that I might also be arrested for not cooperating with the law. We made it back into Postville only to find our school surrounded by the cameras of the media. I will not make a comment about the news media . . . because I do not have anything good to say about them at this point.

I arrived at my classroom to find that our entire computer network crashed at 10 a.m. (the same time ICE came to Postville). It has been running off and on today, with an entire computer tech team unable to find out what is wrong. Call me a conspiracy theorist, but I believe our accounts are being scanned.

After school, all teachers and staff were told to report to the theater. We had one hundred and fifty students with no parents to go home to. We were told that we needed to stay with them until we found out where their parents were or located a relative who would care for them until their parents were found. Many of these kids lost both parents due to the raid, and their parents were now sitting in jail in Waterloo, or in the National Cattle Congress Fairgrounds, until they would be deported.

I guess I don't really care how any of you feel about immigration— we all have our opinions. But I will say that as a human being and a parent, I found it disturbing to see little elementary school kids crying for their parents and asking me to take them home, and all I could say was, "I'm sorry," or "we're looking for them." By the way, we received no information from ICE as to whom they had arrested or whether or not certain parents had been detained. At that point I just wanted to go home and hug my own kids.

I spent the rest of the evening trying to locate family members; helping students "hide" their personal belongings in classrooms, barns, houses, or wherever; and warding off the media. From what I have heard, the story was broadcast on all the news channels and newspapers in the Midwest, with CNN and FOX News also taking up the story. I think we were on the national news that night. It was announced that Postville's raid was the largest immigration raid in U.S. history.

The next day I was missing about half of my students. Some had left for Chicago, others were hiding in town, some had been arrested, and others were at the Catholic Church. I spent the morning in the church helping with food preparation (about four hundred people were seeking refugee in the church) and also trying to locate items like diapers, food, pillows, blankets, and games for the little children. The media reported that about 350 people had been arrested, with 697 more possible arrests; most were Guatemalans (not Mexicans). Only 57 had been released due to child care or medical reasons. They are currently back home wearing ankle monitors. Most will eventually be deported.

The town has literally shut down. Businesses are closed, the school is about half empty, and we are now left wondering if we will have jobs next year. This town was a ghost town fifteen years ago but had managed to build itself up on the backs of our immigrant workers. I have complained many times about the language barriers I encountered at school, but I have always said that the reason I had a job was because we were the only district that actually was growing and able to keep its staff due to the sheer number of students in our school district. Working in the Postville School District makes me eligible to have half of my student loans forgiven over a five-year time period. I only have one more year left. If we lose half of our students, this will not happen.

What frustrates me most is that this raid accomplished nothing positive. It has destroyed families, it will more than likely close some area businesses, some of us will lose our jobs, and the real estate in the area will become worthless overnight—and all this in an already struggling economy.

I know that my account of what happened in Postville has become a long complaint, but those who complain about the immigrants "taking American jobs" don't even want these jobs. Honestly, who wants to work for minimum wage, twelve hours a day, six days a week with no overtime, in cold, smelly conditions, gutting chickens or cows? I know that I don't want to do that for a living.

It's interesting, though, that my students in U.S. history made a direct correlation between what we all witnessed yesterday and our history lesson three weeks ago. We had been studying World War II and the Holocaust. I had them view the movie *Schindler's List*. We had discussed what happened in the movie, with the Nazis rounding up the Jews, having them report their names and the names of their families, then transporting them to unknown places, keeping them in substandard holding areas, and in the end getting rid of them. Some of my students compared this to what happened yesterday, with one exception—the United States has not practiced the use of genocide.

Today ICE is doing house-to-house searches of every home and apartment with a Hispanic name attached to it. It is scary to see search teams go from place to place looking for immigrants. We had agencies at the school a month ago with a subpoena to seize all student and employee files. Any name that sounded remotely Hispanic was flagged. I find this to be a form of racial profiling, and I know that it is happening. Three weeks ago I was asked to bring in a copy of my birth certificate due to the fact that my maiden name (de Julio) was "Hispanic" sounding.

How quickly we forget our own histories. Many of our ancestors came here with nothing to their name and very little to survive on. They wanted a fresh start too. Unless they are 100 percent Native American, our ancestors were also immigrants. So why are we trying to make an example out of those less fortunate? Why not go after the people who really are doing something illegal and wrong? Like drug dealers or child molesters? If we spent as much money on that as we are currently spending on the war in Iraq (which we are losing) or building a seven-hundred-mile-long wall on the Mexican border, which is actually two thousand miles long—we might have a stronger economy and a country that would be safe for our families.

Testimony about Faith
Karen Cotta

Guadalupe bridges the gap! Four of us were on patrol in the Sonoran Desert, somewhere between Mexico and Tucson, Arizona. We

Karen Cotta recently graduated from Iliff School of Theology with a master's of divinity degree. She was among a group of students who traveled to the border with Dr. De La Torre to place water and food along the migrant trails.

were carrying food bags filled with Gatorade, peanut butter crackers, fruit cups, granola bars, small cans of Vienna sausages, and socks. Each of us also carried one or two gallon jugs of water. All these were to be left at a food drop at a common crossing spot in the hills. We hiked about a mile in from the road. It was a beautiful day for a hike, with constant cloud cover and an occasional mist. Being late August, it was near the end of the monsoon season and the desert was in full bloom. We trudged through grasses, some as tall as six feet, surrounded by butterflies of yellow, orange, and black. The cacti and even the ocotillo were in bloom.

In order to reach our destination we had to circumvent a small lake. Because of the heavy rains, the lake was full and completely covered with duckweed. It's at spots such as these that the desperate migrants stop for a drink and often fill any water jugs they are still carrying with them. This may extend their lives another day, but most lakes and water troughs carry so many bacteria that those who drink from them will die in the desert anyway.

We continued to trudge past prickly bushes, stumble over loose rocks, and ease our way up and down arroyos. This is not the flat, desolate terrain that I had pictured. However, you are lucky if all you receive are a few mosquito bites and scratches. The beauty of this season is deceptive. This is the time of year when snakes are hatching from their eggs, when grass hides popular trails, and when you could get trench foot from walking in the rain. And, of course, there is the constant threat of scorpions. However, the most common and debilitating injuries experienced on these trails are foot blisters and ankle sprains, especially on the mountainous terrain that many migrants are forced to cross these days.

That is exactly what we encountered when we happened upon a large group of migrants hiding in a narrow ravine just past the lake. I'm sure they heard us long before we caught sight of them. It is customary to announce our presence when patrolling the migrant trails with a "shout out" like the following:

Compañeras y compañeros, somos amigos de la iglesia. Estamos aquí para ayudarles. Tenemos comida, agua, y asistencia medical. Si necesitas ayuda, por favor, avísanos. No somos la migra.

Companions, we are friends of the church. We are here to help you. We have food, water, and medical assistance. If you need help, please notify us. We are not the Border Patrol.

As we approached the group of migrants, we asked if they were hungry. They all answered with a nod or soft-spoken *sí*. We began to hand out food bags and gallons of water. As we did so, I counted twelve individuals, but over the course of several minutes, a few others emerged from the ravine's crevices in order to grab food or let someone come forward for help. The first to come forward was a young woman with a sprained ankle. She couldn't have been more than twenty years old. She had her ankle lightly wrapped, so our medic gave her a new wrapping, some pain medication, and a cold pack to help reduce the swelling for at least a few hours.

The next woman to come forward was a slightly older indigenous woman who looked like she might have been from Guatemala. We know from the group's own reporting that some of them had, in fact, already crossed one border and made it all the way through Mexico. She had wet feet with a blister forming. The medic bandaged the blister in order to reduce the amount of rubbing this sore spot might incur. It was clear from her hand motions that the woman thought it might help to pop the blister, but medics have found that this often leads to infection and more pain and suffering.

While this woman was treated, everyone ate quietly. I stood back and made only occasional eye contact so that no one felt on display or interrogated. We asked only the necessary questions that would allow us to provide humanitarian aid and gather a few facts about the conditions of the migrants crossing in this area. We did not give out information that might be construed as "furthering their presence," and they didn't ask. Their *coyote* hid silently in the back. Some persons did feel that they were able to sneak in a few smiles here and there. As I made eye contact with a few of them, I began to notice how young they all were. They had to have been in their late teens and twenties.

One young man stepped up and asked if we were members of the Catholic Church. He and his companions had been reading the tags that were attached to each gallon jug of water. On the front of each laminated tag was a picture of Our Lady of Guadalupe and on the back was a handwritten note. Farmers from the central coast of California, some of them U.S. citizens and some of them Central American migrants who had crossed successfully, had put these together in order to show their love and support of those struggling in the desert. The tags included prayers and attestations of the Virgin's love and support of the poor. Others had simple messages about love and unity among peoples. Others included affirmations of the struggles of the migrants and blessings upon them as they fought to provide for themselves and their families. A few of the migrants removed the tags from the jugs and fastened them, with the twist ties, to their clothing.

When we told the young man that we were with a church, he came even closer and lowered his voice to a whisper. Then he began to tell us the story about how their group had come upon a popular shrine during the four-day journey through the desert. At this shrine stood an icon of the Virgin and, below it, one of our gallon jugs with the top removed. As migrants pass through this sacred site of hope, they drop in a peso, just as if they had attended mass at a church back home. Some even bring along candles, rosaries, and small statues to leave at such sites. The extra weight in their backpack is obviously of little importance in comparison to the hope that these ritual sites provide.

The members of this large group decided they would collect the coins and bring them to a Catholic church once they arrived in Tucson. However, they knew of the likelihood of being picked up by the patrol and were afraid that the money would be confiscated if they were captured. Instead, they asked us to take the money to a Catholic church. They didn't care if the money went to Anglo Americans or Central American migrants like themselves, only that the money went to help others. We promised to be good stewards of the pesos and thanks were exchanged. What amazed me was that the group members had such faith in God's bounty that they didn't keep the money for themselves or their families. It was clear to me that their hearts were full of compassion and generosity. My heart swelled with amazement, and tears welled up in my eyes.

This loving spirit was confirmed when the second woman thanked us for helping her. I did not catch every word that she said, but she told us that she would not be able to survive the journey without God by her side. Not only did she have a very strong sense of God's presence, but she professed that we would receive many blessings for the work that we were doing. She said all of this with a bright smile. In fact, others in her group began to make more eye contact and exchanged bashful smiles with us.

True, it could have been a lot worse for this group. For the most part they were young and healthy. The women were well taken care of, unlike those who are too frequently beaten and raped by the more crooked *coyotes* and Border Patrol officers. They had also stayed together in a large group with their guide, which increased their chances of survival. Still, they were probably fifty miles from Tucson, and who knows how far from their final destination. The rains would continue and bring them more challenges. The food and water that we gave this large group was only enough for one day. The dark clothes that they wore confirmed their testimony of only traveling at night, most likely without flashlights or a compass. Their best defense was staying in a large group, but that had already been threatened by Border Patrol agents. A common form of intimidation and sabotage involves landing a Border Patrol helicopter in the middle of a group of migrants, scattering and confusing them in the process. Most *coyotes* will not take the time to find lost group members.

Dehydration, blisters, sunburn, as well as fatigue and fear would certainly be a part of their lives for the next several days, if not months and years, and yet they blessed us with their words and smiles. We did what we could to stay within the *legal* limits of the United States. I would add that there was certainly nothing *alien* about this encounter; however, the faith and generosity the migrants modeled for us was certainly not of this world.

There is much ambiguity in the discussions of immigration. There are individuals on all sides of the issue with selfish motives and violent tendencies *and* there are just as many, if not more, individuals who are simply fighting for survival and a slice of happiness. The day after we encountered this group, I was walking along a rock wash and came upon a small group of black and yellow butterflies. "How sweet and delicate," I thought. Then I noticed that they were feeding on animal scat, probably belonging to a wildcat. Indeed, life is messy and disgusting *and* precious and beautiful.

Postcard Images on the Trail

According to folklore, Jesús Malverde was a Robin Hood–type character who stole from the rich and gave to the poor. After he was killed in 1909 by the police, the public—not the official church—made him a saint. People began to believe that his image offered protection from the

Jesús Malverde

law, and as such he be-came the patron saint of drug dealers. Although he is known as the narco-saint, migrants also venerate the image of Jesús Malverde, praying that he will provide safe conduct into the United States. One finds his image on postcards on the migrant trails.

The trails also display many postcard images of Toribio Romo Gonzalez, a priest martyred by Mexican federal troops during the Cristero Wars and canonized in 2000 by Pope John Paul II. Since canonization, immigrants crossing the Sonoran Desert to get to the United States have claimed that San Toribio has appeared to them, guiding their journey north. As a result, the Shrine of St. Toribio, in Santa Ana de Guadalupe, draws many pilgrims from throughout Mexico who are preparing to make the hazardous crossing into the United States and are in need of spiritual protection. He has quickly become the patron saint of immigrants.

Toribio Romo Gonzalez

Testimony from a Community Organization
Lisa Durán

I am not an immigrant, but I am the granddaughter of immigrants. Because of my grandparents, because I am proud of my Mexican heritage, because I love diversity, and because I fear for the soul of the United States, I work in immigrant rights, directing an immigrant-based organizing project. Three of my four grandparents came from Mexico in the 1920s (the fourth had roots in colonial New Mexico prior to the American Revolution). My parents lived with blatant racism and discrimination: they were allowed to use the public swimming pool only on the day before it was cleaned, and they commonly encountered signs saying, "No Mexicans Allowed." My brothers and I lived with lesser examples, but discrimination was there nonetheless. We were privileged to live in a family that honored and had pride in its Mexican heritage. Growing up in the face of that racism, we were armed with our parents' admonition to always be proud of who we are.

I have worked in issues of immigrant and refugee rights since 1984. My work took on new urgency after the passage of Proposition 187 in California in 1994, a law that was later found to be unconstitutional. Among other things, that law called on health-care providers and teachers to report people they suspected of being undocumented to immigration authorities. Since that time the immigration debate has turned uglier, providing convenient excuses for a sharp rise in nativism and racism.

The deeper truth about why I do this work, and how I know I can continue doing justice work in the future, stems from my family's history, my faith, and my values. An early story can illustrate my point. When I was seven years old, living with my family in Pico Rivera, California, we had just come home from grocery shopping. My mother brought the car to a stop in front of our little house, but then just sat there, keys in the ignition, the radio still playing, with the news droning on. I asked, "Mommy, what's wrong?" She was focused on the radio with her head down, listening. She shushed us and turned it up.

Lisa Duran is the executive director of Rights for All People in Denver, Colorado.

"Oh, no," she said, shaking her head, foreboding in her voice. "Oh, no!" "What, Mommy?" She turned and looked at us, sadness welling up in her eyes, saying heavily, "They shot Martin Luther King. They *killed* him because he was black." And so began my education of what it means to live a good life.

We were six, seven, and nine years old, and my mom continued trying to explain, using words we could understand, that there were people in this world who didn't like other people "*just because of the color of their skin.*" I remember being told that we were not that kind of people, for that was not what God would want us to be. I remember the importance of that moment, that my mother wanted us to hear her, *really* hear her. I felt an answering echo within me that agreed with my mom, that said I *should* care about what happens around me, even if it is to people that I don't know, *especially* when it involves people being preyed upon by grave injustice.

Shortly after, Bobby Kennedy was killed, only a twenty-minute drive from where we lived. The night after it happened, my parents were out of the house and we had a babysitter. She was distraught watching the news coverage, and she left the TV on for what seemed like hours. Without the security of my parents' presence, I remember feeling frightened about what could happen, feeling like something was breaking down and that we couldn't control it. Later, my parents helped me make the connections between myself and the people and events around me. And that drew me into the work, made it a calling for me.

When we were small, my mom bought us a book about the Good Samaritan. I was intrigued by the artwork, a style of torn colored construction paper on a mottled background that was popular then, but I related more to the story. At first I thought there had been a mistake in the telling. How could a *priest*—who was supposed to serve God— and a Levite, a holy man, ignore someone who had been beaten and left for dead at the side of the road? At first the message for me was simply that this good person, this Samaritan, did what we should all hope to do when faced with another's suffering. In later years I learned that Samaritans were despised in those days, that they were the African Americans under Jim Crow laws, the undocumented immigrants of those days. And this story became even more meaningful to me. This recognition of the Samaritan's decency invited us to open our hearts to God in every person and to the possibility that those who are elevated to be our leaders and our role models might sometimes find themselves limited by their humanity in ways that will cost all of us.

When people ask me why I do the work I do in immigrant rights, these early memories often start the story. What came next was that I discovered the inspiring stories about people working together to build community and change the world. I sought as many opportunities as possible to become a part of that history: boycotting grapes and iceberg lettuce for many years in support of the United Farm Workers; becoming active in 1974 in the Chicano movement and Chicano student groups and student newspapers in college; traveling to Mexico and Cuba in 1979 to study liberation theology in Latin America; declaring campus sanctuary at the University of California, Riverside, which sparked a national wave of declarations in response to the United States's horrific, inhumane interventions in Central America.

I could not have imagined the resurgence of xenophobia and racism that has surfaced during the last fifteen years involving immigration. The language used to discuss immigration and immigrants has become hateful. The drumbeat of "they do not have permission to be here" questions the very humanity of immigrants. Legislative proposals would make felons out of millions for civil violations. The explicit aim is to create so much suffering that "undocumented immigrants will voluntarily leave" their homes and communities. The very roots of immigration—*stemming from U.S. laws and political and economic systems*—are conveniently ignored by those who would paint the issue in the simplest of terms. The door is closed to any honest attempt to grapple with common-sense solutions. The insistence that dehumanizing the undocumented is for the common good is frighteningly inhumane. How can I not work to bring about change?

Over time, my faith journey moved from being the impetus to becoming the sustaining foundation of my social justice work. My faith and values provide a vital and relevant guide that helps me transcend the cruelties around us to build something beautiful that can be of service to all. To incorporate such deeply held beliefs into my work appropriately, I have had to mature and find personal healing.

When I was sixteen years old, I gave birth to a son, Nando. The way my family decided to deal with my unwed pregnancy was by giving him up for adoption. On my seventeenth birthday I signed the papers that would give him to his new family. Then I was supposed to go home and "move past all this." I was not supposed to speak of it, because in those days many still believed that a young, unmarried mother was ruined for the rest of her life. My family wanted to forget it so I could get back to growing up and making something of myself. This course of action was heartily promoted by our church. From that church, in many ways, I received the message that I was irredeemable for having become pregnant outside of marriage. I remember a priest taunting me when I went to him for spiritual guidance about my unmarried status. I left deeply scarred.

Having shamed myself and caused my parents pain, I did my best to move forward. I did well in college, earning a B.A. and an M.A. I read voraciously about political and economic systems and how communities were creating change. I was inspired because people who experienced injustice powerfully organized to transform it, to transform their communities, and to transform the way people and institutions related with each other.

I lived with the realization that my son was out there somewhere. I thought of him every day, hurt on his birthday and Mother's Day, but I told very few people about this reality. I coped by becoming intellectually driven. For many years I blocked my heart and spirit out of my work. Organizing was an intellectual pursuit. I was disconnected from my humanity and the humanity of those around me. I was unable to be vulnerable, to bring myself to my work. I rejected faith because of the way I had been treated, without mercy or compassion.

All of this changed when I found my son, who was then twenty-six, in the aftermath of a painful divorce. I was made whole in a way I had never anticipated. I began to see that this wholeness was a form of grace in which divergent paths had converged. Working to alleviate suffering and misery, to improve our communities, had opened my eyes to economic and political structures and institutions that perpetuate inequality. I found a welcoming faith practice that mirrored Christ's loving acceptance of those considered less than desirable. This allowed me to experience the mercy and healing that I needed so I could grow beyond my mistakes and root myself in compassion. I was able to share with my son an open and loving heart.

The immigration issue is personal for me. I find that my work has become truly sustaining only as a result of reconnecting with my faith and values. I look at the moments in my life when I am at peace with my surroundings, when I *know* that I am on the right path, and they involve grace. Grace involves love and acceptance of myself and those around me, mercy and forgiveness, compassion, courage to witness suffering, and sacrifice to help alleviate it. Bringing this approach to the work of building community helps us to be the change we want to see, borrowing words from Mahatma Gandhi. It will help us all become the Good Samaritan.

Voice of the People

Mi Lindo Campo de Arivaca
(My Pretty Camp in Arivaca)

An eight-year-old girl stumbled into the aid camp with her mother. Both were dehydrated and in need of water. Their lives were literally saved by this No More Death site located near the town of Arivaca. In gratitude, the girl drew this picture for the camp that is located at the foot of two hills. Marking the camp are two jugs with the Spanish word for "water" written on them. Above the water jugs is the phrase "My pretty camp in Arivaca."

5

The Politics of Fear

Many who enter the country illegally are just looking for jobs, but others are coming to kill you, and you, and me, and my children and my grandchildren.
—Rep Tom Tancredo (R-CO), 2008 Republican
presidential candidate[1]

In an age of terrorism, drug cartels, and criminal gangs, allowing millions of unidentified persons to enter and remain in this country poses grave risks to the sovereignty of the United States and the security of its people.
—2008 Republican Party Presidential Platform

While being detained by the Border Patrol, fifteen migrants, including three women and two children (ages fourteen and sixteen), were made to run for thirty minutes in the desert. Those who stopped running were kicked by officers and forced to continue running to discourage them from ever attempting to cross again. In another case three young women who were apprehended by Border Patrol agents and walking in custody were pushed by these agents into cacti. They were refused medical treatment for the injuries they sustained.

When a mother of two small children (one six and the other nine) who was being held in detention for two and a half hours begged for water for her children the Border Patrol officer drank water in front of them and refused to give them any. A twenty-one-year-old woman was forced to remove her top and lie on the floor of her cell. A seventeen-year-old girl was "searched" by a male officer who inappropriately touched her chest, thighs, and reached deep into her pockets.

According to Joan Cooney, a retired New York State judge, "I was repeatedly told that water was provided in a single, large dirty bucket with one ladle placed in the middle of a large detention room." Sarah Roberts, a registered nurse, states, "I have spoken with hundreds of migrants who were separated from their family members and repatriated at different times." Joseph Shortall, a First Aid-certified volunteer, reported, "I have witnessed and/or treated dozens of injuries including sprained ankles, injured arms and hands, lacerations, severely blistered feet, sunburns, and dehydration among returned migrants who had received no medical care of any kind while in U.S. custody."[2] And, finally, during my own research, I often heard accounts of migrants who, after crossing a desert and being incarcerated, were given saltine crackers and no water.

These abuses are some of the 345 testimonies collected by medical professionals and trained volunteers working in migrant aid centers during 2006 and 2007. The lack of any uniform regulation by our government for short-term immigrant custody and the total absence of any independent oversight of the treatment of those detained create an atmosphere in which migrants are routinely denied food and water; where they are separated from their families during the repatriation process; where physical, sexual, and verbal abuse are common; where they are addressed by racial epitaphs; and where their possessions are confiscated and not returned—in short, migrants are exposed to widespread and systematic practices that deny their human dignity and abuse their human rights.

Such maltreatment is not a new phenomenon. In the 1980s human rights organizations began documenting violations against migrants committed by Border Patrol agents. The American Friends Service Committee Law Enforcement Monitoring Project documented over twelve hundred human rights violations between May 1989 and May 1991.[3] Amnesty International has also documented continuous denial of food, water, and medical attention in an atmosphere of routine verbal, physical and psychological abuse by the Border Patrol.[4]

Not surprisingly, these habitual practices of law-enforcement agencies, specifically the Border Patrol, have led to unnecessary and senseless deaths of immigrants who were in their custody. A few examples of the many documented incidents should suffice. Victoria Arellano, a transgendered woman suffering from HIV, was denied her medication while being held in an ICE detention center in San Pedro, California. This led to complications and ultimately her death. Edimar Alves Araujo was picked up by ICE for a traffic violation. While in custody at the Providence, Rhode Island, detention facility, he suffered an epileptic seizure. His sister rushed to the facilities with his medication, pleading that it be given to him. Officers refused, leading to his death.

In March 2006 a Border Patrol agent ran down a twelve-year-old girl, Lourdes Torralva, with his SUV after the daughter and her father ran to hide in a bush. She was on her way to Oxnard, California, to be reunited with her mother. Jesús Rivera Cota was shot in the back of the head by a Border Patrol agent when the truck in which he was a passenger drove by the officer in an attempt to *return* to Mexico in May 2005. Francisco Javier Dominguez-Rivera (age twenty-two) was shot and killed at close range by a Border Patrol agent after crossing the border with three family members.[5]

Stereotyping and Abuse

Abuse and brutality at the hands of law-enforcement agencies is not limited to the border area separating the United States from Mexico. To be a Hispanic in the United States today is to be a target. One of the privileges of being white is never needing to be conscious of one's ethnicity or race. For example, what would happen if 10 percent of all Euroamericans were routinely stopped by law-enforcement officers for the sole purpose of checking their Social Security cards? Even if they committed no crime, nor did any suspicion exist that they participated in a crime, they were stopped solely because they had white skin. Or what if 10 percent of African Americans were stopped to make sure they had documentation for being in certain neighborhoods? While African Americans are disproportionately stopped and ticketed for so-called traffic violations, they are not stopped because a law-enforcement officer is suspicious that they might not be Americans. No doubt, there would be outrage. As Americans, we defend our freedom to move about the country without first having to obtain permission from some policing agency. There is the accepted belief that we are all innocent until proven guilty. Yet documented Hispanics, including those born in the United States, are all guilty of *not belonging* until we show proper documentation proving otherwise. According to a 2008 survey conducted by the Pew Hispanic Center, nearly one in ten of Hispanic adults (8 percent of native-born U.S. citizens, and 10 percent of immigrants) reported that in the past year they had been stopped by law-enforcement officials and asked about their immigration status.[6]

Mayra Figueroa's encounter with the law is a typical example. Figueroa, a U.S. naturalized citizen, was pulled over by a Houston police officer. When asked why she was stopped, the police officer responded that he found it suspicious that a Latina was driving a late-model car. Although Figueroa was a licensed driver, the document requested by the officer was her Social Security card in order to prove her citizenship. "I have been living here for the last seventeen years, and to have an officer stop me for no reason and ask for [my identification] papers made me feel like he didn't think I belong here," said Figueroa. "It makes people feel that anytime that something happens to you, you can't call police."[7] Obviously, such racial profiling disproportionately burdens Hispanics, the majority of whom are either law-abiding documented immigrants or U.S. citizens.

The use of language also betrays the racist underpinning of the current debate. Those opposed to immigration consistently use the term *illegal* to describe undocumented migrants. Why? Stereotyping the immigrant as a lawbreaker, by extension, stereotypes all Hispanics as lawbreakers. Figueroa became a suspect only because she made the error of driving while under the influence of being a Latina. Because the police officer falsely assumed that all Hispanics are poor, then simply being Latina and driving a late-model vehicle raised suspicions. The stereotype says that Hispanics aren't part of the middle class.

The use of fear-mongering by politicians has brought a new dimension to racial profiling. Hispanics, including U.S. citizens and resident aliens, can be stopped by law-enforcement officers under nearly any pretense. A practice long suffered by African Americans (and since 9/11 by persons of darker complexions in general) is now being brought full force against Hispanics. While a passenger in a car a few miles from the Mexican border, I realized that I was without my wallet. I had left it in my knapsack back at the camp. During the entire trip I was extremely uneasy and worried. Unlike the others in the car, I was Hispanic, and at that moment I was without proper identification. If pulled over by the Border Patrol or police, I could easily have been detained or arrested until I proved my status, something no other person in that vehicle had to worry about.

But it doesn't stop with just being pulled over by law-enforcement officers. Some Hispanics, according to that same Pew survey, reported experiencing other difficulties because of their ethnicity, including finding or keeping a job—even if they had proper papers—because they were Hispanic, and finding and obtaining housing.[8] Americans are being denied the ability to provide for their families and find shelter because employers and landlords are frightened of what might happen to them if they inadvertently employ or rent to someone who might not have proper documentation.

For those who do find housing or a job, the discrimination continues. Consider what happened to José Sauceda. Smithfield Packing, located in Tar Heel, North Carolina, is the world's largest hog-processing plant. Sauceda was responsible for cutting pork loins with a power saw. An immigrant with poor English skills, Sauceda was abused by supervisors who pushed him to work faster and faster. Attempting one day to meet the supervisor's demand to get the product out quickly, he caught his hand in the saw while reaching for the next slab of loin. His injury required surgery to set pins in his finger. His hand didn't heal properly, leaving him with crooked fingers. When he returned to work, he found he was unable to perform his job adequately. After a while, Smithfield Packing fired him, saying his immigration papers were not in order. While testifying on October 2, 2003, before the Congressional Immigrant Worker Safety and Health Briefing, Sauceda summed up his experience. "This work that we do here in the United States is really hard and the companies take advantage of us as immigrants who don't speak English and who don't know our rights. They intimidate us to keep us in line and fire us when they want to."[9] What Sauceda experienced is not an exception but a widespread practice.

According to a study done by the AFL-CIO, both documented and undocumented Hispanic workers have experienced a sharp increase in workplace fatalities. In 2006 fatal injuries among Latino/as increased by 7 percent, with 990 fatalities, the highest number ever reported. More than two-thirds of these fatalities (667 deaths) were among foreign-born Hispanics, of which several, undoubtedly, were undocumented. Fatal injuries among Latina/o workers were 25 percent higher than those among the population of other U.S. laborers. Since 1992, when these figures began to be collected, job-related fatalities among Hispanics have increased by 86 percent. In the construction industry a Hispanic is twice as likely to be killed by occupational injuries as a non-Hispanic worker. In short, Latino immigrant male workers are disproportionately at greater risk of being killed by occupational injuries than any other gender or racial/ethnic group.[10]

As high as these numbers appear to be, the actual numbers of injuries and fatalities are under-reported. Under-reporting is a problem among laborers with questionable documentation or limited permission to work. They fear being fired or reported to the ICE if they report injuries. When an injury occurs, the worker, especially a day laborer, is often simply dropped off at the emergency room of a nearby hospital.

Ethnicity is the primary determinant in the hazards faced by the undocumented and the treatment they receive from their employers. Indeed, this nation's long history of racism and ethnic discrimination provides the background for the present debate on immigration policies.

If the present demographic trends continue, before we reach the midpoint of this century one in four Americans will be of Latino/a descent. There has been tremendous growth since 1950, when there were only four million Hispanics residing in the United States, about 2.6 percent of the population. The figure rose to 11.3 percent at the start of the twenty-first century, representing more than a 650 percent increase. As of 2007 Hispanics encompassed some 47 million Americans or 15.5 percent of the U.S. population. Now that Census Bureau information indicates that Hispanics are the fastest-growing group within the United States, for many, closing the border becomes a strategy to minimize the "browning" of America.

Yet, according to Kenneth Johnson, senior demographer at the University of New Hampshire's Carsey Institute, "If you close the borders tomorrow, there is still going to be a large Hispanic increase." Between 2006 and 2007, about 62 percent of the increase within the Latina/o population was due to births. The median age of Hispanics is younger than that of the general population, and between 2000 and 2007 there were 8.4 Latino births for each death. African Americans had 2.4 births for each death, and Euroamericans had 1.6 births for each death. To maintain a stable population, women must conceive 2.1 children. While Hispanic women give birth to an average 2.8 children—well above the 2.1 replacement rate—the conception rate of Euroamerican women at 1.8 children is well below it.[11]

Who Are These Hispanics?

Many within the dominant culture see Latina/os as a monolithic group with few or no differences, even though there are Central Americans, Caribbean natives, Mexicans, and Chicano/as. In a culture where some groups still cling to the idea of racial purity, Hispanics are seen as inferior because they represent a *mestizaje* (mixture) of cultures, races, and ethnicities. Latino/as are heirs of several different cultures, including Amerindian or indigenous peoples (the Taíno, Mayan, Aztec, and Zapotec), remnants of medieval Catholic Spain (influenced by Muslims and Jews), and of Africa (primarily in the Caribbean and Brazil), Asia, and due to their continuous presence within the United States, various European groups. There is no such thing as a "pure"

Hispanic, and it is often this mixed ethnic and racial composition that makes all Latina/os suspect to "pure-blooded" Euroamericans. Ironically, the Europeans were the most recent arrivals and as such are the true foreigners. Even though Hispanics are seen as foreigners by the dominant culture, many are actually occupying the native lands of their ancestors. Some have the contradictory distinction of being the first inhabitants and the latest migrants. Yet regardless of the status of Latino/as or where they live or how long their people have lived on U.S. soil, all Hispanics find themselves living on one border or another.

Demographically, approximately 12 million people live along the 1,833–mile border that separates the United States from Mexico, with about 6.3 million living on the U.S. side of the border and 5.5 million living on the Mexican side. Still, the U.S. borderlands are more than a geographical location; they are also the existential reality of Latina/o alienation. A Latina/o does not need to live in one of the towns or villages along the U.S.-Mexican border to experience the alienation of living on the border. Borders exist in every state, county, city, and town that separates Hispanics from Euroamerican-designated spaces. The invisible walls are as real in Kansas City, San Francisco, and Chicago as are the visible walls in Chula Vista, California; Douglas, Arizona; or El Paso, Texas.

To be a Latina/o living anywhere in the United States is to face constantly a border that separates him or her from the benefits that society has to offer.[12] This is evident in the continuing segregation existing in housing, public schools, and employment. Even when Hispanics are actually born in the United States and can boast of generations of U.S.-born ancestors, their Spanish surname, or stereotypical Latina/o ethnic features, or identification with Hispanic culture is sufficient grounds to be seen as foreign. Sadly, even Puerto Ricans who are born legal U.S. citizens (including those born on the island of Puerto Rico) are seen as foreigners and thus relegated, along with all other Hispanics, to the other side of the border.

For many Euroamericans, any fluidity of borders is a frightening prospect. Borders, both physical and invisible, must be maintained. Indeed, the "browning" of America signals the realization of their worst fears, and the recognition that in the future Euroamericans will become a minority population has spurred many initiatives to forestall the inevitable. Many states have passed English-only legislation, imposed restrictions on obtaining a driver's license, and placed restrictions on obtaining emergency medical services. Some states, like Arizona, are even considering legislation that would bar citizenship to those born in the United States to undocumented parents.

The Scourge of Racism

One of the main reasons the current debate on immigration has become so polarizing is because it is based on racist distinctions. Legislation focused on criminalizing a group of individuals along ethnic lines, in this case Hispanics, creates an environment that favors racial profiling. An atmosphere of fear is fostered when employers and social-service agencies, fearing governmental reprisals, find it legally and financially safer to discriminate against those who appear "foreign"—in other words, having a Hispanic name or "features," or speaking Spanish.

Consider the actions of Joe Arpaio, the sheriff of Maricopa County in Arizona, whose jurisdiction includes Phoenix. Sheriff Arpaio has authorized his deputies to arrest undocumented immigrants (using questionable tactics), a responsibility normally reserved for federal agents. Phoenix Mayor Phil Gordon has become so alarmed by the sheriff's tactics that he has asked the Justice Department's Civil Rights Division to examine what he calls discriminatory harassment and improper stops, searches, and arrests. "Sheriff Arpaio's actions," according to Mayor Gordon, "have infringed on the civil rights of our residents."[13] Sheriff Arpaio's jails are notorious for feeding Latino/a prisoners rotten ("green") baloney and forcing male prisoners to wear pink underwear in an attempt to humiliate them.[14] In early 2008 Sheriff Arpaio unveiled a hotline for citizens to report those whom they suspected of being undocumented.[15] This raises the question: Exactly what does an undocumented person look like?

Comments of North Carolina Sheriff Steve Bizzell of Johnston County are also revealing. Sheriff Bizzell came to the attention of the American Civil Liberties Union and other civil rights groups for discriminating remarks made against Hispanics during an interview with *News and Observer*, a regional newspaper in North Carolina. According to Sheriff Bizzell, "Everywhere you look, it's like little Mexico around here." He condemned Mexicans for being "trashy" and "breeding like rabbits," and spreading a culture of drunkenness and violence. A letter to Bizzell written by ACLU legal director Katherine Lewis Parker expressed "alarm" at the sheriff's comments, which "may constitute direct evidence of racial discrimination and animus" toward Latina/os in Johnston County. Nevertheless, the sheriff's rhetoric that undocumented immigrants "rape, rob and murder" American citizens, fail to pay taxes, and drain social services cemented his popularity among conservative voters and ensured his reelection.[16]

It would be easy to dismiss Sheriff Bizzell as an exception, but unfortunately, numerous daily actions experienced by the Latina/o community, documented and undocumented, throughout the United States testify that Sheriff Bizzell is closer to the norm. Of course, you do not need to be undocumented to feel targeted by the police, as was my experience when I was without identification and close to the border; being Hispanic is more than enough. Some of the actions of law-enforcement officers may result from personal bigotry, while others may surface because of the heightened racialization of the immigration debate.

For Latina/os, police brutality as a manifestation of racism was best illustrated in Los Angeles on May 1, 2007, when the Hispanic community held a rally to protest Congress's failure to pass comprehensive immigration legislation. Hispanics met for a peaceful gathering in MacArthur Park, west of the downtown area. Unexpectedly, police in full riot gear showed up, swinging clubs and attacking the Latino/a families, including men, women, children, and grandparents. When the press protested the abuse, Christina Gonzalez from a Fox News affiliate, her camerawoman Patti Ballaz, and National Public Radio reporter Patricia Nazario were among the injured civilians. The police justified their actions by reporting that a band of youths—although *not* affiliated with the peace march—had taunted them over a block away from the park.

Instead of separating and arresting the troublemakers, the police herded them into the park where Hispanic families had gathered and indiscriminately swung and shot at them. After the smoke cleared, Police Chief William J. Bratton admitted that this was the "worst incident of this type [he has] ever encountered in thirty-seven years." According to Victor Narro, an attorney with the National Lawyers Guild, one videotape showed the police firing a round of rubber bullets at what appeared to be a ten-year-old boy, and then "toss[ing] him aside like a piece of meat."[17] These were police actions against documented Americans who happened to be Hispanic.[18]

Not surprisingly, Hispanics, whether they are recently arrived or have lived on these lands prior to there being a United States, have expressed concerns that the present social and political climate caused by the debate on immigration has had negative effects. According to a 2007 report released by the Pew Hispanic Center, 64 percent of Latino/as questioned indicated that the polarizing immigration debate has made their lives more difficult: 12 percent reported having more trouble getting a job, 15 percent expressed difficulty in finding or keeping housing, and 19 percent reported being asked more often for proof of documentation. When asked about discrimination, 41 percent responded that they, a family member, or a close friend had experienced discrimination in the past five years, up from 31 percent when the same question was asked during the 2002 survey. More than half of all Latina/os (54 percent) stated that discrimination remains a major obstacle to succeeding in this country, up from 44 percent in 2002. When asked to list the major causes of discrimination, 46 percent listed language, 22 percent listed immigration status, 16 percent listed low wages and roadblocks to education, and 11 percent said skin color.[19]

The treatment of undocumented immigrants with Latin American ancestry and U.S. documented Hispanics today, spurred on by the anti-Hispanic rhetoric of the immigration debate, constitutes a violation of basic civil rights. A fully documented Hispanic in the United States today should have full acceptance by the society and full access to the society's resources and opportunities. However, such acceptance is usually contingent on how close the Latino/a is to a white ideal. And, unfortunately, the social structures responsible for normalizing, legitimizing, and institutionalizing ethnic discrimination today are strongly compromised by the language of the immigration debate.

Yet, talk of a violation of basic civil rights for Hispanics bothers some Euroamericans. Civil rights, the argument goes, is a term that is restricted to African Americans and the civil rights movement begun in 1960s. However, while focusing on the African American experience, this country's civil rights leaders never limited the need for justice to just that community. As Martin Luther King, Jr., reminded us, the greatest obstacle to full integration into society blacks faced were the same obstacles faced by Latino/a migrant workers, poor Appalachian whites, Native Americans relegated to the reservations, and other marginalized communities—all part of the economic stranglehold of white elites on the entire society. Both Martin Luther King, Jr., and Malcolm X were aware of the role played by poverty. King wanted to lead a Poor Peoples March, a desire unrealized due to his assassination, and Malcolm X spoke and wrote of how the U.S. black experience was related and interconnected to the consequences of colonialism that were also being experienced by other peoples of the world.

According to King, one of the lessons of the civil rights movement is that "justice denied anywhere diminishes justice everywhere." The injustices faced by Hispanics in general, and today's undocumented in particular, would no doubt have attracted the attention of the early civil rights leaders. Unfortunately, by creating a false dichotomy between black and brown people (or red and brown people), racism and ethnic discrimination have triumphed through the old strategy of divide and conquer. Rather than working together for justice, media reports of African American–Latino/a friction reinforce tensions between marginalized communities that otherwise would be natural allies with a greater influence on the political process.

The present immigration debate uses many techniques to mask its ethnic discriminatory foundations. While some groups do use anti-Hispanic rhetoric quite openly in advocating anti-immigration policies, other groups are more nuanced. Some try to avoid appearing intolerant or racist and mask their anti-immigrant sentiments by framing their arguments as a need to protect the environment, to control population growth, to check anti-corporate concerns, and/or to protect access to jobs.

But regardless of how the argument is framed, or which side of the debate people support, the human rights abuses faced by the undocumented and the ethnic discrimination faced by the documented should be repudiated by all. To participate in or be complicit with the institutional violence visited upon the Hispanic community, or to stand silently by as people, due to their ethnicity, are targeted for abuse, only robs the victimized of their dignity and also robs the perpetrators of their humanity. Both need healing, both need salvation, both need liberation. Fear must be overcome so that a more humane approach to immigration issues will benefit native-born and the undocumented.

Testimony about Ethnic Discrimination
"Pablo"

Pablo's clothes and appearance were unkempt. It appeared he had not washed for days. He was in his late thirties, with prominent

---

"Pablo" is Subject #3, interviewed and taped by Miguel A. De La Torre on June 13, 2008. His story was translated, transcribed, edited, and then written by the interviewer.

Aztec features. While we were talking, a contractor looking for laborers approached us. He needed some drywall installed. They were unable to arrive at a fair price, so Pablo turned down the offer to work and stayed to talk to me. He was agitated and frustrated for what he perceived to be an injustice being committed against him.

He had a knife to my throat. I was scared. It was late at night, and I was walking home from work. From the shadows of a building, a tall American appeared out of nowhere. He was easily a foot taller than me. He grabbed me from behind and put the knife under my chin. "Give me your wallet and backpack," he barked. Fighting him would have been futile, so I handed over my bag. The only thing in the bag was a change of clothes, a few pictures, and some food items. My wallet, containing just a few dollars, was also in my backpack. But what that American really stole from me was priceless. I had my alien registration card in my wallet.[20] I am documented. I have my papers. I can legally stay and work in this country. But now I cannot prove it because my card has been stolen. Now I am seen and treated as if I'm garbage.

I used to work as a farmer in Mexico, and I came here to do the same type of work. Because I had my papers, I had no difficulty finding a job. I worked hard, took paid vacations, and paid my taxes. But now, no one wants to hire me without my alien registration card. When I cannot produce it, they just send me away, or pay me a fraction of what I used to make with the card. After a while I lost my steady job. My employer was afraid he would be fined if he kept me without proper documentation.

With time, I became homeless. Now I spend my days here waiting for someone to give me a day job. I'm lucky if I can get a job that pays seven or eight dollars an hour. Usually they just give me thirty dollars for a full day of work. I end up getting the worst jobs available, the jobs no one else wants to do. When I'm out there working, I never see an American working by my side, doing the same type of work I do— so I'm not taking away anybody's job. For the past two weeks I haven't been able to get work for even one day. At nights, I sleep under a bridge or at the park. There I am usually harassed by the local drug dealers. In such a rich nation how can people be forced to live like animals under bridges? We are, after all, humans.

I reported the robbery to the police, but they did nothing. They didn't even fill out a form. When I go to the government to get a replacement, no one helps me. My English is not very good, and I cannot afford an attorney, so I'm treated very poorly. I'm just shooed away. I'm told I need an address to get a new card, but I have no address. I'm homeless. The park bench I sleep on doesn't have an address. So they tell me to get a post office box, but the post office won't give me a box without proper identification, which I can't get because I don't have a P.O. box. If the government wants me to work and provide for myself, then please, give me a replacement card. But they don't. Why? Because I'm Mexican. At the government buildings I see these same clerks treat white people ahead of me in line with courtesy, but when it is my turn, they dismiss me. They don't speak to me; they scold me as if I were some stupid child.

Why the animosity? We did not come to destroy this country, but to build up a nation. I came to this country to work, and no matter how hard it has been, I have never stolen a penny from anyone. I'm only claiming what I have worked for. But the discrimination against Latinos is just horrible. Even when I go to the mission, or to a homeless shelter, they make sure the non-Hispanic people get beds first before they allow us Latinos to enter. Discrimination has been getting worse. If some Mexicans are bad, then there are laws to put them away, but don't punish all of us.

They make fun of me, laugh at me. I hear people say to me, "Go back to Mexico" or they call me "wetback." Maybe I should return to Mexico. No one deserves to be treated this way. No one pays attention to those of us who have become victims. Even if we're documented, because we are Mexican, we are treated as if we were illegal, as if we were some sort of criminal. It's not right; it's not just. I'm not asking for a handout; I'm asking for justice. If I, who am documented, cannot get any help, what hope do those who are undocumented have? How the undocumented are treated is affecting all Hispanics.

As tempted as I am to leave, I will stay. I will get my papers back. I will go to school and learn English. I will become a U.S. citizen and then, maybe, they will recognize my humanity. Ever since Reagan, every president has been worse than the previous one. The racism has only gotten worse. What we need is a president who will help stop this discrimination against Latinos, who will give us a chance and stop blaming us for all that is wrong. We are humans who need to work so that we can feed ourselves. This is a great country to work in, but when you cannot work, it is a terrible country to be in.

Testimony from the African American Community
Vincent Harding

Ever since the earliest days of our current national debate over immigration (and the very real human lives and needs embedded in that word), I began to hear voices from beyond our contemporary time and space. Indeed, I had begun to make contact with these voices a long time ago, in the years when I first set out on my own serious exploration of the lives of my forebears, the enslaved children of Africa who were brought to this continent and this country in times of forced and harrowing migration.

For reasons that I only partly understand, I found myself drawn in a special way to the stories of those thousands of enslaved women, men and children who chose—often at great risk—to break loose from their places of bondage and find their way toward a greater freedom and a new set of human possibilities for their lives and their families. I knew these fugitives from slavery were also defying the national laws of the United States, pursued not only by privately hired slave catchers, but also by the official keepers of American law and order. I read their memoirs, interviews, and later stories of how it was to risk their lives in dangerous woodlands; wading through rushing, unpredictable rivers; desperately searching for food; always listening for the dogs and the men on their trail; dreaming of what it would be like when they reached a "free" place—wondering if they would recognize it.

I remember as well reading their accounts of how absolutely joyous and full of gratitude they were for all the people who helped them along the dangerous paths toward reunion with their loved ones, toward the "promised land" of new beginnings, toward freedom. They appreciated the risks taken by Native Americans and by other slaves who knew the unfamiliar and perilous terrain the fugitives often had

---

Dr. Vincent Harding is a professor emeritus at the Iliff School of Theology. He was a speechwriter for and friend, colleague, and biographer of the Rev. Dr. Martin Luther King, Jr.

to cross. They realized that the free blacks who guided and hid them in the cities were risking their own freedom. And they were forever thankful for both black and white abolitionists who helped them find their way to Canada, to Mexico, and sometimes to the ambiguous—neither slave nor free—American Territories.

Somehow I knew that these enslaved, endangered ancestors in search of freedom were profoundly related to my contemporary sisters and brothers who have been crossing rivers, braving deserts, risking capture and sometimes death in search of new possibilities for themselves and their families. Their freedom-seeking voices clearly merged within my heart, becoming one compelling call—ultimately joining the voice that said, "I was a stranger and you welcomed me."

Not long ago, while seeking confirmation for this sense of deep connectivity that filled my thoughts and dreams, I turned to one of my elder comrades in hope, Phil Lawson, a veteran of the post–World War II African American freedom struggle who now lives in Oakland, California. Like his legendary brother, Jim Lawson, Phil has never allowed himself to be trapped in a narrow, inflexible definition called civil rights activist or one labeled Christian minister. Officially he can be called by either name, but he has always reached out beyond such labels in order to engage the lives of our nation's most rejected and exploited people, organizing with them to transform their broken and misused communities. Because I knew something of the scope and depth of his concerns and commitments, I was not surprised in recent years to hear that Phil, like Jim, was deeply involved in work as a local and national ally of endangered immigrants from Mexico and other parts of Central and South America. (One of his crucial instruments for that work is the Black Alliance for Just Immigration.)

When I asked Phil why he was so urgently involved in such efforts, I received a more powerful affirmation of my medley of voices than I could have predicted. It turned out that the paternal grandfather that Phil had heard about as he grew up in Massilon, Ohio, was Henry Dangerfield Lawson, a fugitive slave who had escaped into Canada and had never forgotten either the dangers or the blessings of that long journey toward freedom. (With a name like Dangerfield, how could he forget? He was surely named after Dangerfield Newby, one of John Brown's faithful companions at Harpers Ferry.) Apparently he never tired of telling the story, and he never forgot all the men and women who helped him on his way. With those shared memories deeply embedded in his own life, Phil spoke firmly when he said, "I would be a traitor to my history if I didn't do everything I could to help these folks on their journey."

So the voices and the journeys were unmistakably one. Ultimately they led to the stranger of Jesus' story and to the marvelous discovery that our best humanity—and our divinity—may be found in the company of the outcasts. (Indeed, I wondered if Jesus was remembering the immigration experience of his own parents when he invited his followers to the privilege of compassionate caring for the strangers and loving companionship with the fugitives, the migrants.)

Perhaps the marvelous wisdom of James Forbes, emeritus pastor of New York's Riverside Church, emerges with great power here. Forbes interprets the Matthew 25 experience to mean that "if you want to enter the gates of heaven you'll need a letter of recommendation from a poor person." And he would certainly allow us to be even more specific, to make that person an immigrant. Such an interpretation seemed very right to me as I remembered our fugitive ancestors and heard Phil Lawson's unmistakable commitment to be faithful to his history—and his master. Indeed, Phil's experience suggested to me that we African Americans, as the writers of many such letters in our past, now have the great privilege of collecting our own commendatory messages from the outstretched hands of our immigrant sisters and brothers. Inspired by such missives we may be moved beyond the narrow confines of a rigid understanding of civil rights, opening our liberating history toward the creation of "a more perfect union."

Grounded in the magnificent freedom of the children of God, seeking to encourage the best possibilities of all our kin, moving from civil rights on to human rights, we press toward the realization of the amazing, creative potentials of all life. Perhaps our freedom-seeking ancestors were moving toward such a hope, planning to take every one of the endangered strangers with them, purposefully walking together until the strangeness becomes a beloved community.

Testimony from the Tohono O'odham Nation: Who Will Speak for the Dead?

Mike Wilson

I am a retired U.S. Army Special Forces master sergeant and now a charter school resource manager. I am also one of the roughly twenty-five thousand members of the Tohono O'odham Nation. Our reservation is comparable in size to the state of Connecticut. Our lands are located within the Sonoran Desert in south central Arizona. The Tohono O'odham Nation encompasses about 2.7 million acres, composed mainly of a wide desert valley with mountains that nearly reach eight thousand feet. Our ancestral land straddles the international border between Mexico and the United States, with our people living on both sides of the border. Several thousand O'odham live in northern Sonora, Mexico. For centuries, before there was a border, the O'odham traveled back and forth. But since the U.S. government began tightening the border, movement of our people has been curtailed. For many O'odham born in Mexico, access to our tribal centers here within the United States is restricted.

We are supposed to be a sovereign nation, but our sovereignty exists only when those who have conquered us allow us to have it. If we are indeed a sovereign nation, why does the Border Patrol run rampant on tribal lands? As far as I am concerned, the United States Border Patrol is an army of occupation. If we were truly a sovereign nation, we would not have an occupying army on our sovereign land.

Since the tightening of the border, both the Border Patrol and the Department of Homeland Security have further divided our land and disrupted migration patterns of the O'odham. They never consulted us. When in four hundred years have Native Peoples ever been consulted? Never, and we never will be. They imposed decisions upon the O'odham that are against our best interests. Not only did they divide our lands, but their unilateral actions to seal the borders redirected the flow of thousands of migrants. We are known for having the hottest desert in North America, thus making the route migrants take through the Baboquivari Valley in our Nation the deadliest migrant trail in the United States. We now have two to four thousand migrants coming through an eighteen-mile-wide swath of mesquite- and cactus-filled land.

Our Nation was simply not prepared or equipped to handle this increased flow of humanity. As a result, thousands have died trying to cross this desert, where temperatures easily reach three-digit figures—thousands who are poor and have brown skin. It is easy to get dehydrated or stranded. Many, not fully aware of the distance, try crossing with a jug of water. That is not enough. Soon they find themselves in a life-threatening situation. Some, out of desperation, fill their empty jugs from stagnant pools of water where animal carcasses are decomposing.

Organizations like No More Death or Humane Borders do not have permission to come onto our lands to place water tanks. However, because I am a member of the Tohono O'odham Nation, I have access. So each Saturday since 2001 I rise long before dawn and drive my Dodge truck to the four water stations in the Baboquivari Valley that I maintain, placing water on what I suspect are the most traveled trails. These stations each have two fifty-five gallon barrels. Each water station has a name: Matthew, Mark, Luke, and John. Not everyone at the Nation agrees with me, but I continue to do it. Why? No one deserves to die in the desert for lack of a cup of water. Placing water for the thirsty to drink is a humanitarian act. I'm simply doing what I can. I just have to keep putting out water. When I started placing water out, I was serving as a Presbyterian lay minister at the tribal capital town of Sells. I told my congregation that we had a moral responsibility to respond to the endless migrant deaths occurring on O'odham land. Unfortunately, my congregation disagreed with me, so I quit before I was fired.

We have always been a hospitable and giving people. There are tribal members in this area who do offer water, food, and humanitarian help. Unfortunately, the Baboquivari District Council in June 2002 passed a resolution forbidding water stations in that district. The problem is that there are so many coming across the border daily that those tribal members who live along this border have become completely inundated. All these people crossing our land are creating a tremendous financial burden. The Tohono O'odham Nation and the State of Arizona pay the major portion of the expenses for border-related law enforcement and emergency medical services. This has pitted brown people against brown people. But isn't this the way the conquerors operate? My fear is that we who were once oppressed are now the oppressors. We would rather let starving, desperate, hungry, and destitute people die on O'odham lands than extend a helping hand and a cup of water.

When I am out here it is common to come across migrants. Many come north looking for work. They come in hope of finding a job to feed their families. I think you and I would do the same thing. I know that I would if my children were hungry. I would definitely cross a desert. But the Nation's attitude is that if I begin to put out water, more migrants will be inspired to cross the desert through our tribal lands. But historically that's not true. They came before the water stations existed, and they will continue to come whether there are water stations or not. Unfortunately, at times I find that my tanks have been confiscated by the tribal authorities, or that my one gallon water jugs have been slashed.

Recently [September 3, 2008] the Baboquivari District Council district chairwoman, Veronica Harvey, ordered me to remove my lifesaving water barrels. She also banned a group of visiting seminary students who were with me from ever setting foot on O'odham land. But my response was simple. I respectfully declined to take down my water station. Migrants are dying, and they need the water. Human beings need water to survive here in the desert, and to remove these water stations from the epicenter of where people are dying is a crime against humanity. It certainly is nothing less than that.

For the O'odham, Baboquivari Mountain is the center of the universe and the home of the Creator I'itoi.

Mike Wilson at the Matthew water station facing a group of Iliff seminary students while being detained by a tribal police officer. We were given a warning that if we ever return to the reservation, we would be charged with trespassing.

MIGUEL A. DE LA TORRE

Voice of the People

Corridos are popular Mexican ballads that date back to the eighteenth century. Historically, they have been used to provide education or relay news. Often, they serve as subversive commentaries on an ongoing injustice committed by the powerful against the people. The *corrido* usually has three parts. It begins with a salutation from the singer who introduces the story that is about to be told; it then tells the story, usually about heroes of the people or famed criminals; and it finishes with a moral principle or truth to be learned.

This particular *corrido* was written by a Salvadorian factory worker from Hempstead, New York, named Saul Linares. He sings about the Maricopa County sheriff, Joe Arpaio, who has been accused by members of Congress of creating a "reign of terror" against Hispanics in Phoenix. On February 4, 2009, Sheriff Arpaio paraded undocumented immigrants who were in his custody, in chains, through the streets of Phoenix.

EL CORRIDO DE JOE ARPAIO
Written by Saul Linares
Music by Francisco Pacheco

Voy a cantarles un corrido a los presentes,
que le compuse a Joe Arpaio de Arizona,
un sinverguenza, desgraciado, anti-inmigrante,
que se ha ganado el repudio de toda la gente.

Es un sheriff que esta gastando mucha plata,
mucho dinero que paga el contribuyente,
Arpaio mete preso al inmigrante,
porque el dice que son unos delincuentes.

THE BALLAD OF JOE ARPAIO
Translated by
Miguel A. De La Torre

I am going to sing a *corrido* to those who are present,
Which I composed to Joe Arpaio of Arizona,
A shameless, disgraceful, anti-immigrant,
Who has earned the repudiation of all the people.

He is a sheriff who is wasting a lot of cash,
A lot of money paid by the taxpayer,
Arpaio imprisons the immigrant,
Because he says that they are criminals.

Pero tan solo buscan un trabajo decente,
que en su pais ellos no lo han encontrado,
y sin sentido y sin razon aparente,
por una calle encadenados los paseaba.

Ya los Latinos ya estan muy cansados,
los inmigrantes que muy organizados,
no tienen miedo al sheriff ni policia,
a Joe Arpaio le dicen y le repiten,
sos criminal deberias estar preso.

But they only look for a decent job,
That in their country they have not found,
And without any apparent sense or reason,
Down the streets while in chains he paraded them.

The Latinos are already very weary,
And the immigrants are very organized,
They are not afraid of the sheriff or police,
To Joe Arpaio they say and they repeat,
You're the criminal who should be in prison.

6

Christian Perspectives

What we'll do is randomly pick one night every week where we will kill whoever crosses the border . . . step over there and you die. You get to decide whether it's your lucky night or not. I think that would be more fun. . . . [I would be] happy to sit there with my high-powered rifle and my night scope.
—BRIAN JAMES, ANTI-IMMIGRANT TALK RADIO HOST WITH
KFYI-AM IN PHOENIX[1]

If we call ourselves disciples of Jesus Christ, what are we expected to do in response to the present immigration crisis? This is not a question related to our American citizenship or our political views or to our concerns for the economy or homeland security. The focus of the question is what we are expected to do in light of our witness to the gospel message.

Whenever women and men of faith ask this question, more often than not they place themselves at odds with the policies of civil leaders and governments, for the question forces believers to choose whom they will serve, Jesus or Caesar. This is not an easy question to answer, because many of us would rather take the easier route of trying to please two masters, of articulating a Christian message while not upsetting the civil or political status quo.

Even a casual reading of the scriptures reveals the prominence of the alien—the stranger within our midst—throughout the biblical narrative. The people of God are constantly reminded to welcome and love the stranger for they too were once aliens in a strange land. The biblical term *stranger* or *sojourner* does a good job of capturing the predicament of an alien in today's world. Aliens live in an in-between space—in a land to which they were not born, yet a land where they now live and work. As such, the alien is "foreign," different from the native-born due to language, customs, history, and traditions. As such, the alien lacks the benefits and protection ordinarily provided to those tied to their birthplace. Vulnerable to those who profit from his or her labor, the alien derives security from the biblical mandate of hospitality.

Sojourners in the Bible

Treatment of the sojourner is based on three biblical presuppositions: (1) the Israelites were once aliens who were oppressed by the natives of the land (Ex 22:21); (2) God takes sides and intervenes to liberate the disenfranchised (Ex 23:9); and (3) God's covenant with Israel is contingent on all members of the community benefiting from it (Dt 26:11).

The Hebrew Bible includes at least thirty-eight verses instructing the Israelites not to mistreat or oppress the alien. The common theme of these verses is summed up in Leviticus 19:33–34: "And when aliens reside on your land with you, you shall not oppress them. The alien shall be like the native-born among you. And you shall love them as yourself, for you were aliens in the land of Egypt."[2] Obviously, the experience of the Hebrews dwelling as slaves without rights in a foreign land profoundly shaped their self-awareness, and thus they designed specific laws on how to care for the undocumented in their midst. Foreigners were to be treated with generosity (Dt 14:29) and with the same rights and protections as the native born (Nm 35:15). The ultimate hope was that these aliens would one day receive an inheritance in the land symbolizing their full inclusion as citizens:

> So you shall divide this land among you according to the tribes of Israel. You shall allot it as an inheritance for yourselves and for the aliens who reside among you and have begotten children among you. They shall be to you as citizens of Israel; with you they shall be allotted an inheritance among the tribes of Israel. In whatever tribe aliens reside, there you shall assign them their inheritance, says the LORD GOD. (Ez 47:21–23)

The Hebrew Bible is unambiguous about belonging: the alien wishing to become "naturalized" by circumcision and following Torah was to be treated with all the rights and privileges of the native-born Israelite.

To be an alien is to live without the societal and familial structures that can provide protection. To be an alien is to be radically vulnerable to those already living in a place. Those living in the land have two real options: they can welcome strangers, or they can refuse them entry.

The story of a city named Sodom in Genesis 19:1–29 describes the consequences of this choice. Abraham's nephew, Lot, welcomed sojourners into his home. But when the people of the city heard that strangers had taken shelter under Lot's roof, they surrounded the house and demanded that the strangers be handed over to them. "Send them out to us that we may abuse and rape them!" they cried out.[3]

Unfortunately, many within the church have read their own biases into the story and concluded that the residents of Sodom were guilty of the "sin" of homosexuality. Yet, according to the prophets, Sodom's sin was taking advantage of the disenfranchised, refusing to seek justice, failing to reprove oppressors, and treating orphans and widows unjustly (Is 1:10–23; Am 4:1, 11). The prophet Ezekiel echoes this belief: Sodom's sin was its unwillingness, due to pride and haughtiness, to share wealth with the marginalized (16:49). The people of Israel had a clear responsibility to protect and care for the vulnerable.

The citizens of Sodom demonstrated their xenophobia in their attempt to humiliate publicly the aliens among them, even resorting to rape. Consider, however, the way in which U.S. policy makers and citizens today attempt to humiliate publicly the aliens among them through unfair practices, including arrest, detention, and economic rape. Genesis 19, which has been greatly misused in the past, is a text that warns nations that God sides with the oppressed aliens over and against the unjust native born.

The gospel texts reinforce the lessons of Genesis 19 and the prophets. Those of us who are or have been undocumented find comfort in Matthew 2:13–14:

> An angel of the Lord appeared to Joseph in a dream, saying "Rise up! Take the child and his mother with you and flee into Egypt, and stay there until I tell you, for Herod will look for the child in order to destroy him." And rising up, he took the child and his mother that night and fled to Egypt.

While most people may not find this text foundational to their faith, those of us who are *not* native born understand how our hope in God actively connects with our despair at being uprooted. Jesus, like me, and like many others, was an alien.

Just as the holy family arrived in Egypt as political refugees, fleeing the tyrannical rule of Herod, I—and many others like me—arrived in this country as a political refugee. Like Joseph, my father returned home to his wife, my mother, with similar news of danger and the need to flee. There was no time to pack personal mementoes; we left as soon as possible, literally with only the clothes on our backs.

Jesus understood the pain of being a foreigner in an alien land. Jesus knew what it meant to be seen as inferior, to come from a culture that is different. I have no doubt that Jesus wept as a child for the same reasons I did. Because Jesus experienced the trauma of undocumented aliens, he is a savior who knows what it means to cross a border.[4] For me, the miracle of the incarnation is not that God became human, but rather that God became an alien. God's ultimate act of solidarity with the dispossessed makes it possible for me to worship a God who knows firsthand what it means to be undocumented.

When Jesus sent his disciples upon their first missionary journey, he specifically told them that those cities that refused to provide hospitality for them would face the same punishment as Sodom (Lk 10:1–12). The authors of the gospel texts clearly connect the care of the alien with the hope of salvation: in a very real sense, how we treat the alien is how we treat our God.

Matthew's description of the Day of Judgment makes this point very clearly. Jesus will return in all his glory, escorted by all the angels, to take his seat on the throne. He will gather all the nations before him and separate their inhabitants like a shepherd separates the sheep from the goats. He will look to the sheep on his right and welcome them to the kingdom prepared for them since the foundation of the world (Mt 25:31–46).

Why are the sheep chosen and not the goats? They enter into salvation not because they professed a certain doctrine or because they held membership in a particular church, or even because of their prayers. According to Jesus,

> I was hungry and you fed me; I was thirsty and you gave me something to drink; *I was an alien and you welcomed me*; I was naked and you clothed me; I was sick and you visited me; I was in prison and you came to see me. . . . For solemnly I tell you, in so far as you did this to one of the least of these, you did it to me. (Mt 25:35–36)

And for those on his left, Jesus sends them to the eternal fire prepared for the devil and his angels. Why? They refused to feed Jesus when he was hungry, provide water when he was thirsty, welcome him when he was an alien, clothe him when he was naked, or visit him when he was sick or in prison. "For solemnly I tell you, in so far as you neglected one of the least of these, you neglected me." For Jesus, salvation is contingent upon interactions with the least within society, those who are excluded from full participation.

In this country the least of these today is certainly the alien crossing the desert who is both hungry and thirsty. Migrants arrive naked and sick, and if caught by the Border Patrol, they are sent to prison. The undocumented is Jesus in the here and now. Those hoping to see Jesus, those craving salvation, will find their savior among the undocumented, today's crucified people. Following the gospel admonitions, this is a path to salvation.

Theologian Jon Sobrino insists that God chooses those who are oppressed in history—the hungry, the thirsty, the naked, the alien, the sick, the prisoner—as the principal means of salvation because they are the face of Jesus.[5] God does not appear to the pharaohs or the caesars of history. Leaders of empires whose policies cause death to God's people are not aligned with the Divine. For this reason God appears to their slaves, their vassals, and those disenfranchised by the empire. This is as true today as it was in the past, and without a doubt, among the most disenfranchised of the land today are the undocumented.

Almost all Christian faith traditions and denominations agree that Christians have a moral duty and responsibility toward the stranger in our midst. While there may be wide disagreement on federal immigration policy, there should be no disagreement that the Christian must feed the hungry, provide water to the thirsty, and clothe the naked. The language of the gospels is very clear, and Christian-based organizations are performing all of these acts in the desert right now. Yet, while such acts are to be commended, our Christian faith requires more from us.

The Sanctuary Movement

For this reason, many Christians are again calling upon churches to provide safe haven for migrants. The Sanctuary Movement of the 1980s found new life in September 2006 when a thirty-two-year-old undocumented cleaning woman named Elvira Arellano walked into Adalberto United Methodist Church in Chicago and requested the right of sanctuary, an ancient practice of seeking refuge in a sacred place. Her actions were a desperate attempt to avoid separation from her seven-year-old son, Saul, a U.S. citizen.

This practice has its roots in the Bible. When the Jews entered the Promised Land, six cities were designated as places of refuge that would provide absolute security to fugitives (Jos 20:1–9). In the event of accidental homicide, the person charged could seek asylum from any avengers. This tradition of setting aside a site of refuge became part of American tradition during slavery, when an underground railroad of safe houses was established to serve as havens for runaway slaves journeying north toward freedom.

During the 1980s U.S. foreign policies pushed Central Americans, specifically refugees from civil wars in El Salvador and Guatemala, to the United States to escape violence and death. Because the Reagan administration supported the regimes responsible for the violence, these migrants were usually denied refugee status and repatriated to their homeland, where they more than likely faced torture or death. In response, Christian ministers began the Sanctuary Movement. Jim Corbett (a Quaker) and John Fife (a Presbyterian) co-founded the movement, which was purposely designed to lack a central command or hierarchical structure. It consisted of loose connections among faith-based communities, human rights groups, and secular organizations. On March 24, 1982, Reverend Fife, then pastor of Southside Presbyterian Church in Tucson, Arizona, along with five churches in San Francisco, declared their worship space a sanctuary for those fleeing the violence in El Salvador and Guatemala. Soon afterward, Corbett asked the Chicago Religious Task Force on Central America to set up an underground railroad that moved refugees seeking sanctuary away from the heavily patrolled border area of the southwestern United States to the less patrolled north.

Elvira Arellano's request for sanctuary in 2006 was reminiscent of the Sanctuary Movement of the 1980s during the height of Central American civil wars. Her act of disobedience sparked formation of a New Sanctuary Movement, creating a possible new path to citizenship for many who are undocumented. Just as religious congregations throughout the United States came together to provide a safe haven for those who faced death if deported in the 1980s, congregations in the new millennium are responding to the injustices faced by the undocumented. Although Elvira Arellano was eventually deported on August 19, 2007, her actions sparked a new discourse concerning the responsibility of churches.

The New Sanctuary Movement is an interfaith coalition of religious leaders and participating congregations that open their church doors to undocumented immigrants residing in the United States. Those associated with the movement attest that all people share basic common rights: to a livelihood, to maintaining family unity, and to physical and emotional safety. Because the immigration policies of the United States violate these rights through unjust deportations that often separate children from their parents and by exploiting immigrant workers, the movement is designed to enable congregations publicly to provide hospitality and protection to a limited number of undocumented families whose cases reveal the moral contradictions of our present immigration laws.

In addition, these congregations commit to support legislation that brings about reform. Support is aimed at those families who will be deported even though they have a good record of employment and have children who are U.S. citizens. Each congregation commits to offer hospitality for three months, at which time the family rotates to another congregation until its case is resolved. The congregations do not violate federal law because the family's identity is made public.

All human beings—regardless of their faith or lack thereof; regardless of their race, ethnicity, gender, or sexual orientation; and regardless of their immigration status—embody the image of God. As such, all have intrinsic worth and should be treated with dignity. Because every life contains the sacred, every life is sacred. What is the meaning of this basic theological principle? First and foremost, basic human rights must be safeguarded. All have the right to be safe from physical harm, to receive basic health care, to work and receive in return a wage sufficient to sustain life. All children have a right to be with their parents. Today our present immigration laws deny these minimal human rights to over 11.9 million undocumented aliens residing in the United States.

Jesus' parable of the Good Samaritan (Lk 10:29–37) teaches us that we must care for all humans regardless of their documentation. To deny preventive health-care services to any person based on that individual's documentation status is inhumane and directly repudiates the teachings of Jesus Christ. The story of the Good Samaritan lies not only in some distant past. Christians today are called to heal the wounds of the strangers within their midst. It's interesting to note that because Samaritans were viewed as the dirty foreigners of Jesus' time, this particular one was singled out as good. If this parable were to be updated for today's audience, it might be titled the parable of the Good

Illegal Alien—a story of someone who doesn't fit the predominant negative stereotype.

A second basic human right for all people is that they not be molested or oppressed. Yet this is exactly what we do when we pay substandard wages for work done by undocumented laborers. Saint Paul reminds the church that "the worker deserves his or her wages" (1 Tim 5:18). For Saint James, cheating laborers of their wages incurs the wrath of God: "Behold, for the wages of the laborers who have worked your fields cry out. You cheated them of their earnings—listen then to the wages you held back and realize that the cries of the fieldworkers have reached the ears of the Lord of Hosts" (Jas 5:4). Refusing to pay a living wage to any worker, regardless of documentation, goes against every biblical principle dealing with justice-based relationships. And our homes are to be open to strangers in our midst. The author of the Book of Hebrews admonishes us: "Do not neglect to show hospitality to strangers, for by doing that some have entertained angels without knowing it" (Heb 13:2). This is a reference back to the story in Genesis 18, which tells how Abraham eagerly welcomed strangers who turned out to be unidentified messengers of God with the incredible news that he and Sarah would have a son who would found a great nation.

The right of children to be protected at all times is the most basic of all human rights. References to children as blessings of the Lord abound in scripture. All children, not just the children of certain people, are to be cared for and protected. When it comes to defending children, God does not check immigration papers, and neither should the members of God's churches. Yet, our present immigration policies break up families—often without warning—an inhumane act with serious future consequences for children who are separated from their parents. When plants and factories are raided to round up the undocumented, those taken, in many cases, leave behind children who are U.S. citizens by birth. Pope Benedict XVI, during his April 2008 visit to the United States, warned that separating families "is truly dangerous for the social, moral and human fabric" of Latin and Central American families.[6] Family values can never focus solely on the families of those privileged with documentation.

Citizens can wait for their government to address the present humanitarian crisis faced by the undocumented, but Christians cannot. Our faith as Christians should never be reduced to a personal piety that abdicates our responsibility for our fellow human beings. To be Christian, by definition, means to stand in solidarity with the same people that Jesus did. To be a Christian means to be willing to take up a cross for the sake of others. To be a Christian means that we continue to abide by the words of the prophet Micah, that we "act justly, love tenderly, and walk humbly before our God, for this is what God asks of us" (6:8).

A Catholic Voice
Kathy Thill

On Tuesday, May 20, 2008, Sister of Mercy Kathy Thill spoke at a press conference organized by the Congressional Hispanic Caucus concerning the events that occurred in Postville, Iowa, when 390 of the approximately 2,300 residents were arrested and detained by U.S. Immigration and Customs Enforcement (ICE).

My name is Sister Kathy Thill, and I am a Sister of Mercy who works with the Latino/a community of Iowa. I am also a U.S. citizen who grew up believing that this is a democratic country in which the dignity of all people is respected and their rights protected. That is not the country I experienced this past week. I share my experience with the hope that it will help lawmakers and my fellow citizens see that our nation's immigration policies and practices are broken and inhumane.

When ICE took over the National Cattle Congress grounds for "training purposes" a week before the raids, we knew something was going to happen. Yet not one of us was prepared for what did happen on Monday, May 12, in Postville. Sister Mary McCauley at St. Bridget's Catholic Church called me that morning, shortly after the raids began. I was one of three staff members from El Centro Latinoamericano, a Hispanic resource center in Waterloo, who went to help in Postville. At St. Bridget's we found hundreds of people in

---

Kathy Thill is a Sister of Mercy who advocates for compassionate immigration reform. For more information, see www.sistersofmercy.org/SAVEAct.

shock and distress, frightened to leave the church for fear of being arrested, and desperate to find out what was happening to their loved ones who had been arrested.

Working with the staff of St. Bridget's we did our best to meet the needs of the families, and at 4:00 p.m. we went to Agriprocessors, the site of the raid, and tried to get information on those detained. We were especially concerned about seventeen minors who had been taken during the raid. We had brought with us a list of names and ages of the minors and requested information about them. We were told to come back later, and that parents with proper identification could then pick up some youths who would be released. ICE officials did not provide any additional information. Later, we returned with two parents, each hoping for word on their sons. Again ICE officials would not provide any information. So we waited. Eventually, some women and youths were released with GPS tracking devices on their ankles to track them until their court appearances. We were told there would be no more releases and that detainees were going to be transferred to Waterloo and held at the Cattle Congress. The parents we brought earlier still had no word on their sons. Their tension, grief, and distress increased as buses began to remove detainees from the site.

Of the seventeen minors arrested, five or six are still in custody as of today [May 20, 2008]. A sixteen year old who was released told me that he kept trying to tell officials his age, but they refused to believe him, cursed at him, and made fun of him for being Hispanic. A seventeen year old who was arrested said, "I didn't come here to rob people or do bad things. I just came to work, to earn money for my family. Why do people hate us so much?" I had no answer. The only bright spot in the day was the generosity of those in the Postville community and throughout Iowa who made donations and volunteered to help their immigrant sisters and brothers. We spent several hours on Monday evening helping family members sign the forms necessary to enable immigration attorneys to see the detainees the next day.

Meanwhile hundreds of men, women, children, and babies remained at the church, sleeping on the floor and church pews, too frightened to go home. This arrangement continued throughout the week despite our efforts to convince them it was safe to go home. During the early morning hours on Tuesday a few women were released at varying times for humanitarian reasons and taken back to Postville. One woman who was released told me it had been her first day at Agriprocessors and she had been working only fifteen minutes when the raid began. While in custody she asked to call her family but was told by officials she did not have the right to make a phone call. Seeing this mother reunited with her child brought tears to everyone's eyes. It lifted my spirits, but not for long.

Throughout the week we encountered one obstacle after another. For example, on Tuesday, after waiting and negotiating most of the day to see the detainees, the attorneys learned that criminal charges instead of immigration charges would be filed, and thus immigration lawyers could not see or talk to the detainees. I learned later that officials from the Mexican Consulate were also there Tuesday morning but were denied access for quite a while.

Much time and effort was spent during the week trying to obtain information about the detainees, confirming exactly who had been detained, the charges filed against them, and where they were taken. ICE had set up a toll-free 800 number to provide this information, but this was very ineffective.

Hundreds of families were torn apart by this raid. In several families both parents were arrested, leaving no one to care for children. One neighbor cared for small children until their mother was released on Wednesday. Even after her release, ICE officials would not allow her to go to the church where her children were staying. Instead, they took her to her apartment, looked around, and, as they were leaving, warned her not to take a step out of the apartment, that if she did she would never see her children again. The mother of another family was released while her husband was still detained. Her children, one of whom is a U.S. citizen, are upset and frightened. The six year old cries continually, asking to see her daddy. The mother cannot work. There is no income, no way to provide for her children.

The humanitarian impact of this raid is obvious to anyone in Postville. The economic impact will soon be evident. Hundreds of families are now left without income, struggling to figure out how to pay the rent and provide food for their children. Some have thought about canceling their phone service to save money, but ICE officials told those with GPS devices they must maintain service to have contact with officials. Other families have decided to share one apartment to save on rent. Those released need to appear in court—some in Waterloo and some in other places around Iowa—but they have no money for transportation, much less for a night's stay somewhere if that is required.

Before the raids the population of Postville was only twenty-three hundred, so the impact on this community is devastating. It is estimated that the population will decrease by one-third to one-half. And the impact goes beyond Postville. In Waterloo we are receiving calls from people too scared to go to work. People are losing their jobs and have received their last paycheck. Others are in hiding. Fear is rampant. I spoke with a Waterloo school official who was concerned about a particular student who had not been in school this week. Her family was too afraid to leave the house after ICE had come knocking at their door.

In Postville half of the children were absent from school this week. Counselors were brought in to assist the children devastated by the loss of a parent or family member. Later in the week counselors were called back to assist non-immigrant children who were having nightmares worrying that their parents would be taken. This past week a mother and daughter, both U.S. citizens, were stopped while shopping at Walmart and questioned by ICE officials for an hour and a half. The tension and fear are not limited to the Latina/o communities. When driving to Postville this Friday with a car full of donations, I received a call about possible checkpoints between Waterloo and Postville. I wondered what might happen to me for delivering the supplies. I no longer felt free. I suddenly felt like I was in a strange country.

The immigration policies and practices of our government are disastrous. The inhumane way these raids are conducted and the negative impact on families and our communities are intolerable. The trauma created is a tremendous injustice. Perhaps an even greater injustice is the exploitation and physical and sexual abuse by Agriprocessors. Those who are willing to risk so much to put food on their table and try to provide a better life for their children are put in jail and labeled criminals. Yet those who commit crimes of violence go free.

It is with urgency that I call on the government to pass comprehensive immigration reform that includes a pathway to lawful permanent residence and citizenship, meets immigrants' basic needs, encourages family unity and reunification, and addresses the root causes of migration. It is time to change our immigration policies and practices so that once again we become the nation in which the dignity of all people is paramount, and the rights of all are protected.

A Mainline Christian Voice
Dana W. Wilbanks

What in the world is happening? Mothers and fathers, wives and husbands are yanked out of work places and put in detention, with no regard for children who are left at home alone. High-school honor students are denied access to in-state college tuition because they were brought to the United States at an early age by undocumented working parents. Migrants die in southwestern deserts as they desperately seek a barely livable low-wage job. Undocumented immigrants are vilified by politicians and armed vigilantes as threats to U.S. security almost as dangerous as terrorists in 2001.

This is not the first time in U.S. history that immigration politics has gotten increasingly hysterical and alarmist, nor is it the first time that immigrants have been callously and brutally treated. But clearly we are once again in the middle of such a period. In these times it is especially important that churches stand up and speak out. In profound ways immigration policy is a spiritual as well as a political and economic issue. The civic spirit is so poisoned by venomous attitudes and rhetoric that it is almost impossible to face the deeply human issues of immigration in a constructive way. In addition to advocating specific policy proposals, churches are called to minister to the spirit of our communities so that thoughtful and humane measures can stand a chance of being adopted.

The theological bottom line for Christians is that undocumented immigrants are, like long-time citizens, created in the image of God. They are persons with gifts and challenges, hopes and dreams, flaws and potentialities. They have a life story. They have parents, brothers and sisters, and friends. They could be my sister-in-law or your son-in-law. They are human beings who laugh and cry, and who yearn for a better life. It is all too easy to forget the flesh and blood persons within the mind-numbing statistics cited so frequently in immigration debates. For Christians, the personhood of undocumented persons must always be at the center of any deliberations. We are to love them as neighbors in Christ, respecting their inherent dignity as daughters

---

Dr. Dana W. Wilbanks is a professor emeritus of Christian Ethics at the Iliff School of Theology.

and sons of God and defending their value as equal to our own within
the expansive grace of God. It is the human faces of immigration that
make it a matter of high priority for Christians.

A Christian perspective on undocumented immigration is clearly in
conflict with a narrow nationalistic gaze. In a nationalistic view immigrants are valued only insofar as they fit within an often shifting set
of national needs and priorities. For many years undocumented persons
have been working low-wage jobs and contributing to the U.S.
economy with little complaint from the citizen population. Employers
needed them, and consumers benefited from this largely invisible work
force. Then, as extremist anti-immigration rhetoric became more influential, they were suddenly labeled undesirables and illegals who
deserve to be treated punitively. Their personhood is disregarded, and
their rights as human beings are frequently violated.

I believe there are three ways that a Christian perspective calls for
a new policy on immigration. First, all persons living in the United
States have a right to that which is necessary to live. It does not matter whether they are undocumented or documented. It does not matter if they are employed or unemployed. By virtue of their personhood
they have a right to food, to shelter, to protection, to basic health care.
They have a right to send their children to school to be educated. These
are fundamental human rights. For Christians, these are based on our
belief that all persons are created in the image of God and that each
of us is equal in value in our relation to the Creator God. Human rights
are not calculated on the basis of who is most or least deserving, or
who is or is not a legal resident. They are God-given birthrights.

This valuation of persons is frequently challenged in current immigration politics. There are proposals to make it illegal to provide ba-
sic-needs assistance to undocumented immigrants. There are proposals to prevent undocumented immigrants from having access to basic
health care. There are proposals to keep the children of undocumented
immigrant parents from attending public school. There are proposals
to expel all undocumented workers from the United States without any
legal recourse or consideration of circumstances. In the anti-immigrant
politics of today, these are the most extreme attitudes and measures.
But they do have an effect. They make it more difficult to adopt policies that are more humane and far more effective in dealing with the
challenges of immigration. Churches dare not ignore these kinds of
views and proposals. It is crucial to challenge them publicly whenever
they are expressed.

Second, Christians have the responsibility to advocate for the most vulnerable persons in our communities. In ancient Israel, laws protected the widows, orphans, the poor, and sojourners who could not count on the security systems that others had. This kind of radical vulnerability is experienced by undocumented immigrants today. They have to be as invisible as possible so that they will not call attention to themselves or betray their undocumented status. They cannot defend themselves if employers exploit them or abuse them.

But we should not assume that they are passive "victims," because in many ways they take remarkable initiative in finding employment, a place to live, and a place where their children can be educated. Frequently they send money back to family in Mexico, which is remarkable when one considers how low their wages may be. Still, their status as undocumented renders them exceptionally vulnerable, and God calls Christians to seek justice for the marginalized, to protect the vulnerable, and to defend the defenseless.

Just treatment for undocumented immigrants requires that they have a way to legalize their status within the United States. The fact is that many have been living and working for years in our communities. They have been making a contribution to the economy through their labor. Their children are growing up in our communities. And they have been paying taxes, including Social Security, which helps support many citizens in their retirement. These highly significant facts show clearly that they are *already* members of the community.

Morally speaking, community membership is not established so much by documents as by functional interrelationships. For this reason, it is misleading to call legalization *amnesty*. Instead, it should be understood as formal legalization of a status already established. If a lack of documents has not been a bar to making meaningful contributions, then it should not be a bar to legalization. The fact is that undocumented workers have not forced themselves on an unwilling society. They have filled crucial occupational niches that are not provided for by our outdated immigration system. Fair treatment requires the legalization of undocumented workers who have established a place for themselves through their labor. It is a grievous injustice to take someone's labor but not to welcome his or her full personhood. As it is, undocumented workers are, in effect, treated as servants who do "our" bidding but are denied membership in our community.

The church's advocacy here is crucial. Undocumented workers are severely constrained in their freedom to advocate for themselves. The loudest political voices oppose justice for the undocumented persons by resorting to a rigid legalism. These voices emphasize that since undocumented workers are not authorized to be in the United States legally, they should not be permitted to remain and eventually become citizens. In the aftermath of 9/11, they tend to feed off the fears and anxieties about national security that many Washington politicians seem more than eager to perpetuate and intensify. Often, indeed, justice is best served by the consistent enforcement of reasonable laws. But today, given that the present immigration policy has clearly become so unworkable, it seems that the purposes of the law are better served by providing an alternative route to legalization and by providing more realistic legal channels to enable needed workers from Mexico to continue to come to the United States.

The third contribution of a Christian perspective is the moral imperative to extend hospitality to the stranger. When we ask, "Who is the neighbor we are to love?" a very clear answer is, "the stranger." In fact, Jesus identifies with the stranger. "As you welcome the stranger, you welcome me" (Mt 25:35). The force of this teaching is that Christians are to relate to the stranger as we would to the Christ. We are called to be open to, indeed to welcome, those who are somehow different. The message is not to keep them out but welcome them in as neighbors in Christ.

In the biblical tradition the stranger was often viewed as a herald, one who brought news. If we receive the stranger, we may get very valuable news. On the other hand, if we do not welcome the stranger, we may not get the news we need to hear. Consider the intriguing text from Hebrews 13:2: "Do not neglect to show hospitality to strangers, for by doing that some have entertained angels without knowing it." For Christians, strangers can be understood as gifts of God. If we close ourselves off from the stranger, we miss out on news from God that is vital for our faithfulness.

It is true, of course, that the hospitality ethic does not mandate a particular immigration policy. But it does mandate our responses to the "otherness" represented by Mexican immigrants. Recent theological and philosophical discussions strongly emphasize the significance of the other. While we are accustomed to think that human beings are basically alike, our experience is that we are quite different, and in fact, difference matters. The question is, how does or how should being different matter?

Differentness has been the basis for terrible forms of racial, ethnic, and gender injustices throughout the ages. Much of the anti-immigrant rhetoric today betrays the hostility and discomfort that are evoked by the presence of an immigrant population that is different in language, customs, and appearance. Not all persons who favor more restrictive policies are racists, but many of the loudest and angriest voices today, as in the past, clearly express racist views of the other. Mexicans are stereotyped in ways that are almost identical to previous immigrant populations of Irish and southeast Europeans.

A hospitality ethic, however, requires that our response to differentness be one of anticipation and appreciation. We do not require others to become like us. We do not love them only as long as they become like us. Instead, we love them precisely in their difference. We treasure their personhood and culture. We cannot truly love the immigrant if our love is contingent on the person becoming like us. We are to respect and reverence others in their difference. Moreover, strangers bring to us the possibility for new relationships, experiences, and understandings. When we close ourselves off from strangers, we can too easily narrow our moral horizon to a very limited range of understanding. We can too easily close ourselves to the new that God is continually making possible.

On the other hand, to welcome the stranger is to be challenged by new possibilities that we could not otherwise have imagined. This is the promise represented by immigration. God is making possible new expressions of community that are to be created through mutual interaction, not through the passive submission of immigrants to the dominant culture. Let us be about creating and re-creating new patterns of relationships that incorporate gifts of both residents and strangers. God's future is surely not bound up in keeping peoples apart but rather in inventing ways of being together that build on the distinctive characteristics of each.

Indeed, immigrant scholars point out that the United States has never been simply a melting pot into which immigrant peoples disappear without a trace. Yes, immigrants are changed by living in the United States, but the United States is constantly changing as well. The United States has always incorporated varied national, ethnic, and linguistic groups as members of society. Each has a transforming effect on the other. And this is still going on today. As Asian, African, Caribbean, and Mexican immigrants become a part of the ongoing story of American history, we are all changed in some way. The current presence of many Mexican immigrants should be welcomed with a readiness to work together on both the challenges and opportunities.

It is important to emphasize that hospitality is not a paternalistic pattern of relationship. While immigrants often need assistance in settling into a new home, they bring their own gifts to the interaction. Hospitality is not primarily "our" responsibility to meet "their" needs. Hospitality is crucial for the church's faithfulness because it is only as we encounter strangers that we open ourselves to the transforming activity of God in our midst. Differentness brings challenges to us all. But there is no place in Christian witness for cleansing the community of differentness. The Christian way of life is not characterized by shoring up boundaries of the familiar but by a readiness to participate in Christ's transforming presence in the world.

In summary, I believe Christians have three very important contributions to make in shaping the U.S. response to Mexican immigrants. First, we are to work to ensure that their basic needs are met and their human rights are carefully protected. Second, we are called to seek a realistic path to legalization for undocumented workers in the United States as a requirement of justice. Third, we are to welcome the cultural distinctiveness of Mexican immigrants and embrace the possibilities for new and creative relationships God is making possible in and through their presence.

An Evangelical Voice
M. Daniel Carroll R.

The presence of millions of Hispanic immigrants, both those with and without proper documentation, raises challenges with which Christians from across the spectrum of theological beliefs and ecclesiastical practices must engage. Debates center on matters concerning the viability of a stable national identity, the rising costs to the health care and educational systems, pressures on job markets, and the overcrowding

---

M. Daniel Carroll R. (Rodas) is the Distinguished Professor of Old Testament at Denver Seminary and an adjunct professor at El Seminario Teológico Centroamericano in Guatemala City, Guatemala.

of prisons. The topic of immigration generates vivid emotions and language no matter where one stands on these issues.

Unfortunately, among those who claim to be followers of Jesus, these arguments and their tone seldom appear to be informed consciously by their Christian faith. Is a Christian perspective on immigration possible? If so, how? Those of evangelical convictions,[7] as well as others within the broader Christian tradition, have several resources pertinent to immigration from which to draw. Those that will be mentioned here are historical, ministerial, and biblical in nature.[8]

The following discussion is divided into two sections. The first reviews ongoing work conducted with Hispanics for over a century and a half. Ministry to Hispanics is not a new phenomenon, and it is growing. The second is an overview of the wealth of insights that the Bible offers about immigration and the life of the immigrant. It is hoped that these observations will encourage those who want to serve the sojourners in our midst and will help provide a more positive direction for the views of those who are suspicious of these newcomers.

Hispanics and Evangelical Ministry

Debates often fall victim to the tyranny of the immediate, and this is true in the case of Hispanic immigration. Statistical data are pitted against each other, controversies are reduced to simplistic talking points, and advocates of different persuasions try to win the moral high ground by sharing moving stories of victims. To the unaware, the impression can be that the immigration "'problem" is a recent one, and an overwhelming one at that. Historical perspective can provide a corrective to this faulty perception.

The Mexican-American War ended in 1848 with the signing of the Treaty of Guadalupe Hidalgo. With this agreement, much of what is known today as the states of New Mexico, Arizona, Colorado, Utah, Nevada, and California were ceded to the United States in exchange for a sum of money. Hispanics, therefore, have had a presence in this country for quite a long time.[9] After that war, this territory was envisioned as a new frontier for mission. Soon, several denominations launched evangelistic and church planting efforts in the Southwest, and their fruit remains to this day.[10]

This historical thread connects Hispanic ministry to the present in a certain part of the country. Now, of course, because of immigration and other factors, the Hispanic presence is a national phenomenon. Once again, evangelical bodies are responding to fresh opportunities

for ministry. Many denominations, even those that are more hesitant
to speak to the socioeconomic and political aspects of immigration, are
investing money and personnel to establish churches in Hispanic communities. Many of these congregations meet in the church buildings of
the majority culture, so Anglo and Hispanic believers are learning to
work together toward the common goal of building up the body of
Christ. In addition, educational endeavors at a range of academic levels, including correspondence courses of Bible institutes and seminary
programs, are springing up across the country to equip Hispanic pas-
tors and church leaders.

The implications of Christian faith for immigration, though, go
beyond local ministries and training programs to touch deeper ethical
quandaries related to the needs of immigrants as people and their
standing before government authorities. Accordingly, evangelical
groups have begun to speak to these issues, too. Denominations, including the Evangelical Free Church, the Evangelical Covenant Church,
and the Church of the Nazarene, have passed resolutions that call for
gracious attitudes toward immigrants and constructive actions on their
behalf. The National Association of Evangelicals (NAE), the largest
coalition of evangelical denominations, organizations, and institutions
in the United States, has also endorsed such a statement and seeks to
work with Hispanic leaders to help push for the modification of existing legislation.

Evangelical leaders of stature from diverse theological backgrounds
are trying to persuade evangelicals to address immigration from an
explicitly biblical lens. These spokespersons range from Leith Ander-
son, pastor of a mega-church and president of the NAE, to seminary
professor and ethicist Ron Sider at Palmer Theological Seminary, to Jim
Wallis, an activist and founder of the Sojourners Community in Washington DC. One of the organizations within the Sojourner network,
Christians for Comprehensive Immigration Reform, provides materials and sponsors seminars to educate Christians about immigration
reform.

Evangelicals need to be aware of these efforts *toward* Hispanics, but
they also must appreciate the growth of evangelical churches, both of
the more traditional and Pentecostal types, *among* Hispanics. Hispanic
evangelicals now number in the millions.[11] It is estimated that the
National Hispanic Christian Leadership Conference represents eighteen
thousand churches and groups. Its director, Rev. Samuel Rodríguez of
the Assemblies of God, a recognized figure in religious and secular

circles, travels the country lobbying church and government leaders. Another association, Esperanza USA, hosts the annual National Hispanic Prayer Breakfast. Evangelical Spanish-speaking publishing houses and music companies continue to develop, and new organizations and ministries are starting up at a quick pace. All of these ministries long to partner with their majority-culture brothers and sisters to further the reign of God.

In sum, there is a long tradition of evangelicals working with Hispanics. These efforts have multiplied exponentially because of immigration, even as Hispanic evangelicalism is becoming a considerable force. What some fear as an invasion of foreigners is actually a surprisingly rich prospect for ministry and cooperation.

Immigration and the Bible

Evangelicals consider themselves to be people of the book. A foundational tenet of evangelicalism is that the Bible is the final authority for faith and practice. Many perhaps would be surprised by the quantity of material in the Bible that is relevant to the immigration debate. I highlight here the most salient points.

Image of God. The image of God in Genesis 1 is fundamental for dealing with immigration, because, at its most basic understanding, immigration is about persons. Theologians have differed over the meaning of the image, but all agree that this doctrine teaches that everyone has supreme value and potential. Immigrants are made in the image of God. They are, then, worthy of respect, but they also are a source of great promise. They have a lot to contribute in terms of their language, customs, and work—in all those areas that are part of what it means to be human. Immigration, above all else, is about people who are precious in the sight of God and only secondarily about national identity, economics, or border security.

Old Testament Narratives. The Old Testament is replete with accounts of the migration of peoples. Motivations vary. Sometimes it is due to hunger; on other occasions people flee armed conflict or are forcibly removed by conquering armies. Abraham journeys to Egypt in a time of famine (Gn 12). Jacob sends his sons there several times looking for food, and eventually the entire clan moves to Egypt under the care of Joseph (Gn 42—50). Naomi and her family leave Bethlehem and settle in Moab because of hunger, but years later, now widowed, she returns with Ruth, her daughter-in-law. For a time Naomi had been the immigrant, but now Ruth becomes the resident foreigner.

The life of immigrants in other lands could be harsh. In time the Israelites in Egypt provided slave labor for Pharaoh's building projects (Ex 1—2). Evidence indicates that some of those in the Assyrian exile became domestic servants, while others were assigned to work on farms or in construction. Psalm 137 reproduces the feelings of anger, shame, and homesickness of those forcibly removed from Judah by Babylon.

Not everyone endured such harsh fates. Joseph and Ruth are praised for their excellent character. Joseph's integrity and wisdom eventually are rewarded with his promotion to be second in command under Pharaoh, while the hard work and chaste disposition of Ruth earn her the affection of Boaz. Each assimilates to the host country: Joseph marries an Egyptian and has children with her, learns the language, and takes on the attire of the Egyptians; even his brothers do not recognize him! Ruth renounces her people and gods to claim the God of Israel. The genealogy at the end of the Book of Ruth reveals that this Moabite immigrant was a key person in the lineage of David. Daniel is deported to Babylon, where he served several kings with wisdom. His assimilation is officially enforced, although he and his friends refuse to surrender their identity as Jews (Dn 1). Esther's uncle, Mordechai, seems to be a man of some means, and this young woman becomes the queen of the Persian Empire. Nehemiah was cupbearer to Artaxerxes, while Ezra ministered among his people as priest and scribe.

It is interesting to track the varied responses of the host peoples—from the Egyptian anxiety about being overrun by foreign workers to the trust Artaxerxes has in Nehemiah. These reactions are accompanied by political decisions and social arrangements. In other words the treatment of immigrants, however they arrived, was an issue in the ancient world.

Old Testament Law. The presence of immigrants always requires legislation to regulate assimilation and to define the rights and obligations of both parties. The law codes of Israel are an example of an attempt to meet this need. In the Old Testament sojourners are listed with widows and orphans as vulnerable people. Immigrants were excluded from the land-tenure system, and as foreigners, they were disconnected from the kinship networks of their home country. Because of these liabilities, they qualified for the gleaning laws (Lv 19:10; Dt 24:19–22), the triennial tithe (Dt 14:28–29), and were to be given rest on the Sabbath (Ex 20:10; Dt 5:14). No prejudice against the sojourner was to be allowed in the courts (Dt 1:16–17; 27:19). They also were allowed to participate in much of the religious life of the nation. In other words, Israel opened the most cherished part of its life to outsiders.

At the Exodus, Israel was born as a nation of despised foreigners. That experience as immigrants was to mark them as a people. Because they had come from immigrant stock, they were to be compassionate to the foreigners who moved to their land. That history defined them, and their treatment of the outsider was to be a measure of their faith in God (Lv 19:34).

The New Testament. Many have not considered that Jesus and his family were refugees for a time. They fled to Egypt when he was a small child to escape Herod's rampage (Mt 2). While Jesus did not speak directly to the issue of immigration, he did deal with how to treat those who were of a different cultural background—specifically the Samaritans, a people despised by many Jews. He spoke with a Samaritan woman at the well in John 4, and in Luke 10 he lifts up a Samaritan as a paragon of righteousness in his response to the question, "Who is my neighbor?"

The epistles teach that all Christians are sojourners. Our citizenship is elsewhere (Phil 3:20; Heb 13:14). The First Letter of Peter speaks of believers as "aliens and strangers" (1:1; 2:11). The recipients of this letter may have been literal exiles. If so, that legal standing in the Roman Empire reflected their spiritual status as Christians. In addition, hospitality is a Christian virtue. We are to be gracious to others (Rom 12:13; Heb 13:2; 1 Pt 4:9), and this quality is to characterize the leadership of the church (1 Tim 3:2; Ti 1:8).

Both testaments have much to teach Christians of the majority culture. This cursory survey reveals the intrinsic worth of immigrants and that some biblical heroes were displaced persons. Israel's law is a paradigm of compassionate legislation; the challenge is to think through what such ideals might look like in contemporary law. Our country's history, like that of Israel, is inseparable from immigration. That memory, as it was designed to do in ancient times, should influence attitudes toward outsiders today. The life and teaching of Jesus encourage Christians to consider the possibility that those who are different may be the very ones who can lead us to a deeper faith. The epistles call their readers to care for the stranger and remind them that every Christian is an outsider is some sense.

Conclusion

How should evangelicals of the majority culture approach the national debate on Hispanic immigration? History and current trends in ministry show that God is at work in interesting and unexpected ways. The Bible—that guide for the journey of faith—has much to teach. What is needed are eyes to see and ears to hear!

A Latino Liberationist Voice

Edwin D. Aponte

Like many church people I thought that I was doing a fairly decent job of being a good Christian. But recent travel to the borderlands of the United States and Mexico and to Mexico City has challenged my unconsciously self-congratulatory Christianity. I am thinking anew about following Jesus in the twenty-first century by taking a closer look at a divisive and contentious issue, the topic of immigration to the United States.

In July 2007 I traveled with the Leadership Now youth program of Lancaster Theological Seminary to Arizona, crossed the border to the Mexican state of Sonora, and continued to Mexico City. People are now moving across borders for all kinds of reasons, some like Mary, Joseph, and Jesus, fleeing for their lives to Egypt as migrants seeking asylum (Mt 2:13–15).

We first arrived at BorderLinks in Tucson, Arizona, after a long trip beginning at 5:30 a.m. in Lancaster, Pennsylvania. At BorderLinks we learned in a new way what the Bible says about a theology of liberation as well as a spirituality of liberation that is lived out through working with undocumented peoples crossing borders out of unfathomable desperation. We discovered more about the vexing history of the U.S./Mexico borderlands and the complex global economic realities. The changes in recent history have caused the extraordinary growth of poverty in Mexico, so rapid and drastic that a new term has been invented for it, *probreza extrema* (extreme poverty).

Edwin D. Aponte, professor of religion and culture, is vice president of Academic Affairs and dean of Lancaster Theological Seminary.

We were challenged directly by these questions: Does the church really believe in the gospel message? Do we really take our Christianity seriously, especially in light of Matthew 25:31–46? In the past when I came to this text I focused on the Son of Man coming in glory, or the fact that this was a story about the future Great Judgment, or on the separation of the sheep and the goats, but never on why the king invited some to share in the inheritance of the reign of God. With new insight I now see the challenge in Matthew's parable of the sheep and the goats.

Engracia, a strong, optimistic woman who was extremely gracious, was one of the people we met in Mexico. She invited a small group of us (Leadership Now youth and two adults) to share a meal in her home, which she shares with her young daughter and son. It was a delightful, delicious, filling meal served with pride, hospitality, and love in a two-room structure with a corrugated metal roof, dirt floors, and cardboard on the walls. Her home was surrounded by other homes that pretty much looked the same as hers as far as the eye could see.

Engracia is a single parent, originally from Oaxaca in the south, who has been living in this *colonia* of Nogales for ten years. She is a skilled seamstress, president of her woman's work coop, and earns a living to support herself and her children. In addition, she contributes to the coop in order to help others and saves money toward the construction of her own sewing shop and a better home. Amazingly, in the midst of all this poverty and hardship, she could be hopeful. One of the reasons she is so hopeful is that someone had helped her by taking seriously the words of Matthew 25:35–36, "For I was hungry and you gave me food, I was thirsty and you gave me something to drink, I was a stranger and you welcomed me, I was naked and you gave me clothing, I was sick and you took care of me, I was in prison and you visited me." We were surprised by the gifts of grace we received from Engracia, who allowed us to see Jesus in her and her children.

We drove south from Nogales on the border through the desolate vastness of the Sonoran Desert, full of cactus and scrub bushes, rattlesnakes, pumas, and Gila monsters, to the small Mexican town of Altar. When the United States clamped down on the international border out of fear of terrorists and undocumented immigrants, it did not stop the flow of those immigrants but only shifted the flow into the desert, where people die daily. Little Altar is now directly on the migrant route through the desert.

We had dinner with three young migrants and learned something of their stories. Two were from southern Mexico, and the third was from Honduras; all were barely older than the LeadershipNow youth. Most of their travel across Mexico to the north was by train, not inside but strapped on top of jostling freight cars. They had already risked their lives, and now they had the Sonoran Desert to cross, all in the hope of finding a job. There is no work where they came from, and they hope for some simple job to support themselves and possibly help their families back home. Strangers to this part of Mexico, soon the young men would be strangers in the United States. The next day we said our good-byes knowing that we would probably never see each other again and hoping that these young men would not die in the upcoming desert crossing. I was reminded again of the words of Matthew 25:35–36; in their three very different faces I saw Jesus and wondered if anyone would invite them in.

In the town of Altar we visited a *casa de huésped* (guest house), but what we saw was far from the usual definition. I was caught off guard by my own emotional reaction. Racks of plywood platforms with a blanket thrown on top of each wooden shelf were the "beds." It resembled a prison or the photographs I'd seen of Nazi concentration camps rather than a guest house.

We spoke with three men who paid to stay there before making the attempt to cross into the United States—two from Chiapas, one from Guerrero. They all said that they did not want to leave home but had no choice because the poverty was so great where they came from that it was impossible to earn a living wage. They told us they just wanted to work to earn a living, and they did not plan to stay long. One man asked, "Why did you build the wall to keep Mexicans out? Do you think that we are terrorists? We just want to work!" Afterward I dashed into the church at the plaza with tears in my eyes, and on my knees cried out to God, "What do you want us to do? What do you want me to do? What can we do?" Again, I was reminded of the words of Matthew 25:35–36, and in my mind's eye I see Jesus as I think of those three desperate young men.

The immigration situation is very complicated, but, like many complex problems, we seem ready to settle for simple, seemingly easy answers. Rather than work through the difficulties and complexities, we settle for slogans, blame games, or quick fixes that make things worse. We erect physical walls or pass local ordinances that target all Hispanics as potential criminals and illegals, or proclaim that the reason people are crossing the desert is to steal U.S. jobs and to get bargains at Walmart and K-Mart. There are global economic issues that affect all of us in the world in a variety of ways, yet many of us want to blame a particular group for our problems. The global economy has resulted in people living in extreme poverty who see no option for survival other than to try to reach the United States in the hope of finding work—any work. As we in the church discern the global roots for this movement of peoples, a clear challenge remains at our own doorstep.

In the midst of trying to sort out global, political, and social conundrums, the words of Matthew 25:35–36 must challenge our self-satisfied, comfortable Christianity. My vision of Jesus in the twenty-first century is revealed more fully through my actions as a Christian than through what I say I believe. If we truly accept Matthew 25, then, surprisingly, Christ becomes the personal object of all our deeds, and those actions are the evidence of our faithfulness. In the past few years some youth and adults have been asking, "What would Jesus do?" and wearing WWJD bracelets as reminders of that question. If we take Matthew 25:31–46 seriously, then the question is not our asking, "What would Jesus do?" but Jesus asking us, "What will you do?"

Indeed, what *are* we doing? In the end, what matters is whether or not our actions are recognized by Christ Jesus. We call Jesus the Good Shepherd, and we name ourselves his sheep, but what is the point if our actions show us to be the self-deluded, hardhearted goats of Matthew 25?

In one sense the face of Jesus for the twenty-first century is what it always has been. His face is in the faces of those who are hungry and whom we either feed or ignore, and his thirst is the thirst of those to whom we either bring a glass of water or deny the reality of their thirst altogether. He is the stranger who appears foreign and whom we welcome with hospitality or whom we shun as a threat. Jesus is the naked child whom we sometimes clothe or whom we pretend we don't see or turn away in pious shame. It is Jesus whose face is the face of the sick we have cared for or whose care we have left to someone else, along with excuses justifying our inattention. Jesus is the prisoner we seldom visit or simply ignore and send off to be warehoused.

All of us can be skillful at interpreting the clear meaning of this gospel text in a convenient way. We say that people who find themselves hungry, thirsty, foreign, naked, sick, or in prison must have done something to deserve their present condition. Yet even if some have made bad choices that have led to their predicament, there are no qualifications in the gospels. No one wrote, "Whatever you do to the least of these *deserving* people." We are not given permission to judge whether or not people in need are worthy of help.

Some may say that God is working out God's divine plan for the lives of the oppressed. Even if that is true, Matthew 25:31–46 makes it clear that action needs to be taken on behalf of those who need help. Jesus, who crossed so many borders, calls those who claim to follow him to be border crossers as well. His followers must cross the boundaries that people inside and outside the church say ought not to be crossed. Jesus asks us to act in ways that polite society, a society that values people who "pull themselves up by their own bootstraps," might not value.

We are to see the face of Jesus in the faces of those rejected by society, "the least of these," whether they are from across the street or across the world. As we look at the people around us with new eyes and take dangerous, radical, unpopular action for the hungry, thirsty, strangers, naked, sick, or imprisoned, we recognize the face of Jesus today in the twenty-first century.

Voice of the People

QUE TE HIZO CAMINAR
HE MADE ME WALK
(DT 8:15, NIV)

He made me walk.
He made me walk in the desert
filled with snakes and scorpions in the desert.

In the giant and vast desert there is great thirst.
There is great thirst.
Send me water for my thirst.
Send me water for my thirst.
In the giant and vast desert, send me water for my
       thirst.

Que Te Hizo Caminar

(Deutoronomio 8:15, "He Made Me Walk")

Deborah De La Torre
© 2009

He sustained me with manna.
He sustained me with manna in the desert
filled with snakes and scorpions in the desert.

In the giant and vast desert there is great thirst.
There is great thirst.
Send me water for my thirst.
Send me water for my thirst.
In the giant and vast desert, send me water for my
      thirst.

But there was no water.
But there was no water in the desert
filled with snakes and scorpions in the desert.

In the giant and vast desert there is great thirst.
There is great thirst.
Send me water for my thirst.
Send me water for my thirst.
In the giant and vast desert, send me water for my
      thirst.

So He brought water out of a rock.
He brought water out of a rock in the desert
filled with snakes and scorpions in the desert.

In the giant and vast desert there is great thirst.
There is great thirst.
Send me water for my thirst.
Send me water for my thirst.
In the giant and vast desert, send me water for my
      thirst.

7

Ethical Responses

Preach the Gospel at all times and when necessary use words.
—SAINT FRANCIS OF ASSISI

What does it mean to be a Christian? Is having the correct doctrine enough? Is salvation obtained by belonging to a church or being baptized in the right church? Is repeating a sinner's prayer sufficient? Is Christianity a belief, or is it an action, a profession of faith, or a call to radicalism? Are we Christians because we talk about Jesus, or is it because we become Jesus, that is, we do what Jesus did? Do we stand with the powerful and privileged or with the hungry, the thirsty, the naked, the alien, the hospitalized, and the incarcerated?

The major failing of many Christians in the world today is that we too often believe that Christianity is a way of thinking rather than a way of living. In an earlier book, *Doing Christian Ethics from the Margins* (Orbis Books, 2004), I argued that the manner in which many Christians practice their faith falls short of the gospel message because they argue over abstract moral frameworks rather than *doing* ethics. Many Christians respond in words to the inhumane conditions forced upon the dispossessed when it is much more important to respond in deeds, in actions, in praxis. When a moral Christian life is reduced to individual piety or virtues, it often fails to result in Christian action.

Ethics is action, action that leads to salvation and liberation for both the oppressed and their oppressors. A "roadmap" leading to Christian action, based on the Catholic social teaching model of *seeing—judging—acting*, can be helpful. It uses five basic steps: (1) observation—to discern why the present moral dilemma exists; (2) reflection—to understand how social structures contribute to and maintain the moral dilemma; (3) prayer—to understand what our responsibility as men and women of faith should be; (4) action—to respond to what we claim to believe as Christians; and (5) reassessment—to ensure faithfulness to the gospel message of liberation and salvation.

Throughout this book, we have moved beyond the rhetorical debate gripping our country as we have observed and reflected on the faces of real people who are immigrants. We have seen their photos and heard their prayers. Now we find ourselves on the threshold of the fourth step, action. If you, the reader, finish this book, are saddened and shaking your head in empathy for the undocumented, and *do* nothing, then I have failed. If you move on to another book, comforted by the fact that you now understand the issues, then I have failed. Empathy and consciousness, without action, are meaningless for Christians. Brother James probably said it best:

> My brothers and sisters, where is the gain for you to say you have faith, if you do nothing? Is faith able to save you? If a brother or sister is naked and lacking in daily food, and you say, "Go in peace, be warm and filled," but do not give the person what the body needs, where is the gain? Even so, faith without works is dead. Yet someone may say, "You have faith, and I have works." Let me see your faith without your works, and I will show you my faith by my works. You believe God is one, and you do well. But even the demons believe and tremble. Do you not see, O foolish one, that faith without works is useless? (Jas 2:14–20)

My hope is that this final chapter of the book becomes a springboard for you to take action. My hope is that you will raise the consciousness of others, that you will contact your political representatives and demand justice, that you will encourage your congregation to become a Sanctuary church, or that you will spend time at the border giving water and food to Jesus disguised as an undocumented. Only then will a book such as this have had any worth.

The New Sanctuary Movement

Alexia Salvatierra

Years ago Rev. Andrew Johnson, a Baptist minister, was the director of public health for the City of Oakland. His workshops often included an exercise in which he asked people to close their eyes and imagine the sounds of a healthy community. Some would report hearing the sound of children laughing because they had enough to eat and a secure place to sleep and the health care that they needed to be well. Others reported hearing the sound of elderly people swapping stories because they felt safe enough to sit in the sun without fear. One teenager said that he heard the sounds of people who didn't agree talking with one another instead of shouting at or about one another.

The dream of Rev. Dr. Martin Luther King, Jr., would have resonated well with Rev. Johnson's vision. King actually went one step beyond the dream of a healthy community. He talked about the Beloved Community—the place where everyone was welcome, where everyone was equally valued, and where everyone's rights were respected regardless of color, regardless of class. Is that the kind of place where you would like to live?

If that is what we all want, what keeps it from happening? Rev. James M. Lawson, Jr., was the man Dr. King called his theologian of nonviolence. Rev. Lawson had lived in India as a young man, learning from Gandhi. He brought this wealth of wisdom and spiritual teaching back to the beginnings of the civil rights movement. Part of what he learned from Gandhi is that in order to create the Beloved Community, we have to resist evil. And evil for Gandhi as a Hindu was always rooted in a lie. Gandhi taught Rev. Lawson that in order to fight evil in a particular society at a particular time, it is important to understand the core lie that is being used to justify evil, and then to identify the clearest manifestation of that lie. That is what must be overcome.

Alexia Salvatierra is executive director of Clergy and Laity United for Economic Justice of California, an alliance of interfaith organizations that bring religious leaders and congregations together to respond to the crisis of working poverty and to build a faith-rooted movement for economic justice throughout the state. CLUE-CA is the lead agency for the New Sanctuary Movement.

At the beginning of the civil rights movement, Rev. Lawson led a group of leaders through the exercise of identifying the lie and its clearest manifestation. They decided that the lie was the false belief that some people are worth more than others. All of our religious traditions teach that we are all equally and infinitely valuable. The lie that some people are worth more than others was used to justify slavery—the belief that some people were born to be served and others were born to serve. During the civil rights movement they decided that the clearest manifestation of that lie was segregation.

Fast forward thirty years, and Rev. Lawson believed that the same lie still affects our society, but its clearest manifestation is now the crisis of working poverty—the growing number of families in which an adult works full-time without receiving sufficient wages to pay for the basics, for rent, food, and health care. Working poverty is also built on the lie because it assumes that some children have the right to health insurance and others don't, which means, of course, that some children have the right to live and others don't.

A couple of years ago Rev. Lawson realized that the immigration crisis is also connected to the same lie. Can you still belong to the Beloved Community if you were originally born in another country? Do your children deserve to live or die because they were born on one side of the border or the other?

Liliana comes from Mexico. Her family came over legally as farm workers. The United States has a guest-worker program for farm workers, but it's very small. Liliana stayed behind to finish high school while her siblings made the trip north. She is very ambitious and has always wanted to become a psychologist. After she finished high school, her parents petitioned for her to join them. They then found out that there was an immigration backlog of twelve years. It's not surprising that Liliana did not want to wait twelve years before seeing her family. She bought a false birth certificate, but when she tried to use it at the border the guards immediately knew that it was false. They laughed at her and turned her back.

Later, when she was able to cross over, she went to live with her family and work in Oxnard. There she met the love of her life, a U.S. citizen. Together, they had two children who were U.S. citizens. He holds two jobs, she holds one, and they own their own home. They are also leaders in their church and community. When she was pregnant with their third child, he petitioned for her to become a legal resident.

They went through the entire process and eventually reached the final interview, very excited, because this would be the day her papers would be approved.

However, when the immigration official looked at her file his face changed. He said, "Liliana, there's a problem. You have falsely claimed to be a U.S. citizen. That's a felony, and the punishment includes a lifetime ban on immigration to this country—no waiver and no appeal. It doesn't matter that you have three citizen children, a citizen husband, that your whole family is here, that you have a job and a home. You are being deported."

Liliana went home in shock. She didn't know what to do, so she just continued to live her life, that is until about six months later. At 6:00 in the morning five immigration agents arrived at her house as she was breastfeeding her baby and preparing her older children for school. They told her that she had to go with them immediately. Her seven-year-old boy began to cry. He said, "They taught us in school that police take bad people away. My mommy is not a bad mommy; she is a good mommy; she is the best mommy for me." Liliana began to cry.

One immigration agent said, "Lady, don't waste your tears. We take away pregnant women, they give birth in detention, we take their babies and send them to Mexico." The other immigration agent winced and asked Liliana how much time she needed to prepare her children for her departure. She asked for a week. When the immigration agents left, she called her church for sanctuary.

The immigration system is a broken system, a Kafkaesque system, a system that makes any Department of Motor Vehicles look really good in comparison. And it is breaking hearts and families every day. How should the members of the Beloved Community respond when someone is suffering unjustly? There are congregations all across the country in thirty-five cities that are accompanying and advocating for these families, and congregational networks that are providing sanctuary.

The concept of sanctuary goes back to a biblical tradition found in the Book of Numbers. It was created as a social and legal mechanism to deal with a situation in which someone had broken the law and faced a cruel and unjust response. In the Book of Numbers the crime committed was manslaughter, but lawbreakers were being treated as if they had committed murder. In that case, the religious community was instructed to provide a safe and sacred space where a lawbreaker could receive protection until it was possible to receive a fair hearing.

This same concept was invoked during slavery, at a time when abolitionists, who were working hard to change the unjust laws that treated people as property, provided safe and sacred spaces and the underground railroad to protect people from the consequences of the unjust law (which included separation of families) until they could receive a fair hearing.

The concept was invoked again in the early 1980s when hundreds of thousands of Central American refugees came to this country, fleeing repressive regimes in their home countries. When they arrived, they found that it was incredibly hard to receive political asylum, even though international human rights organizations were documenting regular massacres. The policy of the U.S. government set different criteria for people coming from countries that were our allies and those coming from countries that were our opponents. The governments of these Central American countries were our allies and were actually using U.S. funds to massacre their citizens.

When these refugees found that they could not get political asylum, they sought help from congregations. Many were people of faith who had been involved in liberation theology. Congregations initially offered humanitarian support and then tried to advocate for them in immigration court. Then, when they discovered that the refugees couldn't get a fair hearing, congregations declared their churches places of sanctuary and risked prosecution to shelter them until the law could be changed. With their moral courage they made visible the families who were suffering, changing hearts and minds, galvanizing civic participation, and giving the refugees the healing support that they needed to keep on struggling.

Fast forward to December 2005 when the Sensenbrenner Bill passed in the House of Representatives. This bill would have made it a felony to be undocumented or to help or serve an undocumented person. (The bill did not pass the Senate and thus did not become law.) The bill's passage in the House was rooted in an image of immigrants threatening our security and draining resources from our systems. It was the final step in a series of legislative acts restricting immigration and punishing undocumented immigrants.

These acts did not recognize the illogical, ineffective, and inhumane patchwork of laws that comprise our current immigration policy. The average American does not know that our immigration system is profoundly broken and that it is breaking apart families. As religious leaders struggled with the question of the most important contribution that they could make as people of faith to the crisis, they brought back the ancient tradition of sanctuary.

Elvira Arellano had already taken sanctuary in her congregation in Chicago. On Ash Wednesday of 2006 Cardinal Roger Mahony called upon the Catholic community throughout the country to continue to serve immigrants regardless of their immigration status, even if they had to go to jail for it if the Sensenbrenner Bill became law. Cardinal Mahony's pronouncement changed the public debate; it made immigrant workers and their families visible as children of God, victims of a broken system, instead of criminals and invaders. Interfaith networks in Los Angeles and New York began to ask whether there was a way that they could accompany immigrant families facing deportation so that their stories would be heard by the general public, awakening the moral imagination of the country on an ongoing basis. At the same time, other groups around the country were struggling with a similar quest.

In January 2006, at a meeting in Washington DC, a national network was formed under the banner of a New Sanctuary Movement. The goal of the New Sanctuary Movement is to bring together clusters of congregations in over thirty-five cities to support "prophet" families—families who are willing to tell their story publicly. These congregations also provide a religious witness and a moral voice on the immigration issue, as they participate in story-based and values-based education and advocacy work and in providing direct services to immigrant families facing deportation. The New Sanctuary Movement gives parents of citizen-children a safe and sacred space until they can receive a fair hearing.

What is an appropriate punishment for being undocumented? Dr. Juan Martinez, dean of Hispanic studies at Fuller University, says that the crime of the undocumented is breaking and entering (when it is not overstaying a visa). He asks what we would do with someone who broke into our home, remodeled our house, took care of our garden, cleaned our house, took care of our children, and cooked us dinner? Indeed, 97 percent of undocumented men work full-time. And the studies show—even studies from such radical organizations as the Social Security Administration and the IRS—that overall (taking into account local, state, and federal costs and benefits) immigrants contribute more to society than they receive.

There are problems with our current immigration system. People ask if we care about those who suffer from the influx of immigrants—and there are people suffering, people who have been economically displaced when corporations chose to give their jobs to immigrants. We respond that there are more effective and humane solutions than mass deportations. Obviously, immigration is a complicated issue, with no simple answers. Everyone, from the president on down, believes that our present immigration policies have created a broken, incredibly flawed system.

What we don't agree on is exactly what is wrong and exactly how to fix it. However, to take seriously the value of every human being is to take seriously the sacredness of all of our stories. We cannot create sound social policy unless we really listen to all of the stories of those who are directly affected by the problem. We cannot afford to ignore any stories. I would like to share a story—a story that is not often heard but is representative of many others.

María was a member of my congregation in Fresno. When I first noticed her, she had big purple blotches on her arms. She was a farm worker, and the blotches came from the chemicals used in the fields. However, María didn't complain about the chemicals and the lack of protection because she was undocumented—one of the 90 percent of agricultural workers in our country who are imported. (Since the beginning of this country we have always imported people to work our fields.)

One day she shared her story with me. María's family had been prosperous corn farmers in Mexico for six generations. They worked hard, and they did well. Then NAFTA was passed, and U.S. agribusinesses (which are highly subsidized by the U.S. government) began selling corn at prices with which her family could not possibly compete. They tried shifting crops, but every crop they could sell, American agribusiness could sell more cheaply. In the end, they lost the family farm.

In order to feed her children, María, a widow, was forced to move north to the border where there were multinational factories. She worked in a factory, a *maquiladora*, and sent the money home to her mother to feed her children. Then the factory closed and moved to Indonesia, where the owners could pay even lower wages than they did in Mexico. María then crossed the border and walked through the desert, risking her life to work in the fields for the same agribusiness companies that had destroyed her family farm. She sent money home to feed her children.

María was a victim of U.S. policy. Subsidies to American agribusinesses, combined with the trade agreement between the United States and Mexico, were responsible for María's incapacity to feed her children while living in Mexico. So she risked the trip to the United States.

According to the Universal Declaration of Human Rights, Article 23 (3), everyone who works has the right to just and favorable remuneration ensuring for himself and his family an existence worthy of human dignity, and supplemented, if necessary, by other means of social protection. Article 25 (1) declares that everyone has the right to a standard of living adequate for the health and well-being of himself and of his family, including food, clothing, housing, and medical care and necessary social services, and the right to security in the event of unemployment, sickness, disability, widowhood, old age or other lack of livelihood in circumstances beyond his control. Article 25 (2) states that mothers and children are entitled to special care and assistance. All children, whether born in or out of wedlock, shall enjoy the same social protection.

Yes, María is undocumented, but she has committed her "crime" in response to the violation of her rights, a violation that threatens the lives of her children. What would any of us do to feed our children? What would any of us not do?

Rev. Donald Wilson has been a chef at a luxury hotel for twenty years; he is African American. Over the years he has watched his company prefer immigrants over African American workers, presumably because they are less likely to demand rights and just compensation. However, over time he learned that these new employees could also be organized to stand shoulder to shoulder with him in fighting for their common rights as workers.

Many of these immigrants were from countries where they had risked their lives for justice, and they were courageous and consistent in the struggle. Rev. Wilson shared his concerns with his new allies about the lack of hiring African Americans, and they worked together successfully to insert a clause in the union contract to require monitoring of diversity, outreach to the African American community, and training for young African Americans and other poor native-born Americans to move into quality jobs in the hotel industry.

Immigration is complex—and a truly comprehensive solution to current problems will take into account international trade and foreign policy. However, we can never come up with a sane solution until we pay attention to the truth that underlies the vision of the Beloved Community. Injustice anywhere is a threat to justice everywhere. An injury to one is an injury to all. We are so connected that the good of each and the common good are the same. May we form our opinions and our commitments with that truth in mind.

Civil Initiative
John Fife

It behooves us North American Christians to realize now what the German churches learned too late . . . it is not enough to resist with confession; we must confess with resistance.
—WILLIAM SLOANE COFFIN[1]

Civil initiative as a term did not exist prior to 1982. Our colleague, Jim Corbett, created it in his brilliant Quaker mind and then defined it for us in the Sanctuary Movement. Civil initiative has been practiced, however, since the very earliest stories that have formed our faith and witness. When Pharaoh decreed that the Hebrew midwives should kill all the male babies of the slaves at birth, the Book of Exodus says they resisted. The resistance of Pharaoh's daughter saved Moses from the waters of the Nile, and Moses then led the Hebrew slaves out of bondage. In American history the Abolition Movement and the underground railroad are classic examples of civil initiatives in practice. Another civil initiative was taken by the people of Denmark who joined together to resist the Nazi occupation and deportation of the Jews. That bright example, however, was overshadowed by the tragic failure of the Christian church in Europe to protect Jewish refugees in the 1930s and 1940s.

John Fife is pastor emeritus of Southside Presbyterian Church. A co-founder of No More Deaths, he now serves as an active volunteer in that movement. He was also a founding member of the Sanctuary Movement in the 1980s.

The term *civil initiative* had its origins in the Sanctuary Movement formed to protect Central American refugees from deportation back to the death squads, torture chambers, and civil wars of El Salvador and Guatemala. In spite of the judgment of the U.N. High Commission on Refugees and every international human rights organization, the U.S. government refused to recognize as refugees people fleeing conditions of violence in Central America. The deportations of those seeking refuge to face death squads and massacres confronted the church of North America with a fundamental question of ethics and faith.

After trying failed strategies of legal aid, court suits, and even shareholder actions against airlines contracted to transport the deported refugees, a few churches determined to declare themselves a sanctuary for refugees. One of those churches was Southside Presbyterian Church in Tucson, Arizona. On March 24, 1982, as pastor of Southside, I sent a letter to the attorney general of the United States stating:

> We take this action because we believe the current policy and practice of the U.S. government with regard to Central American refugees is illegal and immoral. We believe our government is in violation of the 1980 Refugee Act and international law by continuing to arrest, detain, and forcibly return refugees to the terror, persecution, and murder in El Salvador and Guatemala.
>
> We believe that justice and mercy require that people of conscience actively assert our God-given right to aid anyone fleeing from persecution and murder. The current administration of the U.S. law prohibits us from sheltering these refugees from Central America. Therefore we believe that administration of the law is immoral as well as illegal. We beg you, in the name of God, to do justice and love mercy in the administration of your office. We ask that extended voluntary departure be granted to refugees from Central America and that current deportation proceedings against these victims be stopped. Until such time, we will not cease to extend the sanctuary of the church to undocumented people from Central America. Obedience to God requires this of us all. Since the government had threatened the churches who had declared sanctuary with indictment and prosecution, our assumption was that we were engaging in "civil disobedience" in the tradition of Thoreau, Gandhi, and King. In public statements, sermons, and interviews all these prophets of civil disobedience were quoted freely to explain the Sanctuary Movement.

A phone call from a human rights lawyer a month later put an end to all of those eloquent quotations from Dr. King. "You are doing more harm to human rights and refugee law than anyone else I know," he began. "Listen carefully! You are not doing civil disobedience. Civil disobedience is publicly violating a bad law, and assuming the consequences, in order to change an unjust law. We don't want to change U.S. refugee law. It conforms to the international standards. The problem is that the government is violating our own refugee law. The government is doing civil disobedience!"

So Jim Corbett coined a new term for the practice of sanctuary. He called it "civil initiative." The current definition reads, "Civil initiative is the legal right and the moral responsibility of society to protect the victims of human rights violations when government is the violator." Jim pointed to the Nuremberg Principles in international law as the legal foundation for civil initiative. When the Nazi generals and officials were tried for their crimes against humanity, their defense was simple and clear. "We were just following the laws and orders of the state." The court found that was not a defense: "The essence of the Charter (of the Military Tribunal) is that individuals have international duties that transcend the national obligation of obedience imposed by the individual state."[2]

As a founding principle of the United States, the Declaration of Independence recognizes that all people are endowed with certain human rights, and nation-states that violate those inalienable rights have no claim to legitimacy. So Justice Robert Jackson (later to become a U.S. Supreme Court Justice) in his opening statement to the Nuremberg Tribunal said, "The principle of personal liability is a necessary as well as a logical one if International Law is to render real help to the maintenance of peace. An International Law which operates only on states can be enforced only by war because the most practicable method of coercing a state is warfare."[3]

This prophetic statement by Justice Jackson pointed beyond the legal right and led to the moral responsibility of civil initiative. International law can be enforced only by war unless civil society assumes the responsibility for protecting the victims of human rights violations.

This simply points to an unfinished task that was implicit at the tribunal. It proclaimed everyone's right to aid the persecuted but failed to establish a social base for citizens to exercise this right. Sanctuary congregations are now forming that base; from the perspective established by international law, this is exactly what the provision of sanctuary does. Covenant communities' right and duty to protect the victims of government persecution must be conceded by the state if the proceedings at Nuremberg are to have any shred of judicial validity.[4]

According to Corbett, if the legal right established at Nuremberg is to be implemented peaceably, the moral responsibility can be implemented only by faith communities acting faithfully.

Whenever a congregation that proclaims the prophetic faith abandons the poor and persecuted to organized violation, its unfaithfulness darkens the way for all humankind. And when it stands as a bulwark against state violations of human rights, it lights the way. The congregational obligation to protect victims of state crimes extends beyond our individual civic responsibilities, because only in this kind of covenant community can we provide sanctuary for the violated.[5]

And it worked! By 1986 some 567 churches and synagogues had declared themselves a sanctuary and welcomed a refugee family into the protection of the community of faith. A new underground railroad had formed, moving refugees from city to city, across the United States and even to Canada. Seventeen cities, including New York, Chicago, Los Angeles, and San Francisco, had declared themselves "cities of sanctuary" and instructed their public employees not to cooperate with federal immigration agents. Colleges and universities declared sanctuary and moved refugee families onto their campuses in the tradition of the free university. A movement was born!

Of course, the government responded with arrests, indictments, and trials, but the number of sanctuary churches and synagogues doubled during the trial of eleven defendants in Tucson in 1985. By 1987 juries were acquitting sanctuary defendants, and in 1989 the basic aims of the movement were realized. An agreement was reached with the U.S. Department of Justice to:

1. end all deportations to El Salvador and Guatemala,
2. give all refugees from those countries work permits and temporary protected status,
3. reform the political asylum process at the INS [Immigration and Naturalization Service].

Now a new crisis of human rights violations has challenged the faith communities of North America. As you have heard, or perhaps even learned from this book, the Border Patrol has implemented a new border-enforcement strategy since the events of 9/11. Its strategy has deliberately channeled the migration of workers into the most hazardous, isolated, and deadly areas of the borderlands. The resulting deaths of over five thousand poor workers, their wives, and their children, and the suffering of untold hundreds of thousands of migrants in the desert do not simply represent a failed strategy. They also represent a continuing violation of human rights and international law.

In 2003 a six-judge panel of the Inter-American Court of Human Rights ruled unanimously that the deaths of almost two thousand Mexican and some Central American migrants are the strongest evidence that the United States has violated and continues to violate human rights by maintaining Operation Gatekeeper. In subsequent determinations, the United Nations Human Rights Commission, Amnesty International, and other international human rights organizations have reached the same conclusion.

How have communities of faith responded? Churches and synagogues have acted by taking up strategies of civil initiative. Here in the borderlands of southern Arizona, faith communities that were part of the Sanctuary Movement came together in 2000 in response to the increasing death toll of migrant workers in the Sonoran Desert. Since then they have created three faith-based organizations to provide direct humanitarian aid to migrants and to save as many lives as possible in the desert.

In 2000, Humane Borders organized to place water stations in critical areas of the borderlands where deaths were occurring. The primary cause of migrant death is dehydration and heat stroke. Each year between twenty thousand and twenty-five thousand gallons of water are used by migrants from these water stations.

By 2002 the annual death toll had doubled, and so new strategies for civil initiative were required. While the water stations were a passive presence in the desert, it was decided that an active presence was necessary. The Samaritans group was organized to put four-wheel-drive vehicles out in the desert daily with volunteer doctors, nurses, and EMTs. These vehicles carry water, food, and emergency medical gear. Samaritans have found hundreds of migrants with heat stroke, broken ankles, twisted knees and ankles, and rattlesnake bites. They have found victims of heart attack and stroke, rape and beatings, as well as the lost and abandoned.

In 2004, understanding that the annual death toll in the Tucson sector had reached a new record despite all of the lives that had been saved, a third faith-based effort, No More Deaths, was organized. During the hottest and deadliest months of the year No More Deaths sets up 24/7 camps in critical areas of the desert. Volunteers go out from the camps each day with backpacks filled with food, water, and medical gear. They hike the migrant trails and treat migrants in distress. Civil initiative is once again being practiced by faith communities in the borderlands to resist government violations of human rights.

Another form of civil initiative is also under way. Beyond the borderlands and across the United States, churches and synagogues are forming a New Sanctuary Movement to protect undocumented parents of children who are U.S. citizens so these families who are threatened with destruction because of the deportation of one or both parents can find sanctuary and support with faith communities.

A paraphrase of Jim Corbett's ethical call to the churches in 1982 was taken up in 2008. Those of us who want to be faithful in our allegiance to the reign of God cannot avoid recognizing that collaboration with a government that violates human rights is a betrayal of our faith, even if it is a passive or even loudly protesting collaboration that tolerates the deaths of thousands of poor migrant workers.

When a government uses the crucifixion of entire peoples in the desert as a border strategy, there is no middle ground between collaboration and resistance. We can take our stand with the oppressed, or we can take our stand with organized oppression—but we cannot do both.

Testimony from a Scholar-Activist

Miguel A. De La Torre

The borderlands that separate poverty from privilege form a land of ambiguities, paradoxes, and contradictions. The imaginary line reinforced by walls and guns protects the wealth accumulated on one side from those stuck on the other side on whose backs a major portion of that wealth was created. This space we call the borderlands is undergirded by racial and ethnic suppositions that fuel capital-building assumptions geared to justify the transfer of wealth from those forced to live south of this line to those who live to the north. We say that we are a beacon of human rights for the world, yet it is not really exaggerating to say that the borderlands are the epicenter of what is probably the greatest human rights crisis presently occurring within the United States.

For several days eleven of my students and I spent our time exploring the ambiguities, paradoxes, and contradictions of the borderlands. Each day after breakfast we would separate into four groups, making sure that someone with some proficiency in Spanish was in each group. One of those days my group of four headed for the migrant trails assigned to us with our backpacks full of water and food. As we drove toward the start of the trail, we spotted turkey vultures circling overhead, about a thousand feet from the main trail. No one needed to say anything. We all knew that they usually circle once they detect the rancid smell of death. We jumped out of the red Explorer and headed toward what appeared to be the center of the circle, expecting the worst. Today we were fortunate. There was no dead migrant. Some other groups have found a dead cow or some other animal. Not long ago a group found the body of a teenage girl. We say we are the land of plenty, but thousands die in this region because they lack water or food.

As we drove away, headed back to the trail, we came across a few lost migrants. We gave them food and water and pointed them northward. We were giving them directions when the Border Patrol arrived. The migrants were quickly placed in what appeared to be a covered dog cage in the back of a pickup truck. There was certainly no air conditioning there. We say we do not torture prisoners, yet according to the testimonies of some of the migrants and official accusations, at times the Border Patrol places migrants in these overcrowded cages and actually turns on the heat.[6]

The migrants we met were taken away to be "voluntarily" returned to Mexico, yet we knew they would more than likely reattempt the trek. We finally arrived at the start of the trail and headed up into the foothills and through the canyons to leave our food and water. We walked on trails covered with footprints and littered with empty water bottles, plastic jugs, clothing, and other personal effects. Volunteers from our camp have been charged with littering for leaving bottles full of water on these trails, yet we always pick up and bring back to camp as much discarded litter as we can carry to be properly disposed of.

Along the way we pass two shrines, a reminder that there are symbols of the Divine and the life promised in Christ on these trails of

Author at a shrine containing a variety of religious relics.

The Border Patrol removing undocumented guest "Paco el Gordo" from our camp after the raid.

death and terror. After walking a short portion of the trail, I am exhausted, fully aware that I would never survive the entire journey. When we return to camp we find that the Border Patrol is there conducting a raid. We are detained for hours until they get instructions from headquarters about what to do with a group of seminary students. Eventually we are free to go, but only after the officers have taken all of our information and warned us that "this is not over." Our crime is providing humanitarian aid to several undocumented migrants who were receiving medical attention in our camp.

We say we are a nation based on Judeo-Christian values, yet when some of us attempt to follow the example of the Good Samaritan, we are harassed by the agents of this so-called Judeo-Christian nation. Today a "Good Samaritan" can receive up to twenty years in prison for providing transportation to the closest hospital for a dying immigrant. Is this the only country in the world in which providing humanitarian aid is a crime? We can muster our resources to save the whales but not Latino/as.

One of the migrants taken from our camp was named Paco el Gordo (Paco the Fat One). His limbs were so swollen that they bulged through his pants. Because he was no longer able to walk, he was left behind by the group. His only salvation was stumbling into our camp. When we were raided by the Border Patrol, three Latino officers arrested Paco and took him away. Like the Indians who served the U.S. Cavalry as scouts to the detriment of their own people over a century and a half ago, modern-day scouts still assist the authorities to the detriment of their people.

These events demonstrate how the entire immigration debate throughout this nation resides on ambiguities, paradoxes, and contradictions. It is a debate based all too often on rhetoric, and it fails to focus on how to create and implement policies that can bring about humanitarian solutions. Our present policy simply does not work. Our government's failure to implement comprehensive and humanitarian immigration reform has led to oppressive social structures experienced throughout every stage of the journey, the struggle, and the life lived by those we call undocumented.

Ambiguities and Paradoxes Confronting Migrants
The ambiguity of the present immigration crisis begins in the undocumenteds' homeland, where the viability of the economy has been impeded by U.S. foreign policies rooted in the historical concept

of gunboat diplomacy and by present economic policies such as NAFTA. Migrants make the decision to cross the border because we, as a nation, crossed their borders to extract their resources and cheap labor. Today, many ethicists speak of the virtue of hospitality as a foundation upon which to base and implement a moral response to the immigration crises. But doesn't this virtue assume that the "house" belongs to the one practicing the virtue? Similarly, sharing one's resources with the other implies that the other has no claim to them. Employing the virtue of hospitality can ignore altogether the complexity of immigration caused by the consequences of U.S. action throughout history. The "house" of many of today's migrants in the form of land, resources, and labor was taken from them when the United States invaded Mexico in 1845 and appropriated half of Mexico's territory. Perhaps it might be more accurate to speak of the responsibility of restitution rather than the virtue of hospitality.

The border desperate migrants cross is in what we call the southwestern United States. While it is true that this area is located politically in the southwestern region of the United States of America, it is simultaneously located in the northern region of the cultural and historical ethos of a people. Before there were Europeans on this continent, this region was the northern realm of indigenous nations whose people moved north during times of harvest and returned south when the harvest seasons changed. With the establishment of Nueva España (New Spain) the region remained the northernmost point of that empire, far from the center in what would become known as Mexico City. When the undocumented begin their journey north, the borderlands are indeed an area of ambiguity, a place that for them is both north and southwest.

Before many of the migrants begin their journey north, they are told that crossing the mountains will take one day and reaching Tucson, Arizona, will take another. The reality is quite different. Migrants I have spoken with on the trails have said that it can take up to four days to cross the mountains. They have also gotten the impression from the *coyotes* that Tucson is just ten miles away, when in reality it is sixty miles distant, hardly a one day's walk. Many, therefore, are unprepared to cross the desert and have insufficient water and food. Those who do not find water and food that is placed for them by organizations like No More Death or Samaritans will surely perish. Some, out of desperation, drink their own urine. There is a profound contradiction in that many are led to their deaths by fellow countrymen.

There is a contradiction between our own government's rhetoric of creating "a culture of life" while legislating immigration policies that cause death. Funneling migrants to the desert was based on a philosophy that the collateral damage of dead brown bodies would deter others from crossing. Even after recognizing that few were deterred, we continue to implement policies that lead to death. Not since the days of the Jane and Jim Crow South have governmental policies systematically and brutally targeted a group of non-white people.

Ambiguities and Paradoxes of the Border

Those who do cross the border find themselves in a desert that is full of ambiguity and contradiction. In the middle of August one can die of heat exhaustion during the day or of hypothermia because of the torrential rains and the sudden drop in temperature during the night. The desert is a place where one can die of thirst or one can drown because of flash floods that sweep through dry riverbeds in seconds. The land can be barren of life, but it can also be a space where a walker must hack through eight feet of tall green weeds.

The land is hostile to anyone who attempts to cross it, and it is no surprise that thousands fail and die. Not only is the land full of ambiguities, but so are the laws that attempt to prevent thousands from crossing each day. Billions of taxpayers' dollars are spent each year on sophisticated technology and deterrent strategies to stop the flow of immigration, yet there exists no empirical evidence that migration has actually been deterred. Instead desperate people of color are placed into even more life-threatening situations.

These ambiguities along the border are not restricted to a particular location. Those who do succeed in traversing the death-causing obstacles of the border and are disbursed throughout the fifty states still find themselves faced with a border. No matter where they live, they will always live on the border between legitimacy and illegitimacy, the border between "making it" and poverty, the border between acceptance and rejection, the border between life and death.

In addition, no matter where they physically reside within the United States, in a very real sense all Hispanics, regardless of documentation, even regardless of being born in this country, live on the border between privilege and disenfranchisement. The native term *nepantla*, defined as the in-between space, captures the existential ethos of every Latina/o. Documented and undocumented alike live in that in-between border space.

Ambiguities and Paradoxes in Government Policy

Although there are increasing claims that we live in a post-racist society, it is common in cities throughout the United States to hear race-based, anti-immigrant, anti-Hispanic rhetoric. "They" come to use our services and to take advantage of what we have to offer, not wanting to work. Yet city officials consistently attempt to pass legislation that makes it impossible for immigrants to work. For example, the city commission of Aurora, Colorado, passed an ordinance that made it more difficult for day laborers, who are predominantly Hispanics—and of which the majority is documented—to gather to obtain employment. Ironically, prior to the vote on this issue, Aurora celebrated being named an "All American City." Unfortunately, "All American" did not include those citizens who were Hispanic.

The situation was even more complex and paradoxical in that the sponsor of the legislation was an African American woman who a generation ago would have faced a similar city ordinance designed to maintain her people as disenfranchised and marginalized citizens.

What a sad commentary when the formerly oppressed become oppressors. This country continues to pass laws targeted at darker faces. When a white man bombed the Federal Building in Oklahoma City in 1995, Congress responded one year later by passing the first anti-terrorist legislation targeted at foreigners. Billions are spent to defend the southern border from terrorists crossing even though no terrorist has ever been caught crossing or has crossed our southern border to do harm within the United States.

As noted earlier, a further ambiguity is the sealing of the border with Mexico, making it impossible for migrants to return to their homelands. One farmer I interviewed mentioned that in the past many would cross over, work on his farm for the season, make enough money to return to their own farms in Mexico and, with the money they earned, maintain their farms, feed their families, and put their children through school. Sealing the border now makes this impossible.

Another paradox of this debate is that many who support family values have created the laws that destroy families by separating fathers and mothers from their children. Ironically, often men who leave their families to go north and work to provide money for loved ones back home find themselves eventually ending those relationships due to prolonged separations and starting new relationships here.

Even more heartbreaking is what happens to children of immigrants. During the first six months of 2008, 18,249 children under the age of eighteen were repatriated. Of those, 10,000 children were literally dumped, without any adult supervision, on the Mexican border. To make matters worse, it is common to repatriate women and children to unfamiliar cities at night after shelters and other services are no longer available.[7] Abandoned in violent border towns, they become easy prey. So, as we extol our Christian family values, our legislation breaks apart and destroys the families of the undocumented.

While the virtues of human rights are proclaimed loudly abroad, such rhetoric falls short when it concerns the undocumented here at home. A recent report released by the United Nation's Human Rights Council in Geneva showed that the United States has fallen short in its international obligations to protect the human rights domestically of undocumented immigrants. They are denied labor protection and when picked up in an ICE raid, they are commonly denied an appeal process and subjected to long detentions in substandard facilities.[8]

Several immigrants in Mexico who were recently deported reported that they had been packed in an overcrowded cell for days, forced to sleep on concrete floors, and fed nothing but saltine crackers and water. The ill among them received no medical attention.[9] We demand that the undocumented submit to the rule of law, yet when caught, their basic legal rights, according to numerous reports, are steamrollered. Rather than being treated as exploited laborers in need of a fair hearing, they are treated as dangerous criminals who deserve neither fair treatment nor mercy.[10] Undocumented immigrants are told to leave and then return once they receive proper documentation, yet once arrested, they can never legally return. Individuals who are deported or removed and then apply to enter the country with proper papers are permanently barred as undesirables because they have a "criminal" record.

We are a nation of immigrants who benefit from the oppression of immigrants. The exploitation of the more recent immigrants ensures and enriches the lifestyles of earlier immigrants. Where is the justice in such a practice? We ignore or refuse to see the terror we impose on the most recent immigrants so that we can hold on to the illusion of being a compassionate nation. Yet it is often those church members and leaders who are quick to lift their hands to heaven to praise God who are the slowest to lift a finger to help their brothers and sisters in

Christ. The words of the apostle John come to mind: "How can we love a God who we cannot see when we fail to love those around us who we can see?" (1 Jn 4:20).

Ambiguities and Paradoxes among Scholars

After working on this project for over a year as a scholar, I have discovered even greater ambiguities and paradoxes within the academic community. Scholars are trained to be objective, not to become involved with the object of their research. We are to analyze and develop theories from the safety and security of campuses and research centers. Yet, I continue to discover that unless scholarship is rooted in the real life experience of people, such scholarship has little meaning. For me, to be a scholar is to be an activist. Those of us who are theologians have a moral responsibility to use our scholarship to bring about change to improve the quality of human lives and to eliminate injustice.

I have been asked on numerous occasions to join panels on immigration. In the name of fairness I have been told that there must be an opposing voice. Hence, I have found myself on panels that included members of the racist organization known as the Minutemen, as well as representatives from the office of Congressman Tancredo, who has made it a life mission to persecute the undocumented. In the name of fairness I have found myself debating those who insist on maintaining the present structures that bring death and oppression. Over time I have concluded that I am no longer interested in fairness: I am only interested in justice. I have no desire to debate those who are determined to maintain the present structures. I want to interact only with those who out of a deep sense of faith desire to do justice so we can struggle together to bring it about.

What will happen if those of us who are academicians cannot hear the cry of the poor, the cry of the oppressed, and the cry of those who are dying? It is only by listening to those cries that we are able to walk in solidarity on the trails of terror that the oppressed walk upon daily as they seek their own liberation and satisfy their desire to work to support their families.

Voice of the People

This mural is directly across the church on the main plaza in Altar, Mexico—a major gathering place for migrants before venturing into the United States. That is where I met the author of this poem as he prepared to return to the United States. He had been in the States before as an undocumented but was deported to his native Honduras. As a Honduran, he must cross three borders to reach his dream. When he heard that I was part of a group placing food and water in the desert, he gave me this poem to share with my fellow volunteers.

HISTORIA DE UN SOÑADOR	THE HISTORY OF A DREAMER
Martin Lizárdo Dominguez	Translation by
	Miguel A. De La Torre

Fue un dia como hoy
El q'de mi pais yo parti

En busca de una vida mejor
Y tratar de sobrevivir.

It was a day like today
When from my country I
    departed

In search of a better life
And to try to survive.

Con la esperanza de cambiar un
    dia,
A mi familia yo abandoné
Y partiendo a tierra legana
Tres fronteras yo cruzé.

El desierto fue mi destino
Como frontera yo decidi;
Ya q'lleno de peligros
Kilometros recorri.

Camino a la frontera
Un lugar me acobijó
Dandome sustento diario
Con cariño y con amor.

A su gente voluntario,
Q'con cariño ofrece pan
Bendicelos Señor por siempre
Y protegelos de todo mal.

A todos los hermanos
Q'con esperanza y con pasión
Dejalos Señor construir
Sus sueños de ilusión.

Y a ti Señor Jesus
Gracias por tu protectección
Se q'siempre estas a mi lado

Derramando bendición.

One day, with the hope of
    changing,
My family I abandoned
Departing to a far away land
Three borders I crossed.

The desert became my destiny
Like a frontier, I decided;
Since I traversed kilometers
Filled with dangers.

En route to the frontier
A place sheltered me
Providing me daily sustenance
With kindness and love.

To you volunteer folks,
Who with kindness offer bread
Bless them Lord forever
And protect them from all evil.

To all of the brothers
With hope and passion
Lord, let them construct
Their dreams of expectation.

And to you Lord Jesus
Thank you for your protection
I know that you are always at
    my side
Pouring out blessings.

Timeline for Legislation on Hispanic Immigration

1882: *The Chinese Exclusion Act of 1882*

Congress passed legislation barring Chinese manual workers from entering the United States. Until then, immigration was unregulated. This was the first significant restriction on free immigration in U.S. history. This act was renewed in 1902 and 1904, prohibiting all Chinese from immigrating.

1898: *Spanish-American War*

The conclusion of the war with Spain left the United States with several of Spain's colonies, including Puerto Rico and Cuba. Puerto Rico remains a colony to this day. Cuba remained under U.S. political and economic control until 1959. Not surprisingly, Puerto Ricans and Cubans are, respectively, the second and third largest Hispanic groups in the United States.

1917: *Immigration Act of 1917*

Also known as the Asiatic Barred Zone Act, Congress overrode President Wilson's veto and enacted legislation that barred immigration from Asia and the Pacific Islands. The Act also instituted tests (literacy and moral) to limit immigration by excluding idiots, feeble-minded persons, professional beggars, polygamists, and anarchists, to name a few. Mexicans were exempted due to a shortage of agricultural labor.

1917: *Puerto Ricans Granted U.S. Citizenship through the Jones-Shafroth Act*

The need for labor and soldiers during World War I led Congress to grant U.S. citizenship to Puerto Ricans, although they would have no vote in Congress. Citizenship allowed travel from the island to the mainland. Technically, this mobility was not considered immigration but rather the movement of U.S. citizens within the United States.

1921: Immigration Act of 1921

Also known as the Emergency Quota Act, this legislation was a response to news reports that in the preceding year more than 800,000 foreigners migrated to the United States. Congress was concerned that most of this migration came from southern and eastern Europe. In addition, the Harding administration was also concerned with the "red scare" that preceded World War I. As a result, Congress limited immigration to 375,000 persons a year. A quota was established that limited the annual number of immigrants from any country to 3 percent of the number of persons from that country already living in the United States in 1910. The first quota system benefited northern and western Europeans, who were allocated over half of all immigrant slots. Those from eastern and southern Europe experienced a 75 percent reduction.

1924: Immigration Act of 1924

Also known as the Johnson-Reed Act, this bill benefited privileged northern and western Europeans by limiting the number of immigrants from any country to 2 percent of the number of people from that country who were already living in the United States in 1890. The Act also excluded immigration of Asians. The Coolidge administration established this quota system to protect the U.S. national character.

1942: Start of the Bracero Program

Due to a labor shortage caused by World War II, a bilateral agreement, known as the Bracero Treaty, was signed that allowed the importation of 4.6 million temporary workers from Mexico to work on U.S. farms and ranches. The program led to notorious worker abuses.

1945: The Great Puerto Rican Migration

In 1945 there were approximately thirteen thousand Puerto Ricans in New York City. By 1946 that number exceeded fifty thousand. Over the next decade more than twenty-five thousand Puerto Ricans migrated, peaking in 1953 when more than sixty-nine thousand came. By the mid-1960s there were over one million Puerto Ricans living in the continental United States. A depressed economy on the island and heavy recruitment by factories in the northeast United States led to this migration. Most settled in the northeast, with New York City serving as the major center of residence.

1952: The Texas Proviso

Concerned that some of the workers in the Bracero program melted into U.S. Hispanic neighborhoods without proper documentation, Congress passed the Texas Proviso, making it for the first time a felony to harbor (but not employ) an undocumented person.

1952: Immigration and Naturalization Act of 1952

Although the Act was an attempt to abolish previous racial restrictions, the quota system remained and restrictions continued to limit the number of immigrants from certain countries.

1954: Operation Wetback

The Eisenhower administration began an aggressive crackdown on undocumented immigrants, deporting about 1.1 million Mexican and Mexican Americans, including U.S.-born citizens of Latina/o descent.

1959: The Cuban Revolution

The Cuban Revolution led to a major exodus of predominately upper- and middle-class Cubans escaping the leftist turn of Castro's government. By 1973, it is estimated that almost half a million Cubans participated in these "Freedom Flights," with most settling in Miami, Florida; Union City, New Jersey; and New York City.

1964: The Bracero Program Ends

The end of the Bracero program was followed by the formation of the United Farm Workers, which transformed how migrant labor is understood. Activist Cesar Chavez, a prominent critic of the Bracero program, called for its end.

1965: Immigration and Naturalization Act of 1965

The Act abolished the national-origin quotas that were detrimental to non-northern and non-western Europeans and established a preference for skilled workers.

1980: Mariel Boat Lift

Economic turmoil in Cuba led to the opening of the Mariel port for anyone wanting to leave the island. About ten thousand Cubans did.

1980: U.S. Involvement in Central America Results in Waves of Refugees

Immigrants, especially from El Salvador, Guatemala, and Nicaragua, fled to the United States to escape the violence caused by civil wars.

1982: Start of the Sanctuary Movement

Hundreds of churches, college campuses, and cities declared themselves sanctuaries from immigration authorities for Central Americans escaping the violence of their homelands.

1986: Immigration Reform and Control Act (IRCA)

The Reagan administration declared that undocumented immigrants were a threat to national security. In response, Congress passed IRCA to (1) provide legal residency to three million immigrants (2.3 million from Mexico) who resided in the United States prior to 1982; (2) expand the Border Patrol; (3) impose, for the first time, sanctions on employers who knowingly hired the undocumented; and (4) make it a crime to work without proper documentation.

1990: Immigration Act of 1990

The immigration ceiling was raised to 700,000 for the next three years, followed by 675,000 each subsequent year. Additionally, the Act created a lottery program that randomly assigned a number of visas. The Act also increased by three times the quota for employment-based skilled laborers and removed homosexuality as a reason for exclusion.

1993: NAFTA Negotiations

During the negotiations for NAFTA, migration issues were conspicuously absent for fear that the United States would fail to ratify the treaty. Nevertheless, NAFTA does provide visas for a limited number of high-level multinational executives.

1994: U.S. Ratifies NAFTA

1994: Proposition 187

California passed Governor Pete Wilson's ballot initiative that limited access by undocumented immigrants to social services, including emergency health care and public schooling. Immediately after the passing of the proposal a temporary restraining law went into effect. By 1998 a new governor ceased the appeal process, literally killing the proposition.

1994: Operation Hold the Line, Operation Gatekeeper, and Operation Safeguard

The Clinton administration enacted several initiatives to close the popular urban crossing cities along the border, specifically San Diego; Nogales, Arizona; and El Paso, Texas. By increasing the number of Border Patrol agents and building obstacles (fences), the flow of migration was successfully moved to remote and dangerous desert regions. The underlying strategy was that deaths of migrants attempting the hazardous crossing would deter others from crossing.

1994: Wet-foot Dry-foot Rule

Attorney General Janet Reno declared that Cubans would no longer be automatically admitted to the United States. Only those who touched "dry ground" would be allowed to stay. Those caught at sea would be returned.

1996: Illegal Immigration Reform and Immigrant Responsibility Act (IIRIRA)

The Clinton administration doubled the number of Border Patrol agents over five years; began construction of "The Wall" to serve as a barrier; eliminated due process for immigrants; tightened claims for possible asylum; increased penalties for the undocumented; and enacted tougher legislation against smugglers of immigrants.

2001: 9/11 Terrorist Attacks

The Bush administration, in conversation with Mexico's Fox administration, discussed developing another guest-worker program similar to the Bracero program. The events of 9/11 brought an end to those talks.

2002: Enhanced Border Security and Visa Reform Act

Responding to the events of 9/11, the Bush administration increased the number of INS agents; tightened systems to track immigrants; and instructed government agencies (specifically intelligence and law enforcement) to share information about immigrants.

2002: The Homeland Security Act of 2002

Responding to the events of 9/11, the Homeland Security Act created the U.S. Immigration and Custom Enforcement (ICE).

2004: Proposition 200

Arizona passed a ballot initiative that implemented some of the toughest anti-immigration, anti-Hispanic laws in the nation. The laws stipulate that a failure by public employees to report undocumented immigrants will result in imprisonment and that citizens must first provide documentation before receiving public services from the state or being allowed to vote. Arizona's laws spurred similar legislation in other states.

2005: Real ID Act

Congress attached a rider to the supplementary budget for U.S. troops in Afghanistan and Iraq that allowed for the construction of a fence along the Mexican-U.S. border; prohibited the undocumented from obtaining a driver's license; and made the granting of asylum difficult.

2005: Border Protection, Anti-Terrorism, and Illegal Immigration Control Act

Although it was passed by the U.S. House of Representatives, this bill was not approved by the Senate. Also known as the Sensenbrenner Bill, it was considered the most anti-immigrant, anti-Hispanic immigration legislation to go before Congress. One of its most controversial provisions made it a crime to assist an undocumented person to remain in the United States; if apprehended, the offender would receive the same prison term as that of a removed alien.

2006: A Day without Immigrants

Monday, May 1, 2006, was declared a day when the undocumented and those who supported them abstained from engaging in commerce or participating in work or school. The intention was to demonstrate that the U.S. economy relied on undocumented immigrants. About one million people participated in nationwide marches on that day and subsequent days.

2006: Operation Return to Sender

May 26, ICE responded to the May 1 demonstrations by initiating massive raids and deportations throughout the country.

2007: Comprehensive Immigration Reform Act of 2007

Known also as the Kennedy-McCain Bill, this bill failed to be passed by Congress. The bill provided legal status and a path to citizenship for the approximately twelve million undocumented living in the United States. The bill would also have created a temporary guest-worker program.

Resources on Immigration

David Carlson

Where can congregations and other faith-based groups turn for additional resources for deeper understanding of the immigration issue and options for constructive engagement? As a first step, contact the local, regional, or national office of your religious denomination or faith-based organization. Many have developed study guides and other resource materials, policy statements, workshops, and programs to help guide responsible, faith-based approaches to the immigration issue.

Review and reflect upon the stories and narratives in your religious tradition that concretely illuminate relationships—both positive and negative—with the other, the stranger, the alien. You can also access contemporary stories in print and film that reveal the personal, human dimension of the immigration issue in concrete terms. Examine analyses of trends, causes, and consequences of immigration. Seek opportunities to meet and interact with immigrants to share stories, concerns, and hopes. Draw from all of these activities a framework of central questions and faith-based principles to guide ongoing, constructive engagement with this compelling issue.

Selected National Religious Organizations

The groups below are among the more than fifty national faith-based organizations listed as signatories as of June 4, 2008, to the "Interfaith Statement in Support of Comprehensive Immigration Reform." (The complete list of signatories and the full text of the interfaith statement are available at numerous sites online.) The statement calls for establishing "a safe and humane immigration system consistent with our values. Our diverse faith traditions teach us to welcome our brothers and sisters with love and compassion." Most groups have policy statements and offer study guides and related educational resources on their websites.

David Carlson is a Ph.D. candidate at Iliff School of Theology. He was among the eleven students participating in research on the border.

American Baptist Churches USA/National Ministries
American Friends Service Committee
Catholic Legal Immigration Network, Inc.
Church World Service/Immigration and Refugee Program Episcopal
    Migration Ministries
Hebrew Immigrant Aid Society
Hindu American Foundation
Islamic Circle of North America
Jewish Council for Public Affairs
Lutheran Immigration and Refugee Service
Mennonite Central Committee
Presbyterian Church USA
United Church of Christ/Justice and Witness Ministry
United Methodist Church
Unitarian Universalist Association
World Relief/Refugee and Immigration Program

Other Faith-based U.S. Advocacy Groups

The **American Friends Service Committee, Human Migration and Mobility Program** (www.afsc.org/ImmigrantsRights/) website provides educational resources and legislative updates.

The **Disciples Home Mission** (www.discipleshomemissions.org/RIM) website provides educational material for churches exploring the issue of immigration and advocates for immigrant rights.

The **ELCA [Evangelical Lutheran Church in America] Transformation Immersion Program** (www.elca.org/mexico) website provides an eight- to ten-day immersion program to experience the reality of the Mexican poor and causes of migration.

The **Friends Committee on National Legislation, Immigration Issue** (www.fcnl.org/issues/issue.php?issue_id=69) website provides analysis and background information on immigration.

Through **Humane Borders** (www.humaneborders.org) hundreds of volunteers from different faith traditions maintain more than seventy emergency water stations on and near the U.S.-Mexican border.

The **Interfaith Worker Justice (IWJ)** (www.iwj.org/actnow/imm/immigration.html) coalition seeks to educate, organize, and mobilize the religious community around the immigration issue.

Justice for Immigrants (aka **Catholic Campaign for Immigration Reform**) (www.justiceforimmigrants.org/) and in Spanish (www.justiceforimmigrants.org/es/) is a coalition of twenty-one Catholic organizations and groups that seek to educate, enact legislative and administrative reforms, and organize Catholics to help immigrants.

The **Migration and Refugee Services, U.S. Conference of Catholic Bishops** (www.nccbuscc.org/mrs/) website informs the public of the Catholic bishops' commitment to immigration rights and provides resources and advocacy to make those commitments a reality.

The **New Sanctuary Movement** (www.newsanctuarymovement.org/) assists congregations to publicly provide hospitality and protection to immigrant families.

No More Deaths (aka **No Más Muertes**) (www.nomoredeaths.org) volunteers provide food, water, and emergency medical attention in the Arizona desert by staffing aid stations.

The **Religious Action Center of Reform Judaism** (rac.org/advocacy/issues/issueir/index.cfm) website provides resources for Reform Jewish congregations about immigrant rights.

Samaritan Patrol (www.samaritanpatrol.org) volunteers provide food, water, and emergency medical assistance to people crossing the Sonoran Desert.

Sojourners—Christians for Comprehensive Immigration Reform (CCIR) (www.sojo.net/index.cfm?action=action.display&item=CCIR_main) is a coalition of Christian organizations and churches that provides resources for comprehensive immigration reform.

Other Advocacy Groups

American Immigration Law Foundation (AILF) (www.ailf.org/) seeks to increase public understanding of immigration law and policy and the value of immigration to American society.

American Immigration Lawyers Association (AILA) (www.aila.org/) was established to advocate for fair and reasonable immigration law and policy, and to advance the quality of immigration and nationality law and practice.

Applied Research Center (ARC) (www.arc.org) advocates for racial justice through research and journalism.

BorderLinks (www.borderlinks.org) conducts immersion programs in the Mexico-U.S. borderlands region and offers international workshops and conferences.

Coalition for Comprehensive Immigration Reform (CCIR) (www.cirnow.org/) is a campaign led by twenty-five national and twenty state and local organizations to coordinate efforts to pass progressive comprehensive immigration legislation at the federal level.

Detention Watch Network (DWN) (www.detentionwatchnetwork
.org) works toward reforming the detention and deportation of immigrants so that the process can be fair and humane.

Fair Immigration Reform Movement (FIRM) (www.fairimmigration
.org) advocates for immigrant rights at the local, state, and federal levels. Its website lists resources on state-level and local-level immigration campaigns across the country.

Immigration Equality (IMEQ) (www.immigrationequality.org/) works to end discrimination in U.S. immigration law that negatively affects the lives of lesbian, gay, bisexual, transgender, and HIV-positive people.

Latin American Working Group (LAWG) (www.lawg.org) encourages decision makers to adopt U.S. policies toward Latin America that promote human rights, justice, peace, and sustainable development.

The **League of Women Voters (LWV)** (www.lwv.org) recently completed an extensive two-year immigration study that explores the underlying values and principles regarding immigration, reasons for immigration, current federal immigration policy, and the impact of immigration on American society.

National Council of La Raza (NCLR) (www.nclr.org) is a civil rights organization that conducts immigration policy analyses and advocacy activities to promote fair and nondiscriminatory immigration policies.

National Employment Law Project (NELP) (www.nelp.org) advocates on behalf of low-wage workers, the poor, the unemployed, and other groups facing significant barriers to employment and government systems of support.

National Immigration Forum (NIF) (www.immigrationforum.org) advocates and builds support for public policies that are fair to and supportive of immigrants and refugees in the United States.

National Immigration Law Center (NILC) (www.nilc.org) is dedicated to protecting and promoting the rights of low-income immigrants and their family members, focusing on the complex interplay between the legal status of immigrants and their rights under U.S. laws.

National Immigration Project, National Lawyers Guild (www
.nationalimmigrationproject.org) is an organization of lawyers, law students, and legal workers who defend the rights of immigrants.

National Network for Immigrant and Refugee Rights (NNIRR) (www.nnirr.org/) serves as a forum to share information and analysis, to educate communities and the general public, and to develop and coordinate plans of action on immigrant issues.

Progressive States Network, Immigration Project (www .progressivestates.org/content/714) provides support to legislative leaders to counter anti-immigrant groups at the state level.

Southern Poverty Law Center (SPLC) (www.splcenter.org/) tracks "anti-immigration" groups and, through its legal department, fights all forms of discrimination while working to protect society's most vulnerable members.

Immigration/Migration Study Centers

Center for Comparative Immigration Studies (www.ccis-ucsd.org) conducts research on international migration and refugee flows throughout the world.

Center for Migration Studies (CMS) (www.cmsny.org) undertakes research and provides a forum for debate on international migration. The Center publishes scholarly works and organizes conferences and forums.

Mexican Migration Project (MMP) (mmp.opr.princeton.edu/) is a binational research project that gathers and compiles economic and social data on Mexican-U.S. migration.

Migration Policy Institute (MPI) (www.migrationinformation.org) serves elected officials, researchers, state and local agency managers, grassroots leaders and activists, local service providers, and others facing the challenges and opportunities from high rates of immigration.

Migration News (migration.ucdavis.edu/mn) provides analysis of immigration trends of the previous quarter.

Selected Film, Print, and Other Media Resources
Documentaries and Other Films

Crossing Arizona (Rainlake Productions, 2006), DVD, 97 min., examines immigration and border policies through the personal experiences and perspectives of those directly involved—farmers and ranchers, humanitarian organization volunteers, political activists, tribal leaders, and Minutemen.

Dying to Live: A Migrant's Journey (Groody River Films, 2006), DVD, 33 min., draws upon the views of activists, musicians, church and congressional leaders, and immigrants themselves to expose and explore the causes and consequences of undocumented migration in personal and social terms.

Echando Raices (Taking Root): Immigrant and Refugee Communities in California, Texas, and Iowa (American Friends Service Committee,

2002), DVD or VHS (English or Spanish), 60 min., addresses issues of labor and immigrant organizing, and the scapegoating of—and violence against—immigrants. Discussion guide available.

The Invisible Mexicans of Deer Canyon (Gatekeepers Productions, 2007), DVD, 73 min., looks at the daily lives of undocumented immigrants in San Diego, hidden in shantytowns without electricity, running water, or sanitation.

The Line in the Sand: Stories from the U.S./Mexico Border (October Sun Films, 2005), DVD, 60 min., shares the diverse viewpoints and stories of migrants, ranchers, U.S. and Mexican government officials, and church workers on border migration. Discussion questions and suggested web links are included. Available at no charge from www.crs.org/dramaproject/.

La Misma Luna (Under the Same Moon) (Creando Films, 2007), DVD, 109 min., portrays the journey across the Mexico-U.S. border of a nine-year-old boy to be reunited with his undocumented mother who is working in the United States.

Strangers No Longer (Groody River Films, 2002), 16 or 22 min. (two versions), Spanish subtitles, produced in collaboration with the U.S. Conference of Catholic Bishops, places current immigration within the context of U.S. history and portrays how churches in the United States are welcoming those from different cultures and backgrounds. (With Spanish subtitles.) Available from usccbpublishing.org/. An English/Spanish discussion guide is available on the justiceforimmigrants.org website.

Print Media—Narratives

Dahl-Bredine, Phil, and Stephen Hicken. *The Other Game: Lessons from How Life Is Played in Mexican Villages* (Orbis Books, 2008). This book interweaves analyses of global economics and trade policies with vivid descriptions of community life among *campesinos* and their families in Mexico's southern mountains.

Guzmán Molina, Ana Amalia. *The Power of Love (El Poder del Amor): My Experience in a U.S. Immigration Jail* (EPICA, 2003). The author and her husband, immigrant parents in the United States, were arrested and imprisoned. Denied their civil rights under the law, they were separated from their three children, who had to fend for themselves for more than a year.

Hobbs, Will. *Crossing the Wire* (HarperCollins, 2007). Facing the prospect of his family's economic collapse due to low corn prices, a fifteen-year-old boy decides to leave home to find work in the United States and send money home. Teachers' Guide available at the harperchildrens.com website.

Martinez, Rubén. *Crossing Over: A Mexican Family on the Migrant Trail* (Picador, 2002). A poet and journalist chronicles the journey of an extended migrant family from southern Mexico to California, Wisconsin, and Missouri.

Urrea, Luis Alberto. *The Devil's Highway: A True Story* (Back Bay Books, 2005). An award-winning poet, essayist, and 2005 Pulitzer Prize finalist, Urrea traces the tragic journey of twenty-six desperate men from Mexico who cross the border into the desert of southern Arizona.

Print Media—Academic

Amnesty International, "Human Rights Concerns in the Border Region with Mexico," May 1, 1998. Available online.

Bigelow, Bill. *The Line between Us: Teaching about the Border and Mexican Immigration* (Rethinking Schools, Ltd., 2006).

Carroll R., M. Daniel. *Christians at the Border: Immigration, the Church, and the Bible* (Baker Publishing Group, 2008).

Chomsky, Aviva. *"They Take Our Jobs!" And 20 Other Myths about Immigration* (Beacon Press, 2007).

Durand, Jorge, and Douglas S. Massey, eds. *Crossing the Border: Research from the Mexican Migration Project* (Russell Sage Foundation, 2004).

Gill, Jerry H. *Borderland Theology* (Ecumenical Program in Central America and the Caribbean—EPICA, 2003).

Hill, Jacob. *Free Trade and Immigration: Cause and Effect* (Council on Hemispheric Affairs, 2007).

Human Rights Immigrant Community Action Network, *Over-Raided, under Siege*. Available on the nnirr.org website.

Isbister, John. *The Immigration Debate: Remaking America* (Kumarian Press, 1996).

Lakoff, George, and Sam Ferguson. "The Framing of Immigration" (2006). Available on the rockridgeinstitute.org website.

López, Ann Aurelia. *The Farmworkers' Journal* (University of California Press, 2007).

Lopez, Mark Hugo, and Susan Minushkin. *2008 National Survey of Latinos: Hispanics See Their Situation in U.S. Deteriorating;*

Oppose Key Immigration Enforcement Measures (The Pew Hispanic Center, 2008).

Martínez, Oscar. *Troublesome Border* (University of Arizona Press, 2006).

No More Deaths. *Crossing the Line: Human Rights Abuses of Migrants in Short-Term Custody on the Arizona/Sonora Border.* Available on the nomoredeaths.org website.

Rubio-Goldsmith, Raquel, M. Melissa McCormick, Daniel Martinez, and Inez Magdalena Duarte. *The "Funnel Effect" and Recovered Bodies of Unauthorized Migrants Processed by the Pima County Office of the Medical Examiner, 1990–2005* (The Binational Migration Institute, 2006).

Smith, James P., and Barry Edmonston, eds. *The New Americans: Economic, Demographic, and Fiscal Effects of Immigration* (National Academies Press, 1997).

Wilbanks, Dana. *Re-Creating America: The Ethics of U.S. Immigration and Refugee Policy in a Christian Perspective* (Abingdon Press, 1996).

Notes

Preface

1. United Nations Population Fund, *State of Population 2006: A Passage to Hope, Women and International Migration.* Available on the unfpa.org website.

2. JoAnn McGregor, "Joining the BBC (British Bottom Cleaners): Zimbabwean Migrants and the UK Care Industry," *Journal of Migration and Ethnic Studies* 33, no. 5 (July 2007): 809–10.

3. Gervais Appave and Ryszard Cholewinski, eds., *World Migration 2008: Managing Labour Mobility in the Evolving Global Economy* (Geneva: International Organization for Migration, 2008), 2.

4. Ibid., 3–4.

5. Ibid., 394–95, 423.

Introduction

1. Quoted in David Holthouse, Southern Poverty Law Center, "Arizona Showdown: High-powered Firearms, Militia Maneuvers and Racism at the Minuteman Project," *Intelligence Report* (Summer 2005).

2. Jeffrey S. Passel and D'Vera Cohn, *Trends in Unauthorized Immigration: Undocumented Inflow Trails Legal Inflow"* (Washington DC: Pew Hispanic Center, October, 2008), i, iii.

3. Janet Hook, "One in Three Would Deny Illegal Immigrant Social Services," *The Los Angeles Times*, December 6, 2007.

4. "Immigration Theater," *The Wall Street Journal*, May 24/25, 2008.

5. Wayne Cornelius, "Controlling 'Unwanted' Immigration: Lessons from the United States, 1993–2004," *Journal of Ethnic and Migration Studies* 31, no. 4 (2005): 782.

1. Creating Borders and Their Consequences

1. Governor Matt Blunt (R-MO), quoted in Julia Preston, "Employers Fight Tough Measures on Immigration," *The New York Times*, July 6, 2008.

2. Douglas J. Besharov, "The Rio Grande Rises," *The New York Times*, October 1, 2007.

3. Post-millennialism was a prevalent theological concept that dealt with the Second Coming of Christ, a return that would occur a thousand years (hence post-millennial) after God's kingdom was established on earth.

4. Sydney E. Ahlstrom, *A Religious History of the American People* (New Haven, CT: Yale University Press, 1972), 845, 877–78.

5. *Speech of John Quincy Adams, May 25, 1836* (Washington DC: Gale and Seaton, 1838), 119.

6. Ulysses S. Grant, *Personal Memoirs*, vol. 1 (New York: Charles L. Webster and Company, 1885), 54–56.

7. It is interesting to note that the democratically elected Arbenz government of Guatemala, a major producer of bananas for the United Fruit Company, was overthrown in 1954 by a covert U.S.-backed coup d'état called Operation PBSUCCESS because of modest land reform that threatened the United Fruit Company's profits. The three men responsible for orchestrating the overthrow were then-U.S. Secretary of State John Foster Dulles, whose law firm Sullivan and Cromwell secured rail subsidiary agreements for the United Fruit Company; his brother Allen Dulles, director of the CIA, who previously served on the board of trustees of the United Fruit Company; and Walter Bedell Smith, undersecretary of state and trusted presidential aide who was a major shareholder in the United Fruit Company and became president of the company after the success of the operation.

8. It is estimated that in the first ten years after the implementation of NAFTA, approximately 780,000 jobs in textile and apparel manufacturing in the United States were lost (Public Citizen Product ID 9013, *Another America Is Possible: The Impact of NAFTA on the U.S. Latino Community and Lessons for Future Trade Agreements* [Washington DC, 2004], 5).

9. Miguel A. De La Torre, "For Immigrants," *Church and Public Life: An Agenda for Change*, ed. Rebecca Todd Peters and Elizabeth Hinson-Hasty (Louisville, KY: Westminster John Knox Press, 2008), 73–84.

10. Public Citizen Product, *Another America Is Possible*, 5.

11. U.S. Government Accounting Office, "North American Free Trade Agreement: Assessment of Major Issues," vol. 2, GAO/GGD-93–137 (September 9, 1993).

12. In is important to note that in 2008, according to the Pew Hispanic Center, undocumented migration dropped for the first time since the implementation of Operation Gatekeeper due to the worsening U.S. economy, as opposed to any success of the Border Patrol strategy. The undocumented population dropped from 12.4 million in 2007 to 11.9 million in 2008. For the first time, migration with documentation has surpassed migration without. See Bruce Finley, "Giving Up on the American Dream," *The Denver Post*, November 23, 2008.

13. Raquel Rubio-Goldsmith, M. Melissa McCormick, Daniel Martinez, and Inez Magdalena Duarte, *The "Funnel Effect" and Recovered Bodies of Unauthorized Migrants Processed by the Pima County Office of the Medical Examiner, 1990–2005*, The Binational Migration Institute (2006), 30.

14. As reported by Global Exchange. See www.globalexchange.org/countries/americas/unitedstates/california.

15. Rubio-Goldsmith et al., *The "Funnel Effect" and Recovered Bodies of Unauthorized Migrants*, 32, 46–47, 49.

16. Claudine LoMonaco, "Many Border Deaths Unlisted," *Tucson Citizen*, June 30, 2003; U.S. Government Accounting Office, "Illegal Immigration: Border-crossing Deaths Have Doubled since 1995; Border Patrol's Efforts to Prevent Deaths Have Not Been Fully Evaluated," GAO-05–435 (2006), 14.

17. U.S. Government Accounting Office, "Illegal Immigration," 5–6.

18. Field notes, August 30, 2008.

19. As of the summer of 2008, the fee for a *coyote* to guide a migrant from Altar, Mexico, to Tucson ranged from fifteen hundred to two thousand dollars.

20. Since 2004, No More Deaths, a humanitarian organization, has had a continuous presence in the southern Arizona desert, providing aid in the form of water, food, clothing, and medical assistance.

21. Operation Streamline is a pilot program for the Border Patrol. When undocumented aliens are caught within the high-traffic Del Rio Sector, which includes some two hundred miles of border, they are charged with misdemeanors and prosecuted under existing law. Those who are not released due to humanitarian reasons still face prosecution for illegal entry. The maximum penalty is 180 days of incarceration. During criminal proceedings the individuals also are processed for expatriation.

22. This testimony was recorded before the November 2008 election.

2. Economic Realities

1. Jim Malone, "Small Groups Dominate U.S. Immigration Debate," *Voice of America,* June 18, 2007.

2. Darryl Fears, "Immigration Is Snaring U.S. Citizens in Its Raids," *The Washington Post*, August 16, 2008.

3. Public Citizen Product ID 9013, *Another America Is Possible: The Impact of NAFTA on the U.S. Latino Community and Lessons for Future Trade Agreements* (Washington DC, 2004), 4–8.

4. Alexei Barrionuevo, "Mountains of Corn and a Sea of Farm Subsidies," *The New York Times*, November 9, 2005.

5. Ann Aurelia López, *The Farmworkers' Journal* (Berkeley and Los Angeles: University of California Press, 2007), 7–9, 41.

6. Walden Bello, "The World Bank, the IMF, and the Multinationals: Manufacturing the World Food Crises," *The Nation*, June 8, 2008; and Celia Dugger, "Report Finds Few Benefits for Mexico in NAFTA," *The New York Times*, November 19, 2003.

7. C. Ford Runge and Benjamin Senauer, "How Biofuels Could Starve the Poor," *Foreign Affairs* (May/June 2007).

8. Bello, "The World Bank, the IMF, and the Multinationals."

9. James C. McKinley, "Mexican Farmers Protest End of Corn-Import Taxes," *The New York Times*, February 1, 2008.

10. Speech given on April 2, 2001, titled "The Challenge of Globalization: The Role of the World Bank." Available on the worldbank.org website.

11. Quoted in Elizabeth Becker, "Western Farmers Fear Third-World Challenge to Subsidies," *The New York Times*, September 9, 2003.

12. Douglas S. Massey, "Foreword," *Latinas/os in the United States: Changing the Face of América*, ed. Havidán Rodríguez, Rogelio Sáenz, and Cecilia Menjívar (New York: Springer, 2008), xi.

13. "Immigration Non-Harvest," *The Wall Street Journal*, July 20, 2007.

14. NAFTA was implemented in 1994. Although Honduras was not one of the participants in NAFTA, it still must compete with U.S.-subsidized corn, thus also facing the pressures of globalized agricultural trade.

15. Marco is referring to Hurricane Mitch, one of the deadliest and most powerful storms ever recorded. A category-5 storm, it pounded Central America from October 29 through November 3, 1998. Considered the deadliest Atlantic hurricane to date, its total damage amounted to over $5 billion (1998 USD) and a loss of over eleven thousand lives—most of which occurred in Honduras, which reported seven thousand deaths and $3.8 billion in damages.

16. All immigration statistics and data cited in this essay are from Jane Guskin and David L. Wilson, *The Politics of Immigration: Questions and Answers* (New York: Monthly Review Press, 2007).

3. Demythologizing the Immigration Debate

1. Frosty Wooldridge, an anti-immigrant author and activist, summarizing an address by a KABC-AM talk radio host to the Federation for American Immigration Reform (FAIR) directors' meeting (see Frosty Wooldridge, "America Is a Nation Not a Market," November 22, 2005). Available on the newswithviews.com website.

2. Julia Preston, "Immigrant, Pregnant, Is Jailed under Pact," *The New York Times*, July 20, 2008.

3. Benjamin Franklin, *Observations concerning the Increase of Mankind, Peopling of Countries, Etc.* (Whitefish, MT: Kessinger Publishing, 1918), 23–24.

4. Miriam Jordan, "Arizona Seizes Spotlight in U.S. Immigration Debate," *The Wall Street Journal*, February 1, 2008.

5. Travis Loller, "Illegal Immigrants Pay Billions in Taxes," *Houston Chronicle*, April 14, 2008.

6. Andelique Soenarie, "Latino Neighborhood Slowly Disappearing in Central Mesa," *The Arizona Republic*, July 29, 2008.

7. Ron Jenkins, "Oklahoma Immigration Bill Will Cost State," *The Associated Press*, March 25, 2008; Don Mecoy, "HB 1804 Could Hurt State, Study Shows," *The Oklahoman*, March 26, 2008; Dan McFeely, "Immigration Laws Send Hispanics Elsewhere," *The Indianapolis Star*, February 24, 2008.

8. *Special Report: Undocumented Immigrants in Texas* (Austin, TX: Office of the Comptroller, December 2006), 1.

9. The report does not distinguish between documented and undocumented immigrants.

10. Christopher S. Decker with Jerry Deichert and Lourdes Gouveia, *Nebraska's Immigrant Population: Economic and Fiscal Impacts*. OLLAS Special Report No. 5. (Omaha, NE: Office of Latino/Latin American Studies [OLLAS], University of Nebraska at Omaha, 2008), 1.

11. The report does not distinguish between documented and undocumented immigrants.

12. Mariano Torras and Curtis Skinner, *The Economic Impact of the Hispanic Population on Long Island, New York* (Port Washington, NY: Horace Hagedorn Foundation, 2008), iv–v.

13. *U.S. Business and Hispanic Integration: Expanding the Economic Contributions of Immigrants* (New York: Americas Society and Council of the Americas—supported by the Rockefeller Foundation, 2008), 7–8.

14. Loller, "Illegal Immigrants Pay Billions in Taxes."

15. Dr. Card's research is discussed in Rich Jones, Wade Buchanan, Robin Baker, and Daniel Spivey, *Effect on Colorado and the Nation: A Review of Research*, ed. Heather McGregor (Denver: The Bell Policy Center, 2005), 4; Eduardo Porter, "Cost of Illegal Immigration May Be Less Than Meets the Eye," *The New York Times*, April 16, 2006.

16. Porter, "Cost of Illegal Immigration."

17. Paige M. Harrison and Allen J. Beck, *Prison and Jail Inmates at Midyear 2005*, Bureau of Justice Statistics, U.S. Department of Justice (May 2006), 1.

18. Julia Preston, "California: Study of Immigrants and Crime," *The New York Times*, February 26, 2008.

19. "Open Doors Don't Invite Criminals: Is Increased Immigration behind the Drop in Crime?" *The New York Times*, March 11, 2006.

20. Department of Homeland Security, "Fact Sheet: Border Security and Immigration Enforcement," November 6, 2007. Available on the dhs.gov website.

21. "Lou Dobbs This Week," CNN, May 20, 2007.

22. See www.cdc.gov.

23. Leon Kolankiewicz and Steven A. Camarota, *Immigration to the United States and World-Wide Greenhouse Gas Emissions* (Washington, D.C: Center for Immigration Studies, 2008), 1–11.

24. www.cis.org/About.

25. Tom Berry, *Immigration Debate: Politics, Ideologies of Anti-Immigration Forces* (Washington DC: Americas Program, Interhemispheric Resource Center, 2005), 1–5.

26. David A. Lieb, "Panel Links Abortion to Immigration," *The Denver Post*, November 14, 2006.

27. Miriam Jordan, "Huddled Classes Yearning to Learn Free," *The Wall Street Journal*, June 12, 2007.

28. Solomon More, "Justice Department Numbers Show Prison Trends," *The New York Times*, December 6, 2007.

4. Family Values

1. Mr. Turner is now with the Federation for American Immigration Reform (FAIR). http://la.indymedia.org/news/2006/10/182264.php.

2. Teresa Watanabe, "Report Decries U.S. Treatment of Migrants," *The Los Angeles Times*, March 8, 2008.

3. Simon Romero and David Barboza, "Trapped in Heat in Texas Truck, Eighteen People Die," *The New York Times*, May 15, 2003.

4. Focus on the Family website (May 2008). http://www2.focusonthefamily.com.

5. Tom Minnery, "Staying Focused: Why We Don't Address All the Issues," *Focus on the Family Magazine* (September 2007): 20–21.

6. "Border Agents in California Say They Were Given Arrest Quotas," *The New York Times*, February 2, 2009.

7. No More Deaths, *Crossing the Line: Human Rights Abuses of Migrants in Short-Term Custody on the Arizona/Sonora Border*, 19. Available on the nomoredeaths.org website.

8. Miriam Jordan, "Arizona Seizes Spotlight in U.S. Immigration Debate," *The Wall Street Journal*, February 1, 2008.

9. Cindy Rodríguez, "For Deported Swift Worker, Agony over Family in U.S.," *The Denver Post*, December 19, 2006.

10. Fernando Quintero, "Impact of Swift Raid Still Being Felt," *The Rocky Mountain News*, May 12, 2007.

11. Christa Marshall, "Greeley Mayor Urges Changes in ICE Raids," *The Denver Post*, May 18, 2007.

12. Michael Falcone, "100,000 Parents of Citizens Were Deported over 10 Years," *The New York Times*, February 14, 2009.

13. Randy Capps, Rosa Maria Castañeda, Ajay Chaudry, and Robert Santos, *Paying the Price: The Impact of Immigration Raids on America's Children* (Washington DC: The Urban Institute for the National Council of La Raza, 2007), 1–7.

14. Ginger Thompson, "After Losing Freedom, Some Immigrants Face Loss of Custody," *The New York Times,* April 23, 2009.

15. Ibid., 1.

16. William Petroski, "Taxpayers' Costs Top $5 Million for May Raid at Postville," *The Des Moines Register*, October 14, 2008.

17. *Immigrant Workers at Risk: The Urgent Need for Improved Workplace Safety and Health Policies and Programs* (Washington DC: AFL-CIO, 2005), 10.

18. Rabbis are present to ensure that food is prepared according to strict Jewish dietary regulations. It is important to note that since these allegations surfaced, several rabbis are publicizing proposals that would revise kosher certification to include how workers are treated.

19. Julia Preston, "After Iowa Raid, Immigrants Fuel Labor Inquiries," *The New York Times*, July 27, 2008.

20. Ibid.

21. Julia Preston, "Kosher Plant Faces Charges of Violating Child Laws," *The New York Times*, September 10, 2008.

22. Monica Rhor, "Advocates Fear Crackdown on Illegal Immigration Will Backfire," *The Associated Press*, March 29, 2008.

23. Field notes.

24. Dan Frosch, "Report Faults Treatment of Women Held at Immigration Centers," *The New York Times*, January 21, 2009.

25. Amy Goldstein and Dana Priest, "Some Detainees Are Drugged for Deportation," *The Washington Post*, May 14, 2008.

5. The Politics of Fear

1. Dan McLean, "Immigration's Tancredo's Top Topic," *New Hampshire Sunday News*, June 12, 2005.

2. No More Deaths, *Crossing the Line: Human Rights Abuses of Migrants in Short-Term Custody on the Arizona/Sonora Border*, 5, 15, 17. Available on the nomoredeaths.org website.

3. Ibid., 7.

4. Amnesty International, *Human Rights Concerns in the Border Region with Mexico*. Available on the unhrc.org website.

5. Human Rights Immigrant Community Action Network, *Over-Raided, Under Siege*, 14, 27, 30. Available on the nnirr.org website.

6. Mark Hugo Lopez and Susan Minushkin, *2008 National Survey of Latinos: Hispanics See Their Situation in U.S. Deteriorating; Oppose Key Immigration Enforcement Measures* (Washington DC: The Pew Hispanic Center, 2008), 1.

7. Monica Rhor, "Advocates Fear Crackdown on Illegal Immigration Will Backfire," *The Associated Press*, March 29, 2008.

8. Ibid.

9. *Immigrant Workers at Risk: The Urgent Need for Improved Workplace Safety and Health Policies and Programs* (Washington DC: AFL-CIO, 2005), iii.

10. *Death on the Job: The Toll of Neglect: A National State-by-State Profile of Worker Safety and Health in the United States*, 17th ed. (Washington DC: AFL-CIO, 2008), 3, 19.

11. Conor Dougherty and Miriam Jordan, "Surge in U.S. Hispanic Population Driven by Births, Not Immigration," *The Wall Street Journal*, May 1, 2008.

12. Miguel A. De La Torre, "Living on the Borders," *The Ecumenical Review* 59, no. 2–3 (April/July 2007): 214–20.

13. "Crackdown on Immigrants Draws Protests in Phoenix," *The New York Times*, April 14, 2008.

14. Randal C. Archibold, "Challenges to a Sheriff, Both Popular and Reviled," *The New York Times*, September 28, 2008.

15. Miriam Jordan, "Arizona Seizes Spotlight in U.S. Immigration Debate," *The Wall Street Journal*, February 1, 2008.

16. Kristin Collins, "Tolerance Wears Thin," *The News and Observer*, September 7, 2007.

17. Jennifer Steinhauer and Julia Preston, "Action by Police at Rally Troubles Los Angeles Chief," *The New York Times*, May 4, 2007.

18. On September 16, 2008, four police officers were terminated and eleven were either suspended from active duty (no more than ten days) or simply reprimanded. See Joel Rubin, "15 LAPD Officers Face Discipline in May Day Melee," *Los Angeles Times*, September 17, 2008.

19. Pew Hispanic Center, 2007 *National Survey of Latinos: An Illegal Immigration Issue Heats Up, Hispanics Feel a Chill* (December 13, 2007): http://pewhispanic.org/files/reports/84.pdf.

20. An alien registration card, also known as an immigrant visa, permanent visa, permanent resident card, and permanent resident visa, is an identification card that must be carried, at all times, by permanent residents. Although permanent residents are not U.S. citizens, they reside as legal aliens and are granted permission to work in the United States on a permanent basis.

6. Christian Perspectives

1. "Officials: Radio Host's Call to Kill Border Crossers Dangerous," *Mohave Daily News*, April 8, 2006.

2. All scriptural quotations are translations by the author from the original Hebrew or Greek.

3. It should be noted that Lot's response to his neighbors is an example of what Phyllis Trible would call "a text of terror" for women.

4. Miguel A. De La Torre, *Reading the Bible from the Margins* (Maryknoll, NY: Orbis Books, 2002), 112–13.

5. Jon Sobrino, *Jesus the Liberator: A Historical-Theological Reading of Jesus of Nazareth*, trans. P. Burns and F. McDonagh (Maryknoll, NY: Orbis Books, 1993), 259–60.

6. Daniel J. Wakin and Julia Preston, "Speaking Up for Immigrants, Pontiff Touches a Flash Point," *The New York Times*, April 20, 2008.

7. The label evangelical is disputed and can be applied to a wide range of groups. I am using the term to refer to those who subscribe to the "Statement of Faith" of the National Association of Evangelicals. Available on the www.nae.net website.

8. I have dealt with all of these matters more extensively in *Christians at the Border: Immigration, the Church, and the Bible* (Grand Rapids, MI: Baker Academic, 2008).

9. Gregory Rodríguez, *Mongrels, Bastards, Orphans, and Vagabonds: Mexican Immigration and the Future of Race in America* (New York: Pantheon, 2007).

10. See Juan Francisco Martínez, *Sea La Luz: The Making of Mexican Protestantism in the American Southwest, 1829–1900* (Denton: University of North Texas Press, 2006).

11. For details, see Gastón Espinosa, Virgilio Elizondo, and Jesse Miranda, "Hispanic Churches in American Public Life: Summary of Findings" (Notre Dame, IN: Institute for Latino Studies, University of Notre Dame, 2003), available online; "Changing Faiths: Latinos and the Transformation of American Religion," Pew Hispanic Center and Pew Forum on Religion and Public Life (April 25, 2007), available on the pewhispanic.org website.

7. Ethical Responses

1. William Sloane Coffin, "Acting Our Conscience, April 15, 1984," *The Collected Sermons of William Sloane Coffin: The Riverside Years,* vol. 2 (Louisville, KY: Westminster John Knox, 2008), 155.

2. United States v. Goering, Judgment of the International Military Tribunal, 6.F.R.D.69, 110 (1946).

3. *The Nuremberg Case as Presented by Robert H. Jackson* (New York: Cooper Square Publishers, 1971), 88.

4. Jim Corbett, "The Covenant as Sanctuary," in *Sanctuary: A Resource Guide for Understanding and Participating in the Central American Refugee Struggle*, ed. Gary MacEoin, 183–97 (New York: Harper and Row, 1987), 193.

5. Ibid., 196.

6. No More Deaths, *Crossing the Line: Human Rights Abuses of Migrants in Short-Term Custody on the Arizona/Sonora Border*, 18. Available on the nomoredeaths.org website.

7. "Mexicans Deported from U.S. Face Shattered Lives," *The Associated Press*, August 25, 2008.

8. Teresa Watanabe, "Report Decries U.S. Treatment of Migrants," *The Los Angeles Times*, March 8, 2008.

9. Field notes, August 29, 2008.

10. "The Great Immigration Panic," *The New York Times*, June 3, 2008.